Picking Winners

Picking Winners

*Citizenship, Central Banks,
and Consumer Finance*

Edited by

LAWRENCE R. JACOBS
DESMOND KING

OXFORD
UNIVERSITY PRESS

OXFORD
UNIVERSITY PRESS

Oxford University Press is a department of the University of Oxford.
It furthers the University's objective of excellence in research, scholarship,
and education by publishing worldwide. Oxford is a registered trade mark of
Oxford University Press in the UK and in certain other countries.

Published in the United States of America by Oxford University Press
198 Madison Avenue, New York, NY 10016, United States of America.

CIP data is on file at the Library of Congress.

ISBN 9780197831793

ISBN 9780197831786 (hbk.)

DOI: 10.1093/9780197831823.001.0001

Paperback Printed by Marquis Book Printing, Canada

The manufacturer's authorized representative in the EU for product safety is
Oxford University Press España S.A. of Parque Empresarial San Fernando de Henares,
Avenida de Castilla, 2 – 28830 Madrid (www.oup.es/en or product.safety@oup.com).
OUP España S.A. also acts as importer into Spain of products made by the manufacturer.

MIX
Paper | Supporting
responsible forestry
FSC
www.fsc.org   FSC® C103567

Contents

Acknowledgments

Picking Winners contributes to the growing fields of American and comparative political economy and the distributional effects of central banks and consumer financial regulation. One of its distinctive contributions is to bring together scholars in the United States along with Europe.

The volume is the result of a two year-long collaboration of sharing research and a conference at Oxford University that invited commentary from European experts on finance and social policy (Benjamin Braun, Matthias Thiemann, and Ursula Hackett) as well as American scholars of historic development and racial and ethnic disparities (James Morone and Jason Casellas). We are grateful to the valuable insights shared by the participants in the Oxford Conference and the sustained and generous engagements by the contributors to this volume.

The collaboration was supported by Nuffield College and the Mellon Professorship held by Professor King. Nuffield College was a gracious host of the research conference. Professor Jacobs was aided by the Mondale Chair at the University of Minnesota.

List of Contributors

Lawrence Jacobs is the McKnight Presidential Chair and Walter F. and Joan Mondale Chair for Political Studies at the University of Minnesota, United States.

Desmond King is Andrew W Mellon Statutory Professor of American Government, University of Oxford, United Kingdom.

Brian Libgober is Assistant Professor, Political Science, Northwestern University, Evanston, IL, United States.

Manuela Moschella is Professor of Political Science, Department of Political and Social Sciences, University of Bologna, Bologna, Italy.

Alice Pearson is Leverhulme Early Career Fellow, Centre for Research in Arts, Social Sciences and Humanities, University of Cambridge, United Kingdom.

Mallory SoRelle is Tony and Teddie Brown Associate Professor of Public Policy, Sanford School of Public Policy, Duke University, Durham, NC, United States.

Chloe Thurston is Associate Professor of Political Science, Northwestern University, Evanston, IL, United States.

1

Political Economy, Central Banks, and Consumer Finance

Lawrence R. Jacobs and Desmond King

Recurrent crises strangle capitalism. In the citadel of capitalism, six domestic breakdowns of finance since the 1980s have rattled Americans' affluence. The promise of affluence for all in advanced capitalist societies is hobbled by sharp inequalities, enduring poverty, and persistent financial and economic breakdowns that disproportionately hurt the working and middle classes.

Central banks and, most prominently, the Federal Reserve Bank have become the handmaiden of capitalism, rushing to its rescue in the full view of citizens with massive, government-funded packages to stabilize financial operations and steady private firms teetering on bankruptcy. The Bank also props up the international financial system and national central banks.

Many economists—following on the analyses of Finn Kydland and Edward Prescott—continue to treat central banks as neutral servants of the "public good" that follow time-proven principles such as the "time-inconsistency principle." A cornerstone of the treatment of central banks by orthodox economists is the assumption that politicians manipulate financial markets: they promise low inflation to attract loans and then later change directions to accommodate the pressure of voters and lobbyists by printing money, which in turn increases the danger of inflation and reducing the real value of the earlier loan. By contrast, independent central banks are motivated, it is claimed, to modulate the money supply efficiently to stabilize inflation with minimal impacts on employment and the output of goods and services.[1]

The redefinition of central bank operations to quell recurrent capitalist crises contradicts, however, the "public good" accounts. Instead, research find that central banks accelerated inequality by inserting themselves into selecting winners and losers, often at the expense of low income households

Lawrence R. Jacobs and Desmond King, *Political Economy, Central Banks, and Consumer Finance*.
In: *Picking Winners*. Edited by: Lawrence R. Jacobs and Desmond King, Oxford University Press.
© Oxford University Press (2026). DOI: 10.1093/9780197831823.003.0001

and communities of color. They became the "primary driver of the upsurge of top incomes" as a result of their interventions to lower interest rates and contain capital market breakdowns through quantitative easing (namely, the purchase of massive quantities of government bonds and other financial assets).[2] Hopeful claims that central bank independence produces low inflation and economic growth are now challenged by a number of studies.[3]

Picking Winners: Citizenship, Central Banks, and Consumer Finance introduces innovative theoretical frameworks and new research about political institutions and organized interests to demonstrate that central banks and financial regulators are not neutral servants of the "public good." According to the research they are swayed instead by deeply resourced financial interests, the values and perspectives of capital over those of wage earners, and institutional designs that are biased to favor the already advantaged.

The contributors to this volume use diverse methods and sources of evidence to penetrate the cloistered operations of central banks and finance regulation to reveal the "subterranean world" of political conflict and influence-seeking. Homing in on central banks and the regulation of consumer finance, these studies variously employ empirical, qualitative, and ethnographic methods directly to challenge the dominant technocratic treatment of central banks and finance. The Trump presidency's efforts to roll back government agencies may result in lasting dilution of regulatory capacity; these impacts were unclear as this volume went to press soon after his inauguration.

1. Political Economy and Central Banks

This opening chapter leverages the frameworks of American and comparative political economy to analyze a critical facet of public policy—financial market operations—that has too often evaded adequate scrutiny for its distributional effects.[4] The original focus of these political economy analyses was social and labor policy. We adapt their insights and frameworks—along with an emerging body of comparative research on central banks—to identify two general models of financial governance that differ from but also approximate established patterns in comparative public policy: neoliberalism and social democracy. Our analysis focuses on three core features of central banks and consumer finance: *organizational combat and coalitions*, *institutional structures*, and *cultural expectations*.

Conflict and Coalitions: High Asset Investors versus Wage Earners

Decades of research trace welfare state development to "institutional class struggle" arising from the competing preferences of employers and their associations versus wage earners and organized labor.[5] The conflict is grounded in the organization of the economy and the distinct locations of those who own large enterprises compared to those who rely on the sale of their labor.

A new body of research directly challenges the technocratic perspective by revealing the political nature of central banks and the regulation of consumer finance.[6] Manuela Moschella's important book identifies political "contestation" as a factor driving the post-2008 shift by central banks away from orthodox monetary policy to large asset purchases and huge lending programs to banks and non-banks.[7]

Wealth and ownership of financial firms is concentrated among high-asset investors (HAIs) and partners in affluent banks and non-banks. Concentrated wealth and control over private financial institutions are systemically important to government officials charged with economic stability and growth as well as central banks who rely on them as buyers and sellers of assets and bonds. The "structural power" of finance rests on its direct pressure as well as the threat of automatic disinvestment from the real economy and nonproductive speculation to reap higher rates of return.[8] Although there are cross-national variations and particularities of import, the general pattern is that the dependence of central bank and regulators on banks and non-banks and HAIs generates incentives to accommodate privately controlled finance.

Resourced organizations representing HAIs and associated firms leverage the government's dependence on them to advance their preferences when feasible. While HAIs and large financial firms differ considerably, their interests converge in favor of lobbying domestic and international regulators to loosen restrictions to pursue increased profits. When markets crash, they reverse direction to seek government intervention to forestall catastrophic losses with little or no conditions. The two-way dynamic resists government intervention during non-crisis periods to widen their leeway to pursue profits and during crises demands government intervention to gain privileged access to credit (on generous terms) thereby mitigating losses.[9]

Wage earners challenge the distributional consequences of economic decision making when able to leverage their political rights and organize alliances with elected representatives, political parties, and associated interests.[10] Social Democratic and Labor parties with long-time connections to mass-membership unions may amplify the preferences of wage earners for employment, personal assets, and access to affordable credit and loans. These preferences require regulations to restrict financial risk-taking from generating economic instability and to oversee the consumer credit firms.

The history of Australia's Labour Party—the first to form a national government in the world—profiles the impact of mobilizing workers and a broad slice of wage earners. Its election campaigns done during the 1890s and early 1900s prevailed on the promise of establishing a "People's Bank" to attack "Money Power" and the private banks that "bleed the people." They offered wage earners an alternative: "chang[e] the capitalist system in the interests of workers," and serve the "national interest. . .above profit." Banks and their allies countered that the socialist attack on finance would damage the economy and trigger unemployment as investors pulled back.[11]

The Australian Labour Party's Commonwealth Bank Act of 1911 struck a compromise that would persist: politically forceful populist appeals to create a bank that "belongs to the people and directly managed by the people's agenda" and policies attuned to banking as a "business concern pure and simple" in response to the lobbying of domestic and, more recently, global finance.[12]

Although contemporary Australia reversed direction in some respects, its history of mingling egalitarianism and accommodation expresses the enduring conflict that is fundamental to political economy frameworks: wage earners threatened by finance and investors intent on operating with minimal restraints.[13]

The deployment of the rights of citizenship in consumer finance and central bank operations has been sharply contested in America's neoliberal structures. While wage earners outside the United States have been able to draw on the collective power of labor unions and political parties, the weakness of encompassing organizations encumbers American consumers. Important research by Chloe Thurston and Mallory SoRelle reveals the historic struggles of wage earners with banks to gain access to credit to purchase homes on favorable terms.[14]

During the nineteenth century, borrowers organized based on their shared interests to gain government protections against bankruptcy.[15] By the twentieth century, however, banks and other lenders countered to remove these protections in the United States and expand their political power. The terms of consumer finance are now under the sway of bank holding companies who work backchannels to advance their interests over that of consumers and have defused what had been a potentially landmark set of regulations passed by Dodd-Frank in 2010.[16]

United States financial interests have exercised a potent form of political power: concealed influence. Shaping regulations in obscure subterranean processes has depressed the political articulation of the HAI–wage earner conflict as a focal point of mainstream politics and depressed both the awareness of the favoritism and engagement by citizens in pressing Congress to intervene.[17] With the exception of extraordinary market upheavals, changes in financial operations and central bank policies lack regular salience in party competition and elections; their tangible impact is less routinely observable than programs and developments directly related to wages, employment, and social assistance.

Financial Governance and Institutional Structures

The conflict between wage earners and banks and non-banks is mediated by nationally distinct institutions, which we refer to as "financial governance." The formal institutions for governing capital markets and consumer finance involve Finance ministries or the Treasury Department as well as regulators. Central banks have become "key pillars" in the administration of capital markets due to their direct interventions in asset and bond markets and institutional interests to sustain them. Their rationale is to forestall the collective action problems associated with competitive, free-riding private firms by intervening as a "last resort" during financial crises and by adjusting the supply of money and credit to avoid inflation and damaging economic downturns that disrupt capital markets.[18] Formal rules and procedures are refracted through the agency missions and personal ambitions of agency actors.[19] While components of this institutional structure may be similar cross-nationally, there are critical variations that reflect and contribute to distributional struggles over capital markets and consumer financing.

The Bifurcated American Governance
The Janus-faced administrative structure in the United States systematically advantages finance. The first face is the familiar Madisonian structures of multiple and competing lines of authority among federal and state decision

makers and regulators, which dulls the significance of citizen demands and favors the organized interests of finance with the capacity to show up and exercise influence across multiple decision making arenas.[20] In her insightful chapter in this volume, SoRelle connects administrative feebleness to the lack of concentrated oversight of consumer financial regulation in the United States, as evident in the weak or nonexistent limits on the terms of personal debt and disruptive risk taking by investors. The effect, she argues, is to elevate the costs of public engagement, reward the aggressive participation of lobbyists for finance in the dispersed subterranean regulatory process, and bias rule makers toward the profitability of banks and non-banks over protecting consumers. Regulation of finance was similarly vulnerable to lobbyists hired by high finance who capitalized on their expertise with arcane judicially enforced procedures and the deference of authoritative regulators to networks of finance. The private meetings of regulators with lobbyists for finance produce "excess returns" in terms of concessions.[21] Donald Trump's aggressive agenda—notably diluting the Consumer Finance Protection Bureau—will further advantage financial interests by weakening the administrative capacity of regulators through reductions in budgets and the government workforce.

The second face was on display during the market breakdowns that banks and non-banks precipitated: strong, responsive, and concealed administrative processes that supplied effective, generous, and quick rescues. The Federal Reserve Bank stands out cross-nationally and in American domestic politics as an institutional behemoth. The Fed enjoys a comparatively high degree of anonymity from public scrutiny and wields unparalleled power on domestic policy. It is largely free of the traditional system of checks and balances that routinely grind down presidential and congressional proposals. The Fed's privileged institutional position is bolstered by funding that is independent of government appropriations: the Bank's operations in capital markets generates interest on its investments and the revenue from buying and selling them.[22]

During the 2008 and 2020 crises, the Fed exercised unrivaled authority, resources, and autonomy to rescue banks and non-banks with unprecedented "facilities" extending credit on favorable terms, and several rounds of quantitative easing.[23] Even its normal operations stood out by leveraging its exceptional institutional positions in relation with the Treasury Department and a roster of agencies.

Canadian Financial Governance

Organized financial interests face their stiffest resistance in Canada's financial governance, which is institutionally centralized and coordinated. Parliament limited the Bank of Canada to monetary policy and set up a separate regulatory body with responsibility to minimize risk and speculation. The Office of the Superintendent of Financial Institutions (OSFI) is a well-resourced independent agency whose coordination with the Bank of Canada, the Ministry of Finance, and federal financial regulators equips it to conduct effective oversight of banks, capital markets, private pensions, and insurance. Interviews with Canadian officials from different parts of the government unearthed a consensual view about the force of scrutinizing investors and creditors. Several senior regulators shared with us that the "Bank of Canada, Ministry of Finance, and regulators create a coordinated system and work together;" and hold a "collective mind-set and recognition of the shared interest to work toward common good." Based on their interactions with and observations of the US regulatory approach, they report that Canada has "one regulatory supervisor instead of the multiple agencies and agency heads that exists in the U.S."

Economic Imaginaries, Central Banks, and Varieties of Financial Governance

Conflicts about the material stakes and institutional configurations are not predetermined but unfold within national contexts of socially shared meanings.[24] Distinctive national histories and experiences create "cultural toolkits" that voters and governing elites draw upon to assign meaning and design policy solutions.[25] Economic anthropologists and ethnographic scholars argue that cultural norms and socially shared meanings may not predict policy detail or outcomes but do set the parameters for choice and "conceivable" options with regard to a wide range of political and policy developments.[26]

Acknowledging the role of cultural norms and beliefs challenges the assumption of orthodox economics that the "facts" of capital markets "speak" for themselves, supplying clear and commanding information that dictates policy and market operations. This "materialist approach" to political economy omits the significance of norms and socially shared meanings related to how the economic dynamics are interpreted and disputed.

By contrast, anthropology and ethnographic scholars argue that "economic imaginaries" and cultural beliefs ascribe meaning to policy choices and shape expectations.

In her chapter, Alice Pearson applies the analysis of "economic imaginaries" and their "distinct material effects" to how economists use the Phillips Curve to justify "wage suppression" as the primary tool for lowering inflation and stabilizing prices. The outcome of these macroeconomic models, Pearson argues, are "not merely abstract neutral representations" but privilege profits over labor.

Drawing on this tradition of research, in this chapter we incorporate nationally distinctive understandings of private bankers, regulators, and officers in central banks into the framework we develop by conducting twenty-six interviews with senior individuals in the United States, the United Kingdom, Canada, and Sweden. More than half of these interviews were with current or former individuals who ran government finance offices, central banks, regulatory bodies, banks, and hedge funds. Our interviews with financial elites covered three critical areas of capital markets and their governance: profit-maximizing firms (namely, investment banks, hedge funds, and private equity funds); large institutional funds that pursued modest returns in exchange for minimal risk; and current or former officials who work in central banks or regulate finance. The identity of our interviewees is anonymous to allow them to speak candidly about sensitive topics.

Our in-depth interviews with financial elites, along with research by the contributors to his volume, supply critical evidence about comparative domestic political configurations within finance and "economic imaginaries." Eminent officials in banking and government frequently dwelled—as we discuss below—on "how things are" and "expectations" about these seemingly technical operations, revealing distinctive patterns of beliefs, norms, and perceptions.

The cultural mindsets among US elites reinforce the organizational advantages of finance and high-asset investors. United States regulators and Federal Reserve officials perceive these interests as "sophisticated" and "innovative" and welcome their overlapping networks of colleagues and mentors. Instead of identifying these interests as adversarial, as is the case in Canada and elsewhere, US officials in positions of authority tend to "agre[e] with the bankers' view of the world" and assume that markets work best when government regulators avoid interventions (unless they entail rescues).[27] Nobel Prize–winning economist Joseph Stiglitz distills the mindset: "What's good for Wall Street is good for America."[28]

Cultural predispositions cement US officials' accommodation to resourced financial interests. Rapid and widespread securitization is one distinctive result. The 2008 financial crisis was preceded by the largely unfettered shift by bankers from the long-standing "originate and hold" management of mortgages to a model of converting these loans into (poorly) graded assets that were traded. The Fed and regulators were comparatively deferential.

By contrast, government officials in Canada adopted a more skeptical mindset toward private banks and resisted the uncritical regulatory catering that prevails in the United States. A senior Canadian regulator reports that, "we talk with business and finance and recruit from both because they bring information and perspectives that are highly beneficial to our decision making." But this official continued, "decisions are made by public servants, Ministry of Finance or Bank of Canada [to serve the public interest]." Canada's culture of financial operations is revealed, according to another official, in the decisions of business and finance to "accept oversight and government decisions." Regulators severely restricted the scope of securitization and required higher capital to loan ratios. Financial firms cringed at the lost opportunity for profit but accepted the restrictions.

2. Social Rights and the Meanings of Citizenship

The contending interests of HAIs and wage earners reflect the broader "conflict between [the] opposing principles" of capitalism and citizenship rights that differentially equip citizens to confront the prerogatives of employers and capital. T.H. Marshall's notion of social rights, which focused on education, social insurance, pensions, and health care, creates a conceptual foundation to make two advances in the analysis of central banks and consumer financial regulation in representative democracies.[29]

Winners and Losers

Orthodox economics assumes that everyone gains when the country is spared financial disaster or inflation because of central bank policy decisions and interventions. But the rates of return are unequal: individuals and firms with massive assets gain more from central bank policies compared to working or lower-income citizens and people of color, as vividly demonstrated by the aftereffects of the 2008 financial crisis in the United States.[30]

The social rights framework challenges orthodox economics for its claim that central bank independence deliver "superior" results without asking: For whom? The principle of central bank independence is particularly inappropriate for the new generation of central bank interventions that exercise authority over fiscal policy reserved for elected lawmakers, effecting distributional consequences and selecting winners and losers.[31] Even under non-crisis conditions, wage earners pay exorbitant and often obscure fees for consumer credit that generate substantial profits for banks and non-banks.[32]

The distributional skew is obscured from public scrutiny by widespread consumer borrowing, investment in equity for savings, and profit sharing. This invisibility creates the perception that the interest of wage earners aligns with the financial system as currently organized. The perception of converging interests contributed, for instance, to the opposition of organized labor to financial regulation in the Netherlands.[33] Even as wage earners integrate into contemporary finance, however, banks and non-banks exercise control over consumer credit and pension funds, which they structure to generate profit.[34]

Neoliberal and Social Rights Governance

We draw on Marshall's framework of citizenship to distinguish between the deferential neoliberal approaches to financial operations and the comparatively interventionist social rights model.[35] Figure 1.1 displays three dimensions of central bank and consumer finance and their variations across the two models, which we illustrate with reference to Western Europe, North America, and Australia.

Access to Affordable Credit

The first dimension of the social rights framework suggests that citizens have *access to affordable credit* as a necessary requirement to be a participating member of a modern community. Marshall argued that "social rights in their modern form imply. . .the subordination of market price to social justice, the replacement of the free bargain by the declaration of rights."[36] The implication is that robust citizenship entails altering or supplementing private control over access to credit and creating favorable conditions for its availability.

	Social Rights Model (Canada)	Neoliberal Model (United States)
Access to credit	Inclusive and stable access to credit	Defer to market allocation of credit
Exposure to Risk	Right to broad protection against risk	Risk is individual responsibility
Stratification	Offset inequalities generated by finance markets	Accept financial market distributions

Figure 1.1 Central Banking, Consumer Finance, and Models of Financial Governance

The *neoliberal governance model* features deference to private banks to determine who gets access to capital and on what terms. Robert Hockett and Saule Omarova argue that the Federal Reserve Bank effectively cedes its management of the faith and credit of the United States to private firms for the latter's gain.[37] Under these circumstances, high-asset investors find ample opportunities to acquire or leverage capital. By contrast, wage earners, low-income individuals, and people of color face significant costs.

The sway of finance in the United States is evident in the political snare and delusion of consumer finance. In her chapter, SoRelle demonstrates that consumer finance is politically constructed to lure consumers with increased access to credit, which in turn boosts profits for banks and non-banks, and then traps millions of Americans in unaffordable personal debt and the hazard of personal bankruptcy. Andreas Wiedemann's comparative research finds that consumer "credit markets interact with welfare regimes and social policies."[38] The relative gaps in US social policies leave families scrapping to pay for their basic needs such as housing, transportation, and education as well as to compensate for drops in income due to illness or unemployment. Americans make ends meet by becoming extraordinarily dependent on loans and credit cards. Compounding that dependence, financial services charge exorbitant fees while lax regulations fail to protect citizens against predatory lending (including subprime mortgages and payday lending). Consistent with the neoliberal model, wage earners and especially people of color and low income carry enormous debt and are at significant risk of personal insolvency and bankruptcy. Historically, banks and non-banks benefited from the reversal of New Deal protections for debtors, which elevated the power of lenders to impose ruinous repayment terms, according to Thurston's astute chapter and her prior research.[39]

By contrast, the *social rights governance* approach to consumer credit features an active role for representative government to widen access to credit on favorable terms and steps to encroach on private capital dominance of consumer credit in order to create opportunities for inclusive economic opportunity.

The Australia's Commonwealth Bank foreshadowed—in a truncated form—the political and institutional commitment to deploy public authority to extend credit. The Commonwealth Banking Act of 1945 sustained a "discourse of community service" and pushed the government toward becoming the largest lender for housing by offering rates that were significantly below those of private banks. It was particularly committed to ensuring access to capital for populations that faced obstacles—people with low income, Aboriginals, and other vulnerable groups.

The Bank's commitment to community service and equitable access to financial services established a rival logic to the market principles guiding the private banks. Clause 8 of the 1945 Commonwealth Banking Act directed the Bank to "pursue a money and banking policy directed to the greatest advantage of the people of Australia." In addition to requiring the standard central bank mandates to stabilize the currency and maintain full employment, the Act insisted on a broad obligation to improve the "economic prosperity and welfare of the people of Australia."[40]

In time, the community logic was challenged by the market logic of private finance and the pressure of central banks to operate within global financial markets. By the 1980s, the Commonwealth Bank was privatized, deregulation started, and many banks closed, which diminished financial services for certain communities. By 2009, the proportion of mortgages originated by the big four private banks increased by 50 percent (from 60 percent to 90 percent).

While the market logic came to dominate by the twenty-first century, the logics of community and "association" continued to invite a "conflict of principles," as TH Marshall would have put it. Between 2007 and 2013, Labor governments promoted financial "mutuals"—especially credit unions—to sustain the cultural expectations of financial services for the community and, especially, those facing hurdles in accessing credit.[41] The persistence of community and associational obligations was showcased in the 2019 Royal Commission; the Commission's authors castigated private banks for conduct that "fell below community standards and expectations."

Risk Exposure

The second dimension of central bank and consumer finance is Marshall's overriding concern with the *"general reduction of risk and insecurity"* and its uneven distribution.[42] The general concept of risk protection is not static but dynamic. When Marshall wrote in the 1940s and 1950s, economic risk and insecurity referred to the travails of postwar capitalism and the impacts on working people.

Global financialization links the well-being of workers and prospective retirees to capital markets at a time when speculation may disrupt the economy, convince businesses to slow or reverse investments, and freeze credit. Initial financial regulations focused on fraud; today, the rights of citizenship is expanding to encompass risk with regard to pension funds; borrowing for housing, credit cards, and student loans; and investments marketed to consumers that require sophisticated knowledge and experience.

The cornerstone of the *neoliberal governance model* in the United States is the belief among financial and political elites that the country's economic growth depends on risk taking and individuals assuming responsibility for their financial decisions. A former senior Treasury Department official who works in finance told us that risk was necessary to foster economic innovation and that it was the individual's responsibility to guard themselves. "America's risk and entrepreneurial culture is the source of America's economic success with Apple, Amazon, Silicon Valley, shale energy production, and more." America's "risk culture" invites "friskiness," overleveraging, and periodic crises but the benefits are extraordinary. "Canada and UK create less risk in financial markets and therefore have weaker economies." A European investor tied the American approach to the fact that "the Fed is super friendly" to risk takers: "There is a strong risk taking because American investors anticipate a friendly Fed and…are complacent." A former senior US official conceded that "households often don't invest well but I don't think they can be protected without [us] becoming too paternalistic."

The neoliberal values of American elites translated into a series of reforms that relaxed restrictions on finance. During the 1980s, Federal Reserve Chair Alan Greenspan weakened government regulations in favor of "private market regulation" on the assumption that the "self-interests of organizations" would unleash "free, competitive markets" to produce innovation and "unrivaled" success. By 1999, Bill Clinton and Congress repealed the Glass-Steagall Act, which cleared the way for investment banking to expand and mingle with commercial banking for the first time since the Great Depression.[43] US financial institutions subsequently changed their business models from seeking yields on credit for consumers and businesses to converting loans into securities that were re-sold—as was the case with the bundling of subprime loans for home mortgages, the trigger to the 2008 economic crisis. Without the government safeguards found in other western countries, debt was aggressively marketed to consumers and corporations, investments were made without adequate cushions to withstand inevitable credit crunches, and new markets for securities and shadow banking flourished outside regulatory constraints. Greenspan conceded—and the congressional financial crisis inquiry reported—that limited regulation was a "flaw, which did little to dampen elite embrace of risk and hostility to restrictions on finance."[44]

After 2008, the Dodd-Frank reforms were enacted but then hobbled by lobbyists for finance; the new rules that were implemented left in place America's high-risk model and the assumption that the collective rewards of this model outweighed the potential burdens. A former official who developed financial regulations after the 2008 crisis normalized the nearly catastrophic economic breakdown: "Risk is prevalent in markets and in life. Nothing ventured, nothing gained." The senior US financial elites we interviewed agreed—without exception—that the costs of regulations to restrain risk taking were greater than benefits of financial risk taking—the opposite conclusion from UK, Australian, and Canadian officials and bankers.

The wide elite acceptance of risk in the United States coincides with comparatively weak protections for consumers. To a degree that stood out cross-nationally, consumers converted pensions into investment accounts, took on significant debt, and overmortgaged. SoRelle traces the lock-in of American financial regulations that placed the onus on individuals—rather than government institutions—to protect against risk in increasingly complex systems of lending. The failure to create stringent federal protections has, in turn, depressed citizens from demanding government intervention to create safeguards. This pattern of elite deference to finance and acceptance of exceptional risk by consumers is consistent with neoliberal politics.[45]

By contrast, Canada embraces the rights of citizens for protection against financial risk by designing central bank operations and financial regulations to minimize the destructive impact of capital market speculation and unaffordable consumer debt—the *social rights governance model*. This commitment guided the institutional design of financial governance after the bank crises in the 1980s and 1990s: regulation shifted to a centralized coordinating body—Office of the Superintendent of Financial Institutions—while the Bank of Canada's primary responsibility was monetary policy.

Current and former figures in the Canadian government and finance accepted, according to our interviews with senior officials, the "paternalistic" tradition that put a premium on prudence and a commitment to risk protection owed to citizens. Reversing the priorities in the United States for investor latitude over risk abatement, Canadian elites widely accept—according to a well-placed financial regulator—an approach to finance that is "risk averse and avoids getting exposed to risk even if it comes with less innovation [and lower short-term profits]." Canadian regulators put a priority on protecting citizens from a broad range of risks in the belief that the significant hazards of finance were often the "fault of a flawed system instead of individual mistakes."

Compared to the United States, Canadian corporations and households carry less debt; banks face limits on their investments in risky ventures such as securitization. Consumers are barred from getting mortgages that outstrip their ability to repay and, instead, are required to place a significant down payment and choose among loans with fixed rates for relatively short periods (five years instead of the twenty or thirty-year duration in the United States). Regulations also protect consumers from investing in products aimed at sophisticated investors. The Canadian expectation of risk protection is enshrined in the energetic Financial Consumer Agency of Canada, responsible for consumer protection laws, guidelines, and concessions by banks.

While the Americans we interviewed uniformly focused on the costs of policies to restrain risk, Canadians stressed the benefits of risk protection over the costs of "failure." The biggest upside of a financial system that "works well" is avoiding the waves of financial crises and economic downturns that afflict the United States. Several Canadians disapprovingly pointed to the American mistake of "taking to the extreme the idea that more risk unleashes animal spirits and produces greater economic growth."

The assumption among Canadian financial elites that risk protection is a social right extends to private banks. "Canada's prudence is embedded," according to a senior official in a Canadian pension firm who previously worked for a European hedge fund devoted to finding high profits. Risk is managed because "Ottawa has created regulations and guidelines to restrain risk taking," and citizens expect the Government to prevent bank failures. This, in turn, shapes the personal motivations of bankers: there is a "fear of losing money [because of the]. . .risk of losing one's job and career . . . . We are afraid of financial risk." Canada's "culture accepts oversight" and banks comply. Private financial firms do something that is rare in the United

States: they infrequently lobby government officials to overturn oversight and restrictions.

Similarly, Australian financial elites and lawmakers recoil at the disruptive consequences of risk. Popular and elite expectations—along with the historic reliance on government institutions—set the context for checking the inroads by globalization. Although Australia deregulated during the 1980s and 1990s and allowed competition to secure market shares in commercial and consumer lending, its lawmakers and watchdogs remained attuned to the signs of systemic trouble. They sounded the alarm with the growth of suspect debt, speculative investments in asset markets that created an artificial boom in the commercial property markets, and the collapse of the giant insurance firm, HIH.[46]

By the late 1990s, lawmakers recommitted to Australia's legacy of distrusting financial institutions and policing them to prevent financial speculation. As part of this re-regulation, the Reserve Bank of Australia (RBA) was stripped of the authority to oversee banks and financial institutions in 1998 and the Australian Prudential Regulatory Authority (APRA) adopted—according to its executive general manager—a "skeptical, questioning, and, where necessary, aggressive regulatory stance" toward banks, non-banks, and superannuating funds.[47] In addition to imposing capital adequacy controls to test bank resilience if faced with the shock of unexpected financial upheavals, APRA steered banks to adopt risk management principles. This strategy deterred Australian institutions from the degree of investment in securitization and derivatives that swelled the highly leveraged subprime mortgages in the United States and triggered its financial implosion in 2008. The cultural expectations and values of low risk and regulation prompted APRA's former chairman to stress that Australia was "untouched" by the Asian financial crisis and global financial crisis during the first decade of the twenty-first century, even though it faced the "same set of global rules" as the US.[48] Banks accepted the norms and ideas about traditional "boring but safe" commercial and consumer lending; regulators supported this culture and practices by banning takeovers within the bank sector to deter hostile purchases geared to improving profits by engaging in speculative investments and securities trading.[49]

Britain is a mixed case of greater financial regulations than the United States but fewer effective safeguards than Canada. During the early twenty-first century, British finance tilted away from neoliberalism[50] and limited central bank independence toward a more activist role in restraining risk following the 2008 economic upheavals. A senior government official in England explained that "citizens enjoy the right to government regulations to reduce risk associated with everyday savings and investments." Five years after the US crisis, Parliament created a new, independent regulatory authority—the Financial Conduct Authority (FCA)—to institutionalize a government commitment to reducing the systemic risks facing citizens as investors and consumers. The motivation for creating the FCA was the realization that citizens remained vulnerable to "making mistakes or being taken advantage of in complicated financial markets where they often don't know what they are doing." While financial restraints expanded after 2008, the timeliness, efficacy, and transparency of the FCA has been threatened by insufficient institutional capacity as well as a backlash by banks, non-banks, and their lawyers.[51]

The assumptions and policy responses to capital market and consumer debt risks demonstrate a significant variation across neoliberal and social rights models of financial governance. A London hedge fund manager captured a consistent response from our interviews with key regulators and officials in banking and non-banking: "Across countries, there are different attitudes to risk. The United States is fine with risk; after all, the Federal Reserve Bank bailout provides a safety net and the fear from 2008 is a long time ago. By contrast, the Europeans [and Canadians] are more conservative."

Economic and Racial Stratification

The third dimension of financial governance concerns *economic and racial stratification*. Marshall argues that social services such as pensions and housing increase the social wage of citizens. "[A]spirations [to build civilized life] have in part been met by incorporating social rights in the status of citizenship and thus creating a universal right to real income." He continues: "Class abatement is still the aim of social rights, but it has acquired a new meaning. It is no longer merely an attempt to abate the obvious nuisance of destitution in the lowest ranks of society. It has assumed the guise of action modifying the whole pattern of social inequality. It is no longer content to raise the floor-level in the basement of the social edifice, leaving the superstructure as it was. It has begun to remodel the whole building."[52]

Marshall's concept of citizenship elevates questions about the significance of central bank and regulator activities for stratification. The United States and its selective responses to the 2008 crisis exemplifies the *neoliberal model*.

First, it reduced interest rates to near zero starting in 2007; then it turned to two unorthodox approaches—neither of which were authorized by Congress or the President. One of these responses were three rounds of large asset purchases known as "Quantitative Easing" (QE). Their purpose was to buy financial assets from banks and other financial institutions in order to expand the money supply. At a time when capital markets were frozen, the Federal Reserve Bank created a market that paid cash to large institutional investors unable to sell financial stocks, bonds, and more. In addition to funneling money to large investors, QE supplied yet another selective benefit: it purchased corporate bonds and shares. In contrast, the European Central Bank (ECB) purchased large amounts of mortgage debt in order to inflate housing prices.[53]

The Federal Reserve Bank's second unilateral invention was as radical but submerged. It invented nine "facilities" in 2007–2009 that delivered concrete payoffs to finance—and itself. The facilities extended loans and guarantees that were ten times the size of the federal government bailout known as the Troubled Asset Relief Program.

Financial elites justify these extraordinary measures as creating a shared benefit—borrowers and working people gained from the stabilizing of the economy. One official explained: "Did we have to respond to the arsonists and reward them? Yes, the house was on fire and everyone had to be saved."

The gain was shared but the gain to individuals and firms with substantial assets was higher. The Federal Reserve Bank's supply of inexpensive credit during a credit freeze was of incalculable value to large banks and non-banks. A series of studies found that the response of the Federal Reserve Bank and US regulators revived finance, ratified its disproportionate place in the US economy, increased bank profits, and restored the concentration of wealth and income among the richest that had been dented by the 2008 crisis.[54]

By contrast, direct support was unavailable for the 13 million homes that faced foreclosure proceedings from 2008 to 2013 and the millions of people who lost savings and assets. Citizens of color were hit particularly hard and for longer. Black subprime borrowers experienced disproportionate wealth loss and lower disposable income compared with comparable white borrowers. This pattern is consistent with American political economy: the Federal Reserve Bank's selective policies accentuated the "race-laden institutional arena" that relegates people of color to subordinate positions in the labor market, depressed levels of wealth, and excluded them from investment networks.[55]

Even the normal operation of financial markets disproportionately favor finance. America's system for consumer finance through credit cards like VISA and Mastercard vividly displays the stratifying effects of neoliberalism. With the Federal Reserve's deferential regulatory regime, US banks established a payment system that permits them to generate enormous profits by charging comparatively high fees to merchants. The costs are passed along to the losers in this system—consumers. Brian Libgober's excellent chapter traces the obscure but potent rules of America's credit card system to reveal its significant distributional effects.

The reaction of American elites to economic and racial stratification epitomizes the values and priorities of neoliberal financial governance: disinterest and denial. "I haven't given it much thought" was the response of a former senior government official affiliated with the Democratic Party. The more common response was to insist that "inequality and the Fed [and financial regulators] are not connected" and Fed policies "did not impact inequality at all." When the stratifying effects were acknowledged, the response was muted and mixed. Some US financial elites insisted that, "inequality can only be addressed through fiscal policy and Congress" while more adopted the familiar neoliberal dismissal of government intervention as "reducing the incentive to work" and worsening inequality. One banker (associated with the Democratic Party) insisted that government programs to assist the economically vulnerable and encourage work with programs like the Earned Income Tax Credit were part of the problem by "encouraging people to take off the summer and collect unemployment checks."

Social rights governance—exemplified by Canada—uses regulations, central bank policies, and regulatory interventions to scrutinize sources of stratification and prevented the sharp rise in inequality that occurred in the United States after the 2008 crisis. Its regulation of credit cards protects consumers (no fees are charged to merchants or consumers) and the profits of banks are limited. Canada's policies also sustained economic security among the mass of citizens by restricting securitization that the United States welcomed and encouraging defined-contribution pensions and investments. The results delivered steady returns and basic income security.

In contrast with US financial elites, all the current or former senior Canadian government officials we interviewed reported that their institutions and regulators "look at inequality and discuss the implications for monetary policy and regulations." Several Canadians disapprovingly pointed to the impacts of the US model for leaving "unsophisticated investors to pay a huge price" for the subprime crisis and earlier Savings and Loan implosion.

Although the Australian and British approaches to finance lack Canada's activism, they were more explicitly aware and on guard against the risk of finance increasing stratification than the United States. Australia's macro-prudential regulation prevented—as intended—the 2008 financial crisis and its disproportionate damage to the less well-off. Australian officials also publicly highlighted the distributional consequences of their financial system. The 2019 Royal Commission on financial misconduct publicly scrutinized the deeper "asymmetry of power and information between the financial services and their customers" that "caus[ed] substantial losses to many customers [and] yield[ed] substantial profit." Bonuses and commissions based on sales and profits, the incentive system of financial firms, were identified as the source of the inequality.

The Bank of England paired its financial rescue starting in 2008 with demands that the rescued banks and investment firms relieve the freeze in credit facing homeowners and businesses. (The Federal Reserve Bank rejected this approach.) In addition, the Bank explicitly monitored and highlighted inequality. For instance, in May 2019, the FCA drew attention to the greater affluence of Baby Boomers (those born between 1946 and 1965) than Generation X (born between 1966 and 1980), proposing new rules and financial products to narrow the generational gap. These ideas got lost in the Covid pandemic fog.

In short, the national vulnerability to finance-driven stratification consists of differential products of embedded institutions, cultural expectations, and dueling interests and organizational coalitions. The Federal Reserve Bank acquiesced to the preferences of high-asset investors and banks; they either ignored stratification or dismissed it as unavoidable. By contrast, Canada most clearly used central bank policies and regulatory interventions to scrutinize sources of stratification to avoid risk and safeguard the assets of citizens.

3. Picking Winners: Generalizations and Departures

Picking Winners shifts analysis of central banks and consumer finance in several significant respects. First, the essays in this volume demonstrate that central banks and consumer finance regulators are not passive technocrats, reflecting fundamental economic principles. Instead, they are institution builders whose efforts are conditioned by their political contexts and the relative power of organized financial interests. In the most permissive environment, the Federal Reserve Bank intervenes in capital markets to serve its interests and those of high asset investors, banks, and non-banks. The Fed's privileged institutional position and accommodation of finance generates reliable political support as well as the revenue to function and reward private banks.[56] By contrast, the ECB is constrained by its institutional and political contexts. For instance, its initial efforts after 2008 to sharply limit securitization by imposing a financial transaction tax was defeated by "infrastructural entanglement"—the dependence of treasuries and central banks on these capital markets.[57]

Second, national patterns of financial governance vary based on distinctive institutional structures, cultural expectations, and the relative power of wage earners and high-asset investors. Neoliberal politics are anchored in a pattern of accommodating large, well-organized economic interests while the redistributive politics of social rights models leverage the broad exercise of political rights and encompassing organized alliances with elected representatives, political parties, and associated interests.

The varieties of financial governance may not mirror the familiar patterns of social policy given differences in institutional and coalitional circumstances. For instance, Sweden's redistributive social policies of the 1970s reflected the coalition of the Social Democratic Party (SAP), the powerful labor organization (Landsorganisationen or LO), and parts of the business community. The cross-class coalition that linked labor and business behind redistribution also obstructed, though, the extension of social democracy to financial governance, which radical elements in the labor movements proposed. In particular, the plans for a social democratic financial policy aimed to use worker pensions and "wage-earner funds" to replace the capitalist ownership model. Unified business opposition was joined by resistance from LO and its political allies, who tied their electoral ambitions to cross-class electoral support. In his interview with us, a senior economist for LO was scornful toward his organization's lack of commitment and the SAP's deference to capital markets. Their "focus is restricted to wages, social policy, educational policy, [and] training policy," he complained. There has been "no interest in capital markets and banks among Social Democrats." As a consequence, "monetary policy has never been on the radar of social democrats even though it should have been." The result is that Sweden's response to inequality has been bifurcated: Social Democrats in power favored redistributive social policy and readily "joined the mindset of international bankers [on monetary policy.]"[58]

A question hangs over the turbulent dynamic of capitalism and financial markets. "What comes after capitalism?"[59] Martin Wolf, columnist at the *Financial Times*, shares the skepticism, concluding that "capitalism is substantially broken."[60] Our analysis reveals an important distinction created by neoliberal financial governance: capitalism is not broken for high net worth investors or banks but it is for many modest wage–earners and low income households experiencing inflated debt levels, poor access to credit, and weakly regulated financial institutions that implode. Is the generation of inequality by the government in neoliberal regimes sustainable economically and politically?

Will the variation in financial governance shield countries with social democratic models from the breakdown of capitalism? The global reach of financialization may leave these countries—as in 2008—vulnerable to epic crises in US markets due to its unparalleled shift toward risky investments in securities. The financial sector swelled from 2.8 percent of the US economy in 1950 to 7.3 percent of US gross domestic product in 2023. A similar pattern characterized profits. The financial sector made up 10 to 15 percent of profits in the 1950s and 1960s; by 2023, finance accounted for 25 to 30 percent of all corporate profits. The drive to earn outsized profits in finance is crowding out more productive sectors: exchanging capital to generate interest, dividends, or capital gains pays more than the familiar production and trading of goods and services. These circumstances are tinder for the next global financial crisis that will threaten to inflame even countries with prudent financial markets.

4. Plan of the Book

The volume is organized to connect themes of political economy with the tangible operations of central banks and consumer finance.

The historic development of American institutions loads the dice against consumers. Chloe Thurston anchors a discussion of citizen access to capital and vulnerability to financial risk in the historic transition in the American neoliberal order from "consumer" capitalism before the New Deal to "investor" capitalism by the 1970s. This political development, Thurston demonstrates, accentuated exposure to higher levels of debt and personal insolvency, climaxing in 2007 and 2008 when "subprime" mortgages imploded at great cost to millions.

Mallory SoRelle builds on Thurston's historical analysis of citizen risk in the American neoliberal model by investigating the severe limits of consumer finance regulation due to the fragmentation across federal and state agencies. The Consumer Finance Protection Bureau (CFPB) was created by the Dodd-Frank Act to redress consumer risks after the 2008 crisis but has been compromised by "a decentralized and fluid system of consumer protection that generates significant inequalities with respect to who has protection and who does not." SoRelle reports that the historic legacy of fragmentation makes it unlikely that the CFPB will succeed in creating uniform consumer protections across the states. Donald Trump's targeting of the CFPB will further diminish its force as an force for consumers.

Thurston's and SoRelle's chapters are exemplary accounts of how neoliberalism became embedded into American political development, exposing citizens to heightened risk and compromising their access to consumer credit.

Brian Libgober's chapter reveals the stratifying effects of America's neoliberal model on contemporary financial operations. The chapter uses a close comparative analysis of payment systems and credit cards to illuminate the organizational advantages of banks. Libgober contrasts the exorbitant fees and hefty profits that US banks reap in the United States to the more restrictive plastic payment models in Australia and Canada.

Alice Pearson expands the volume's attention to Europe, drawing on extensive ethnographic research to investigate the use of the Phillips Curve by economists and central bankers to justify their focus on the "role of employment and wages in inflation" and their "placing of 'profit 'margins' at the margin of concern." "Economic imaginaries," Pearson argues, create a "wilful blindness" that foregrounds "labour as a concern over profits." Although economists present the Phillips curve as a "neutral" method, Pearson insists that it is a "device" that mobilizes a particular set of assumptions and beliefs with "distributive implications."

Complementing Pearson's chapter, Manuela Moschella develops a strikingly innovative synthesis of central bank operations and the deployment of economic imaginaries, arguing that the ECB and the Federal Reserve Bank responded to citizen concerns by expanding their discursive repertoires to appear attentive in an effort to deflect criticism while leaving unchanged their underlying distributional commitments and institutional autonomy. Strategic maneuvering by central banks, Moschella argues, shapes societal conflict and influences the balance of power among social groups.

References

1. Finn Kydland and Edward C. Prescott. 1977. "Rules Rather than Discretion: The Inconsistency of Optimal Plans." *Journal of Political Economy* 85 (June): 473–492; Gregory Mankiw. 2004. *Principles of Microeconomics*. 2004. 3rd ed. (Mason, OH: Thompson/South-Western); Robert Barro. 1973. "The Control of Politicians: An Economic Model," *Public Choice* 14 (Spring 1973): 19–42.

2. Emmanuel Saez and Gabriel Zucman 2016, "Wealth Inequality in the United States since 1913." *Quarterly Journal of Economics* 131 (2): 519–578; Thomas Piketty. 2013. *Capital in the Twenty-First Century*. (Cambridge: Harvard University Press).

3. Of the more than 9000 studies of developed and developing countries, most find that the association of central bank independence with economic stabilization are statistically insignificant, weak, or uneven. For instance, Bodea and Hicks (2015) report that central bank independence exerts no statistically significant effect on economy while there are significant relationships among some countries outside the OECD; see Cristina Bodea and Raymond Hicks. 2015. "Price Stability and Central Bank Independence: Discipline, Credibility, and Democratic Institutions." *International Organization* 69: 35–61; Philipp E. Baumann, Michael Schomaker, and Enzo Rossi 2021, "Estimating the effect of central bank independence on inflation using longitudinal targeted maximum likelihood estimation." *Journal of Causal Inference* 9: 109–146; Jeroen Klomp and Jakob De Haan. 2010. "Inflation and Central Bank Independence: A Meta-Regression Analysis." *Journal of Economic Surveys* 13 (August): 593–621; but see Alberto Alesina and Lawrence H. Summers 1993, "Central bank independence and macroeconomic performance: some comparative evidence." *Journal of Money, Credit and Banking* 25 (2): 151–162.

4. Theda Skocpol. 1985. "Bringing the State Back In," in *Bringing the State Back In*, ed. Peter B. Evans, Dietrich Rueschemeyer, and Theda Skocpol (New York: Cambridge University Press) 3–30; Theda Skocpol, Margaret Weir, and Ann Shola Orloff AS. 1988. *The Politics of Social Policy in the United States*. (Princeton, NJ: Princeton University Press); Jacob Hacker, Alexander Hertel-Fernandez, Paul Pierson, and Kathleen Thelen, eds. 2021. *The American Political Economy: Politics, Markets, and Power*. (New York: Cambridge University Press); Peter Hall and David Soskice, eds. 2001. *Varieties of Capitalism*. (Oxford: Oxford University Press).

5. Gosta Esping-Andersen. 1985. *Politics against Markets*. (Princeton: Princeton University Press); Jane Gingrich. 2015. "Coalitions, Policies and Distribution: Esping-Andersen's Three Worlds of Welfare Capitalism." In *Advances in Comparative-Historical Analysis* eds. James Mahoney and Kathleen Thelen. (Cambridge: Cambridge University Press), 110–130. Cathie Jo Martin and Duane Swank. 2012. *The Political Construction of Business Interests: Coordination, Growth and Equality*. (Cambridge: Cambridge University Press).

6. An extensive body of research has persuasively investigated the institutions and distributional effects of central banks and consumer finance. Benjamin Braun. 2020. "Central Banking and the Infrastructural Power of Finance: The Case Of ECB Support For Repo and Securitization Markets." *Socio-Economic Review* 18 (April): 395–418; Pepper Culpepper and Raphael Reinke. 2014. "Structural Power and the Bank Bailouts in the UK and US." *Politics and Society* 42: 427–442; Erik Jones. 2019. "Do Central Banks Dream of Political Union? From Epistemic Community to Common Identity." *Comparative European Politics*. 17: 530–547; Matthias Thiemann and Jan Lepoutre. 2017. "Stitched on the Edge: Rule Evasion, Embedded Regulators, and the Evolution of Markets." *American Journal of Sociology* 122: 1775–1821; Matthias Thiemann. 2024. *Taming the Cycles of Finance? Central Banks and the Macro-Prudential Shift in Financial Regulation*. (Cambridge: Cambridge University Press); Erik Jones and Matthias Marrhijs. 2019. "Rethinking Central-Bank Independence." *Journal of Democracy* 30: 127–141; Sheri

Berman and Kathleen McNamara. 1999. "Bank on Democracy: Why Central Banks Need Public Oversight." *Foreign Affairs*. 78 (March and April): 2–8; Adam Posen. 1993. "Why Central Bank Independence Does Not Cause Low Inflation: There Is No Institutional Fix for Politics." In John Calverley and Richard O'Brien eds. *Finance and the International Economy* (EDITORS?) (Oxford: Oxford University Press), 40–65; Kathleen McNamara. 2002. "Rational Fictions: Central Bank Independence and the Social Logic of Delegation." *West European Politics*. 22: 47–76; Paul Tucker. 2019. *Unelected Power: The Quest for Legitimacy in Central Banking and the Regulatory State.* (Princeton, NJ: Princeton University Press); Jerome E. Roos. 2019. *Why Not Default? The Political Economy of Sovereign Debt.* (Princeton, NJ: Princeton University Press); and Charles Calomiris and Stephen Haber. 2014. *Fragile by Design.* (Princeton, NJ: Princeton University Press).

7. Manuela Moschella. 2024. *Unexpected Revolutionaries: How Central Banks Made and Unmade Economic Orthodoxy.* (Ithaca, NY: Cornell University Press); Manuela Moschella, Lucia Quaglia, and Aneta Spendzharova. 2023. *European Political Economy: Theoretical Approaches and Policy Issues.* (New York: Oxford University Press).

8. Florence Dafe, Sandy Brian Hager, Natalya Naqvi, and Leon Wansleben. "The Structural Power of Finance Meets Financialization." *Politics and Society* 50 (2022): 523–542; Pepper Culpepper and Raphael Reinke. "Structural Power and the Bank Bailouts in the UK and US." *Politics and Society* 42 (2014): 427–454; Roos, *Why Not Default?*; Zsofia Barta. 2016. *In the Red: The Politics of Public Debt Accumulation in Developed Countries.* (Ann Arbor: University of Michigan Press).

9. Matthias Thiemann. 2024. *Taming the Cycles of Finance?* (New York: Cambridge University Press).

10. T.H. Marshall. 1977. "Citizenship and Social Class." In *Class, Citizenship, and Social Development*, ed. T H Marshall, 23–76. (Chicago: University of Chicago Press); Gosta Esping-Andersen, *The Three Worlds of Welfare Capitalism* (Princeton: Princeton University Press, 1989) Gosta Esping-Andersen and Roger Friedland, "Class Coalitions in the Making of West European Economies." *Political Power and Social Theory* (1982) 3: 1–52; Mark Wickham-Jones. 1995. "Anticipating Social Democracy, Preempting Anticipations: Economic Policy-Making in the British Labor Party 1987–1992." *Politics and Society* 23: 465–494.

11. Selwyn Cornish. 2010. *The Evolution of Central Banking in Australia.* (Sydney: Reserve Bank of Australia); Robin Golan. 1968. *The Commonwealth Bank of Australia: Origins and Early History.* (Canberra: Australian National University Press), 57, 95, 107; Jocelyn Pixley. 2018. *Central Banks, Democratic States, and Financial Power.* (Cambridge, UK: Cambridge University Press), 201.

12. Quoted in Cornish, *The Evolution of Central Banking in Australia.*

13. Leanne Cutcher and Caezilia Loibl. 2015. "Which Bank? Competition and Community Service Obligations in the Retail Banking Sector." In *Markets, Rights and Power in Australian Social Policy*, eds. Gabrielle Meagher, and Susan Goodwin (Sydney: Sydney University Press.), 169–190.

14. Chloe Thurston. 2018. *At the Boundaries of Homeownership: Credit, Discrimination and the American State.* (New York: Cambridge University Press); Mallory SoRelle. 2023. "Privatizing Financial Protection: Regulatory Feedback and the Politics of Financial Reform." *American Political Science Review* 117: 985–1003; Mallory SoRelle. 2020. *Democracy Declined: The Failed Politics of Consumer Financial Protection.* (Chicago: University of Chicago Press); Jamila Michener, Mallory SoRelle, and Chloe Thurston. 2022. "From the Margins to the Center: A Bottom-up Approach to Welfare State Scholarship." *Perspectives on Politics* 20 (2022): 154–149.

15. Emily Zackin and Chloe N. Thurston. 2024. *The Political Development of American Debt Relief.* (Chicago: University of Chicago Press).

16. Brian Libgober and Daniel Carpenter. 2024. "Lawyers as Lobbyists: Regulatory Advocacy in American Finance." *Perspectives on Politics*) (2024), vol 23 no 2: 1–20; Brian

Libgober. 2020. "Meetings, Comments, and the Distributive Politics of Rulemaking", *Quarterly Journal of Political Science.* 15: 449–481.

17. Mallory SoRelle. 2023. "Privatizing Financial Protection: Regulatory Feedback and the Politics of Financial Reform." *American Political Science Review* 117: 985–1003 and 2020 *Democracy Declined: The Failed Politics of Consumer Financial Protection.* (Chicago: University of Chicago Press).

18. J. Lawrence Broz. 1988. "The Origins of Central Banking: Solutions to the Free-Rider Problem." *International Organization* 52 (Spring): 231–268.

19. Christopher Adolph. 2013. *Bankers, Bureaucrats, and Central Bank Politics.* (New York: Cambridge University Press).

20. Agencies with responsibilities for financial regulation include the following: Securities and Exchange Commission, Commodity Futures Trading Commission, Office of the Comptroller of the Currency, Federal Trade Commission, Federal Deposit Insurance Corporation, National Credit Union Administration, and potentially fifty state regulators. Research on the deadening effects of the America's multiple and competing lines of authority includes Peter B. Evans, Dietrich Rueschemeyer, and Theda Skocpol, eds. 1985. *Bringing the State Back In.* (New York: Cambridge University Press); Chloe Thurston. "Racial Inequality, Market Inequality, and the American Political Economy" in *The American Political Economy: Politics, Markets, and Power*, eds. Jacob Hacker, Alexander Hertel-Fernandez, Paul Pierson, and Kathleen Thelen (New York: Cambridge University Press); Jacob Hacker, Alexander Hertel-Fernandez, Paul Pierson, and Kathleen Thelen. 2021. "Introduction: The American Political Economy: A Framework and Agenda for Research" in *The American Political Economy: Politics, Markets, and Power*, eds. Jacob Hacker, Alexander Hertel-Fernandez, Paul Pierson, and Kathleen Thelen. (New York: Cambridge University Press).

21. Brian Libgober and Daniel Carpenter. 2024. "Lawyers as Lobbyists: Regulatory Advocacy in American Finance." *Perspectives on Politics.* 1–20, and Brian Libgober. 2020. "Meetings, Comments, and the Distributive Politics of Rulemaking," *Quarterly Journal of Political Science* 15 (4): 449–481.

22. The interest and revenue that the Fed generates covers its expenses and those of the twelve regional banks as well as a dividend paid to the over 2900 private banks that are members of the Fed's twelve regional banks. This payout is legally guaranteed, often tax-free, and generally larger than the average dividend on the Stock Market's main index. This business model is sufficiently robust that the Fed generates a sizeable surplus—after distributing payouts to the banks—to the US Treasury. Lawrence Jacobs and Desmond King. 2021. *Fed Power: How Finance Wins.* 2nd Edition (New York, NY: Oxford University Press).

23. Jacobs and King *Fed Power.*

24. Richard Scott. 2001. *Institutions and Organizations* (Thousand Oaks, Sage); Colin Hay. 2004. "The Normalizing Role of Rationalist Assumptions in the Institutional Embedding of Neoliberalism." *Economy and Society* 33: 500–527.

25. Ann Swidler. 1986. "Culture in Action." *American Sociological Review* 51: 273–286; Michèle Lamont and Laurent Thévenot. 2000. "Introduction." In *Rethinking Comparative Cultural Sociology*, ed. Michèle Lamont and Laurent Thévenot. (Cambridge: Cambridge University Press), 4–22; Cathie Jo Martin, Dennie Oude Nijhuis, and Erik Olsson. 2022. "Cultural Images of Labor Conflict and Coordination Literature and the Evolution of Industrial Relations Systems." *European Journal of Sociology.* 62 (3): 45–66.

26. Martin, Nijhuis and Olsson. 2022. "Cultural Images."

27. James Kwak. 2014. "Cultural Capture and the Financial Crisis," in *Preventing Regulatory Capture*, ed. Daniel Carpenter and David Moss (New York: Cambridge University Press), 71–98; Simon Johnson and James Kwak. 2010. *13 Bankers: The Wall Street Takeover and the Next Financial Meltdown.* (New York: Pantheon Books).

28. Quoted in Joe Becker and Gretchen Morgenson. 2009. "Geithner, Member and Overseer of Finance Club." *New York Times*. April 26.
29. T.H. Marshall. 1977. "Citizenship and Social Class."
30. Piketty, Saez, Zucman. 2016; Thomas Piketty. 2013. *Capital in the Twenty-First Century* (Cambridge: Harvard University Press); Jamila Michener. 2019. "Policy Feedback in a Racialized Polity." *Policy Studies Journal* 47: 423–450.
31. Peter Dietsch, Francois Claveau, and Clement Fontan. 2018. *Do Central Banks Serve the People?* (Cambridge, UK: Polity); Alexander Reisenbichler. 2020. "The Politics of Quantitative Easing and Housing Stimulus by the Federal Reserve and European Central Bank, 2008–2018." *West European Politics* 43: 464–484; Jens van't Klooster. 2019. "Central Banking in Rawls's Property-Owning Democracy." *Political Theory* 47: 674–698; Jacobs and King. 2021. *Fed Power.*
32. Andreas Wiedemann. 2021. *Indebted Societies: Credit and Welfare in Rich Democracies.* (New York: Cambridge University Press); Michael Dawson and Megan Ming Francis. 2015. "Black Politics and the Neoliberal Racial Order." *Public Culture* 28: 23–62; Devin Fergus. 2018. *Land of the Fee.* (New York: Oxford University Press).
33. Kathleen Thelen. 2019. "Transitions to the Knowledge Economy in Germany, Sweden and the Netherlands." *Comparative Politics* 51 (2): 295–315; Enwald Engelen, Martijn Konings, and Rodrigo Fernandez. 2008. "The Rise of Activist Investors and Patterns of Political Responses." *Socio-Economic Review.* 6 (4): 611–636.
34. Michael McCarthy. 2017. *Dismantling Solidarity: Capitalism Politics and American Pensions since the New Deal* (Ithaca, NY: Cornell University Press).
35. Gosta Esping-Andersen. 1990. *The Three Worlds of Welfare.* (Princeton: Princeton University Press); Jacob Hacker, Alexander Hertel-Fernandez, Paul Pierson, and Kathleen Thelen, eds. 2021. *The American Political Economy: Politics, Markets, and Power.* (New York: Cambridge University Press); Peter Hall and David Soskice, eds. 2001. *Varieties of Capitalism.* (Oxford: Oxford University Press).
36. T.H. Marshall. 1977. "Citizenship and Social Class," p.68.
37. Robert Hockett and Saule Omarova. "The Finance Franchise." 2017. *Cornell Law Review.* 102: 1143–1218.
38. Andreas Wiedemann. 2021. *Indebted Societies: Credit and Welfare in Rich Democracies.* (New York: Cambridge University Press).
39. Emily Zackin and Chloe N. Thurston. 2024. *The Political Development of American Debt Relief.*
40. Leanne Cutcher and Johann Loibl. 2015. "Which Bank? Competition and community service obligation in the retail banking sector." *Markets, Rights and Power in Australian Social Policy* vol 1 (1): 169–191.
41. Cutcher and Loibl. 2015. "Which Bank?"
42. Marshall. 1977. "Citizenship and Social Class," p.56.
43. Greta Krippner. 2011. *Capitalizing the Crisis: The Political Origins of the Rise of Finance.* (Cambridge: Harvard University Press).
44. Edmund Andrews. 2008. "Greenspan Concedes Error on Regulation." *New York Times,* 23 October, 2008; Financial Crisis Inquiry Commission (FCIC). 2011. *Final Report of the National Commission of the Causes of the Financial and Economic Crisis in the United States.* Washington, DC: Government Printing Office, pp. xviii, 23, 28, 35.
45. Esping-Andersen. 1990. *The Three Worlds of Welfare*; SoRelle. 2023. "Privatizing Financial Protection" and 2020. *Democracy Declined*; Gary Gerstle. 2022. *The Rise and Fall of the Neoliberal Order* (New York: Oxford University Press).
46. Stephen Bell and Andrew Hindmoor. 2019. "Avoiding the Global Financial Crisis in Australia." In *Successful Public Policy* ed. Joannah Luetjens, Michael Mintrom, and Paul Hart. (Canberra: Australian National Press); Selwyn Cornish. 2010. *The Evolution of Central Banking in Australia.*
47. Quoted in Bell and Hindmoor. 2019. "Avoiding the Global Financial Crisis in Australia."

48. John Laker quoted in Bell and Hindmoor. 2019. "Avoiding the Global Financial Crisis in Australia."

49. Bell and Hindmoor. 2019. "Avoiding the Global Financial Crisis in Australia"; Cornish. 2010. *The Evolution of Central Banking in Australia.*

50. Colin Hay. 2004. "The Normalizing Role of Rationalist Assumptions in the Institutional Embedding of Neoliberalism." *Economy and Society* 33 (November): 500–527.

51. Upmanyu Trivedi. "UK FCA Doubles Down on Naming Financial Firms Under Probes." *Bloomberg News.* 26 April, 2024; Laura Noonan. "UK Spending Watchdog Slams Delays at FCA." *Financial Times.* 7 December, 2023; Kalyeena Makortoff. "National Audit Office Launches Review of Financial Regulator's Effectiveness." *Guardian.* 16 July, 2023.

52. Marshall. 1977. "Citizenship and Social Class," p. 47.

53. Alexander Reisenbichler. 2020. "The Politics of Quantitative Easing and Housing Stimulus by the Federal Reserve and European Central Bank, 2008–2018." *West European Politics* 43: 464–484.

54. Juan Montecino and Gerald Epstein. 2014. "Have Large-Scale Asset Purchases Increased Bank Profits?" Political Economy Research Institute: Working Paper No. 5, #372. December; Thomas Piketty, Emmanuel Saez, and Gabriel Zucman. 2016. "Distributional Account: Methods and Estimates for the United States." National Bureau of Economic Research, Working Paper 22945. https://www.nber.org/system/files/working_papers/w22945/w22945.pdf.

55. Jacob Rugh, Len Albright, and Douglas S Massey. 2015. "Race, Space, and Cumulative Disadvantage: A Case Study of the Subprime Lending Collapse." *Social Problems* 62: 186–218; Douglas Massey, Jacob S Rugh, Justin P Steil and Len Albright. 2016. "Riding the Stagecoach to Hell: A Qualitative Analysis of Racial Discrimination in Mortgage Lending." *City and Community* 15: 118–136; Chloe Thurston. 2021. "Racial Inequality, Market Inequality, and the American Political Economy"; Rogers M. Smith and Desmond King. 2024. *America's New Racial Battle Lines: Protect versus Repair* (Chicago: University of Chicago Press).

56. The Fed earns sums of money from operating on Wall Street by collecting interest on its investments and the revenue from buying and selling them. Jacobs and King. 2021. *Fed Power: How Finance Wins.*

57. Benjamin Braun. 2020. "Central Banking and the Infrastructural Power of Finance: The Case of ECB Support for Repo and Securitization Markets." *Socio-Economic Review.* 18: 395–418.

58. Proposals for "economic democracy" in Sweden were further side-lined by SAP's limited 1983 reforms and its electoral defeats in 1976 and 1991; see Kathleen Thelen. 2020. "Transitions to the Knowledge Economy in Germany, Sweden, and the Netherlands." *Comparative Politics.* 51 (January): 295–315; Jonas Pontusson. 1994. *The Limits of Social Democracy: Investment Politics in Sweden.* (Ithaca, NY: Cornell University Press).

59. Olivier Blanchard, Tweet, 12/6/18. Blanchard has been the normally cautious former chief economist of the International Monetary Fund. https://twitter.com/ojblanchard1/status/1070776221741580288.

60. Martin Wolf. 2018. "We Must Rethink the Purpose of the Corporation." *Financial Times.* 11 December, 2018; Martin Wolf. 2023. *The Crisis of Democratic Capitalism* (New York: Penguin Press).

2

Building a Nation of Investors

Chloe Thurston

1. Introduction

In 2021, Americans' home values grew by 30 percent, while older citizens saw their 401(k) balances increase by an average of 20 percent, and younger individuals by 33 percent. During the same period, incomes rose by 11 percent.[1] While the year 2021 may have been notable for the stark divergence between wage growth and asset growth, it also reflected a longer-term shift in the significance of assets for many American households' economic well-being. This shift correlates with what scholars have described as the transition in the American political economy from the New Deal to a neoliberal order, wherein a political economy characterized by wage-led consumption, Keynesian demand management, and welfare state protections was replaced by the 1980s with one marked by attacks on organized labor, welfare state restructuring, and an embrace of the disciplining power of markets across seemingly all domains.[2] The New Deal order in the United States also encompassed a set of normative ideas about the linkages between citizens and the political economy, which the historian Lizabeth Cohen terms "a consumers' republic."[3]

As this chapter argues, as the New Deal settlements gave way to a neoliberal order, policymakers, economic elites, and many citizens continued to recognize the importance of consumption to the US growth model. However, the beliefs that underpinned the "consumers' republic" were

---

[1] Jessica Dickler, "Home Prices Are Now Rising Faster Than Incomes, Studies Show." *CNBC.* 10 November, 2021, at https://www.cnbc.com/2021/11/10/home-prices-are-now-rising-much-faster-than-incomes-studies-show.html.

[2] Out of these observations have come a host of efforts to pin down just what has changed in the American political economy since the 1970s: a "great risk shift," the rise of a "rentier economy," the transformation of "asset manager capitalism," and of course financialization.

[3] Lizabeth Cohen. *A Consumers' Republic: The Politics of Mass Consumption in Postwar America* (Cambridge, MA: Harvard University Press, 2004).

Chloe Thurston, *Building a Nation of Investors*. In: *Picking Winners*. Edited by: Lawrence R. Jacobs and Desmond King, Oxford University Press. © Oxford University Press (2026).
DOI: 10.1093/9780197831823.003.0002

transformed—in an environment now characterized by stagnating wages—to embrace the belief that mass participation in financial markets and asset building could fulfill the goals of full economic, social, and political citizenship. Policymakers hoped that by promoting asset building, citizens would find a non-labor path into the wealth stream, thereby reducing the demand for public provision and alleviating the burdens on the federal budget. This approach might even spark widespread acceptance of more market-friendly policies, regardless of one's partisan orientation. Furthermore, policymakers associated this investor republic with broader social goals of opportunity and inclusion. Similar to the postwar vision of consumer citizenship, policies, institutions, private sector practices, and cultural norms evolved together, although never completely coherently and never fully achieving their aspirations.

The place of investment in middle-class prosperity—especially as a potential remedy for wage stagnation—varied significantly in its impact across different countries facing similar challenges during that period. All rich democracies faced pressures to liberalize, but not all neoliberal reforms depended on unlocking mass investment, and not all welfare states had features suitable for the types of reforms seen in the United States. Instead, these were tied to specific policy and regulatory changes, new political commitments from both sides of the aisle, and evolving cultural norms regarding the use of homes as investments and participation in the stock market. These developments build on longer traditions in the American political economy, some established before the New Deal and others following its implementation.

This chapter is organized as follows. Section 2 describes the features of the New Deal order as it developed in the 1930s, leading to its unraveling—a period beginning in roughly the late 1960s and culminating in the election of Reagan. It argues that this transformation involved a shift from wage-oriented consumption toward investment and asset accumulation as the key link between citizens' new political-economic commitments and national growth objectives. Section 3 then examines how an investment-oriented view of citizenship supplanted a wage-oriented view of consumer citizenship, particularly the specific ways it took shape institutionally and culturally. Despite their differing agendas and aims, both political parties ultimately endorsed aspects of an investment based idea of social citizenship by the late 1990s and early 2000s. Section 4 discusses broader and current implications of this shift: the significant role played by financial regulators, particularly the Federal Reserve; the new divisions that have emerged in an investment-oriented society, including both insiders and outsiders, as well as among differently situated insiders; and the ongoing questions regarding whether the shift toward investment actually achieved any of its anticipated outcomes. As the conclusion (Section 5) argues, recent debates as to whether the US economy is "beyond neoliberalism" and in some as-of-yet-unspecified new economic order must continue to contend with questions of how citizenship norms are connected to political economies, and how earlier legacies continue to shape future developments.[4]

2. Political Orders, American Political Development, and the Consumers' Republic

Political orders are foundational to the study of American political development.[5] Broadly defined as "constellations of rules, institutions, practices, and ideas than hang together over time," as well as alliances of actors that mobilize in defense of or opposition to these constellations, orders have proven useful for their ability to describe a political environment constituted by multiple, competing, and sometimes contradictory institutional logics—forged at different points in time and with different purposes—to draw attention to the existence of these multiple competing arrangements,

[4] See, for example, Larry Kramer, "Beyond Neoliberalism: Rethinking Political Economy," 26 April, 2018, at https://hewlett.org/library/beyond-neoliberalism-rethinking-political-economy/; See also, the Democracy Journal's symposium, Felicia Wong, "Overview: Post-Neoliberalism at a Crossroads," *Democracy Journal* 64 (Spring 2022) at https://democracyjournal.org/magazine/64/overview-post-neoliberalism-at-a-crossroads/.

[5] See for example Karen Orren and Stephen Skowronek, *The Search for American Political Development* (New York: Cambridge University Press, 2004); Karen Orren and Stephen Skowronek, "Pathways to the Present: Political Development in America," in *The Oxford Handbook of American Political Development*, eds. Richard Valelly, Suzanne Mettler, and Robert Lieberman (New York: Oxford University Press, 2016); Karen Orren and Stephen Skowronek, *The Policy State: An American Predicament* (Cambridge, MA: Harvard University Press, 2017); Eric Schickler, *Disjointed Pluralism: Institutional Innovation and the U.S. Congress* (Princeton, NJ: Princeton University Press, 2001); Paul Pierson and Theda Skocpol, "Historical Institutionalism in Contemporary Political Science," In *Political Science: The State of the Discipline*, eds. Ira Katznelson and Helen Milner (New York: W.W. Norton, 2002), 693–721.

Desmond King and Rogers Smith, "Racial Orders in American Political Development." *American Political Science Review* 99(1): (2005): 75–92; Desmond King and Robert Lieberman, "The American State," In *The Oxford Handbook of American Political Development*, eds. Richard Valelly, Suzanne Mettler, and Robert Lieberman (New York: Oxford University Press, 2016); Adam Sheingate, "Institutional Dynamics and American Political Development." *Annual Review of Political Science* 17 (2014): 461–477; George Thomas, "Political Thought and Political Development." *American Political Thought* 3(1): (2014): 114–125.

as well as for their ability to explain change as generated by these conflicts over governing authority.[6]

Orders provide a valuable framework for understanding the tremendous changes that transpired in the 20th-century American political economy. The 1930s witnessed a seismic shift in the scope of federal power and in the federal government's role in the economy, along with new supportive coalitions and legitimating ideologies.[7] This New Deal order was set in motion by the crisis of the Great Depression, spurred by the Democratic landslides in the 1932 elections, which ushered Franklin D. Roosevelt into the presidency; consolidated in the postwar decades, it began to unravel in the late 1960s and Carter era, and was finally repudiated by Reagan's election in 1980.

The New Deal order was characterized ideologically by the rejection of laissez-faire and a belief among Democratic economists and policymakers that government could and should play a role in smoothing business cycles, including through regulating banking and securities, making use of deficit spending to induce demand during downturns, and supporting organized labor as a counterbalance to corporate power and force in helping to distribute the fruits of the industrial economy more equitably. This "vernacular form of Keynesianism"[8] manifested institutionally in a massive expansion in federal power and the proliferation of new laws and regulatory agencies. In banking, the Glass-Steagall Act of 1933 separated investment from commercial banking and introduced depository insurance through the FDIC. Together, the Securities Act of 1933 and the Securities and Exchange Act of 1934 regulated the disclosure of securities information and helped to stabilize the stock market through the creation of the Securities and Exchange Commission. Meanwhile, newly created entities like the National Labor Relations Board (1935) helped to institutionalize class compromise in the workplace, strengthening labor's hand and ensuring a potentially fairer distribution of profits. The National Housing Act of 1934 created federal mortgage insurance through the FHA, popularizing the 30-year fixed-rate mortgage and making homeownership attainable to millions more households. Though nominally about housing, lawmakers at the time saw the FHA

[6] Orren and Skowronek, *The Search for American Political Development*, 19.

[7] Steve Fraser and Gary Gerstle, *The Rise and Fall of the New Deal Order, 1930–1980* (Princeton NJ: Princeton University Press, 1989); Gerstle, *The Rise and Fall of the Neoliberal Order*; Cohen, *A Consumer's Republic*.

[8] Gerstle, *The Rise and Fall of the Neoliberal Order*, 22–23.

as a way to stabilize construction employment through stabilizing home mortgage lending.[9]

This shift in governance thoroughly and durably reshaped the contours of postwar American politics and the scope of political conflicts. The expansion of state capacity and the adoption of new governing ideologies began as a partisan project led by a diverse Democratic coalition, capable of securing lasting electoral victories. Early attempts to roll back some of its key gains resulted in only partial successes; for instance, Congressional Republicans' efforts to reduce labor rights through Taft-Hartley (1947) during the Truman Administration. Ultimately, even Republican politicians of that era had to accommodate the changed ideology, expectations, and institutional landscape: the boundaries of what was considered acceptable to challenge had shifted. Eisenhower's presidency offers perhaps the best illustration of the dominance of the New Deal order. Failing to articulate an alternative, the president largely ceded to the presence of a strong central state in domestic affairs, including the use of government economic policy tools to mitigate the impact of business cycles, accepting the role of unions, the expansion of Social Security in both generosity and reach, and a regime of high marginal tax rates on the highest income earners.[10]

Consumption, Wages, and Citizenship in the New Deal Order

While much scholarship of the New Deal focuses on elite efforts to remake the economy, a related strand of scholarship examines how the New Deal order also constituted a remaking of social citizenship. In Lizabeth Cohen's rendering, the architects of the New Deal order (the nation's political, business, and labor leaders) sought to develop "a Consumers' Republic":

> [A] political economy and a political culture that expected a dynamic mass consumption economy not only to deliver prosperity, but also to fulfill American society's loftier aspirations: more social egalitarianism,

---

[9] Chloe Thurston, *At the Boundaries of Homeownership: Credit, Discrimination, and the American State* (New York: Cambridge University Press, 2018), Chapter 2.

[10] Gerstle, *The Rise and Fall of the Neoliberal Order*, 42–43. As Gerstle argues, geopolitics also played a major role in shaping this commitment to the New Deal order and (as Gerstle argues somewhat more controversially) may have helped to secure the business–labor compromise and basic social protections because of the threat of communism.

more democratic participation, and more political freedom. In their ideal America, a mass consumption-driven economy would provide jobs, purchasing power, and investment dollars, while also allowing Americans to live better than ever before, to participate in political decision-making on an equal footing with their similarly prospering neighbors, and to exercise their cherished freedoms by making independent choices in markets and politics.[11]

Many have observed the expectations that policymakers had regarding stimulating mass consumption through homeownership, increasing wages, and expanding retail credit, aiming to foster consistent economic growth and prosperity while reducing political conflict during this time period.[12] Mass consumption, driven by "mortgage Keynesianism," was seen as a path towards social peace and also a fundamental component of the United States' postwar growth model.[13]

A 1959 Department of Labor report titled "How American Buying Habits Change" summarized the transformation of the United States from a landscape characterized by tenements and scarcity at the beginning of the century. It marveled at the markedly increased standard of living and plethora of consumer goods available to the ordinary household:

> Within the worker's home in the mid-1950's was an abundance of modern equipment. Typically, there would be no less than electricity, running hot and cold water, at least one fully equipped bathroom, central heating, a vacuum cleaner, a washing machine, a telephone, a radio and a

---

[11] Cohen, *A Consumers' Republic*, Kindle loc 7319.

[12] Gerstle writes that "In their efforts to make possible (and to measure) the pursuit of personal fulfillment, New Dealers increasingly defined the good life in terms of the quantity and variety of consumer goods that citizens were able to purchase. This marketplace orientation entailed more than materialism, however. For one, it carried a strong egalitarian message: Participation in the marketplace was to be made available to all Americans regardless of class, race, gender, religion, or nationality." (Gerstle, *The Rise and Fall of the Neoliberal Order*, 26); Monica Prasad, *The Land of Too Much: American Abundance in an Age of Plenty* (Cambridge, MA: Harvard University Press, 2012); Sarah Quinn, *American Bonds: How Credit Markets Shaped a Nation* (Princeton, NJ: Princeton University Press, 2019); Alexander Reisenbichler, "Housing Finance Between Social Welfare and Growth Strategies," in Anke Hassle and Bruno Palier, eds., *Growth and Welfare in Advanced Capitalist Economies: How Have Growth Regimes Evolved?* (Oxford University Press, 2021); Gunnar Trumbull, *Consumer Lending in France and America: Credit and Welfare* (New York: Cambridge University Press, 2014); Louis Hyman, *Debtor Nation: The History of America in Red Ink* (Princeton, NJ: Princeton University Press, 2011); Meg Jacobs, *Pocketbook Politics: Economic Citizenship in Twentieth Century America* (Princeton, NJ: Princeton University Press, 2004).

[13] Reisenbichler, "Housing Finance Between Social Welfare and Growth Strategies"; Prasad, *Land of Too Much.*

television set, a gas or electric cooking stove, a refrigerator, and completely furnished rooms. In many instances the heating would be automatic and the kitchen would contain a dishwasher, a garbage disposal unit, and an exhaust fan. Electric air conditioners, blankets, fans, and mixers, and a multitude of other aids to housekeeping and home living, not excepting the power lawnmower, were within the range of the worker's family budget.[14]

The report was not blind to the role that consumer debt played in helping households to achieve a standard of living unimaginable a generation earlier. "Of course, the personal debt outstanding on the house and on much of what was in it, as well as on the automobile parked outside, might be considerable." The report mentioned. "But the chief breadwinner's income, with increasing frequency augmented by the earnings of a working wife, plus relatively cheap credit, carried the burden. In this respect, as in so many others, the worker's family differed little from many in higher income groups."[15]

In addition to the increased availability of credit, the report noted that a changed policy landscape had alleviated workers' fears of being unable to repay such debts. These changes included a system of unemployment insurance and state workers' compensation, workplace collective bargaining agreements with procedures for layoffs and work-sharing, as well as federal social security and disability insurance. In an environment with abundant jobs, workers' willingness to pursue new opportunities also contributed to making debt service more manageable.[16] Crucially, the expectation of employment stability and income growth transformed credit into a budgeting tool, enabling younger households to expect that they could repay these upfront goods over a period of years. Not only was credit at the time closely tied to wage expectations, it was also closely tied to the consumerist political economy: many manufacturing firms and retailers extended credit to their customers not because it was profitable in itself (credit was a loss-leader) but as a way to ensure healthy demand for durable goods.[17]

By the 1970s, numerous indicators suggested the fracturing of the New Deal order. The high costs of the Vietnam War and Great Society began to wear down the nation's fiscal health. The fall of Bretton Woods in 1971, the

---

[14] US Department of Labor, "How Americans Buying Habits Change," 1959, pp. 4–5.
[15] Ibid., pp. 4–5.
[16] Ibid., pp. 4–5, 33.
[17] Hyman, *Debtor Nation*; Trumbull, *Consumer Credit in France and America*.

OPEC oil shocks and energy shortages, wage and price controls under the presidency of Richard Nixon, stagflation during the Ford and Carter administrations, the overall climate of slow growth and declining productivity, and the long-term trend toward deindustrialization and increasing competition from abroad all placed enormous pressure on the system's ability to continue delivering promised prosperity and growth.[18] Stagnant wages and high inflation eroded the promise of rising prosperity and improved living standards, while credit controls left the government in an increasingly tenuous position between households and businesses.[19]

If the New Deal order's failure to meet new economic challenges was becoming apparent by the 1970s, its failures to achieve the loftier aspirations of a consumer's republic had been longer apparent.[20] Despite the hard-fought policy gains of civil rights reformers, the impact of the minority rights revolution on material opportunity remained frustratingly limited. The eruption of riots in cities across the United States over multiple summers highlighted the ongoing challenges. The Kerner Commission Report, tasked with looking into the contributors of continued unrest, identified inadequate housing, persistent racial discrimination, and limited employment opportunities. A rising feminist movement also highlighted the shortcomings of the New Deal model by contesting the male breadwinner assumptions embedded in social and economic policymaking that limited women's full economic citizenship.[21]

The Rise of the Neoliberal Order

These heightened economic, social, political, and distributional conflicts paved the way for the embrace of neoliberalizing reforms by the late 1960s, the ascent of the neoliberal order with Reagan's 1980 election, and its consolidation during the Clinton presidency as both parties came to embrace its core policy commitments.[22]

---

[18] See, for example, Cohen, *A Consumers' Republic*, chap. 8.

[19] Greta Krippner, *Capitalizing on Crisis: The Political Origins of the Rise of Finance* (Cambridge, MA: Harvard University Press, 2011); Quinn, *American Bonds*.

[20] Thurston, *At the Boundaries of Homeownership*; Robert Lieberman, *Shifting the Color Line: Race and the American Welfare State* (Cambridge, MA: Harvard University Press, 1998).

[21] Thurston, *At the Boundaries of Homeownership*; Hyman, *Debtor Nation*.

[22] Gerstle, *The Rise and Fall of the Neoliberal Order*, 1.

The transformation was characterized by several contrasts. While the New Deal order was ushered in by a new Democratic coalition that then enjoyed enduring electoral majorities for decades, the coalition that propelled neoliberalism into power was a Republican Party that began its transformation in the late 1960s as parties realigned around race. This coalition embraced the reduction of New Deal economic regulations during the Reagan era, and its economic policy commitments gained acceptance among Democratic leaders, including Clinton, by the 1990s. These included a shift in ideological orientation from an active government role in managing the economy through regulation, union bargaining, taxation, and transfers to a focus on low taxes and an aversion to budget deficits. This also involved loosening some regulations, alongside the development of new frameworks and mechanisms to encourage certain behaviors, as well as scaling back earlier commitments to the welfare state and social policies, all in an effort to reduce budget deficits and promote "personal responsibility."[23] It also involved presidential efforts to increase homeownership (especially for low-income and minority citizens) during both the Clinton and second Bush administrations, including through "tax credits, down payment assistance, vouchers, financial education, regulatory reforms, and pressure on the private sector."[24] Looking beyond housing, the Bush administration heavily promoted college and health savings and retirement accounts, along with support for small businesses.

With these shifts in policy targets came a change in the key policy actors and tools. The Federal Reserve, led by Alan Greenspan from 1987 to 2006, adopted an implicit policy of responding to stock market downturns by lowering short-term interest rate targets to stave off "credit and liquidity problems in the broader financial markets."[25] Known as the "Greenspan Put" after the chair's responses to the October 1987 stock crash and 1998 long-term capital management crisis, it had by 2001 become widely recognized as part of the conventional toolkit, as a *Financial Times* article confirmed: "it's official: there is a Greenspan Put option."[26] Although not

[23] Steven Vogel, *Freer Markets, More Rules: Regulatory Reform in Advanced Industrial Countries* (Ithaca, NY: Cornell University Press, 1998); Steven Vogel, *Marketcraft: How Governments Make Markets Work* (New York: Oxford University Press, 2018).

[24] Marc Goldwein, "The End of the Ownership Society," https://www.hnn.us/article/the-end-of-the-ownership-society.

[25] John Mullin, "The Fed, the Stock Market, and the 'Greenspan Put.'" Federal Reserve Bank of Richmond, Econ Focus, First Quarter 2023, at https://www.richmondfed.org/publications/research/econ_focus/2023/q1_federal_reserve.

[26] Ibid.

officially recognized, scholars have found evidence that market participants were justified in treating the Greenspan Put as policy. FOMC minutes and transcripts indicate a shift since the mid-1990s in discussions about stock market conditions that were "more frequently cast in the context of consumption, with the consumption-wealth effect highlighted as one of the main channels through which the stock market affects the economy."[27]

The Rise of an Investment-Oriented Political Culture

The New Deal order bolstered and depended on a mass consumerist political culture, serving both as the foundation of the US growth model and in the pursuit of more philosophical aims such as democratic participation, freedom, and egalitarianism.[28] In an Investors' Republic, ideally, citizens would be asset holders in a new financialized global economy, offering them a non-labor path to participate in the "wealth stream" generated by an economy rapidly transitioning from industrial production to a nontangible, service-oriented knowledge economy.[29] Having a hand in this new wealth stream could create new demands for economic stability and increase citizens' stake in the shift towards a market-friendly form of governance. In his second inaugural address, President George W. Bush articulated this vision:

> In America's ideal of freedom, citizens find the dignity and security of economic independence. . . .To give every American a stake in the promise and future of our country we will. . .build an ownership society. We will widen the ownership of homes and businesses, retirement savings and health insurance – preparing our people for the challenges of life in a free society. By making every citizen an agent of his or her own destiny, we will give our fellow Americans greater freedom from want and fear, and make our society more prosperous and just and equal.

While on his road tour promoting his proposal to let citizens invest a portion of their Social Security contributions, Bush echoed some of these ideas, honing in on the stakeholder dimension: "At the same time that you manage

---

[27] Anna Cieslak and Annette Vissing-Joergenson, "The Economics of the Fed Put." NBER Working Paper No. w26894, June 2023, at https://papers.ssrn.com/sol3/papers.cfm?abstract_id=3563962.

[28] Cohen, A Consumers' Republic, Kindle loc 7319.

[29] Torben Iversen and David Soskice, Democracy and Prosperity: Reinventing Capitalism Through a Turbulent Century (Princeton, NJ: Princeton University Press, 2019).

your own account, you own your own account. I love promoting ownership in America.... Promoting ownership in America makes sense to me to make sure people continue to have a vital stake in the future of our country."[30] Bush and other Republican supporters may have hoped that having this kind of stake would also translate into electoral support for the Republican Party, or at the very least foster more commitment to market principles. Additionally, the ability to invest could be seen as a salve or compromise—as jobs became less secure, unions came under attack, regular pay increases became less certain, and policymakers sought to move away from social policy. Expanding ownership of assets that could serve as financial resources offered people an entry into sectors of the economy that could generate wealth for them.

Finally, in the wake of political assaults on earlier civil rights advances, advocates from both the left and the right sought to link policies that promote investment to a broader initiative for including racial minorities, many of whom have long been denied access to essential avenues of economic mobility and stability promised by the 'consumer's republic.' There was a strong foundation for policies aimed at aiding homeownership—the Black-white homeownership gap had improved only slightly since the 1950s and has remained persistent in the decades following the Fair Housing Act, contributing to widening intergenerational wealth gaps. By the mid-1960s, raising the homeownership rate among Black Americans, in particular, was viewed by proponents on both sides as crucial to addressing ongoing material racial inequality, as well as the perceived failures of government social spending in achieving the same goals by the 1970s. For the private providers engaged in the effort, low-income and minority Americans also represented a significant untapped market opportunity.[31] Occasionally, the goal of linking investment and inclusion reached disturbing conclusions. As he tried to sell citizens on a plan to partially privatize Social Security in 2005, George W. Bush touted the proposal's particular benefits for Black men, by emphasizing that their shorter life expectancies relative to their white counterparts meant they could expect to draw from traditional Social Security for a shorter duration.[32] Still, politicians came to view the promotion of investment as a way to promote the economic advancement of minority groups.

[30] "President Participates in Conversation on Social Security Reform," Washington, DC., January 11, 2005. https://georgewbush-whitehouse.archives.gov/news/releases/2005/01/text/20050111-4.html.

[31] Thurston, *At the Boundaries of Home Ownership*, chapter 6.

[32] As Bush said during a conversation on reform, "African American males die sooner than other males do and that means the system is inherently unfair to a certain group of people." See "President Participates in Conversation on Social Security Reform," Washington, DC., January 11, 2005.

3. Open for Investment: Institutional and Cultural
Repurposing of the Consumers Republic

In short, the transformation away from New Deal commitments and the embrace of neoliberalism entailed not only a shift in economic policy but also a reorientation of ideas about proper citizenship—how citizens should behave, what they should aspire to in order to help fuel the economy.[33] This reorientation was not inevitable. There are many ways that citizens can become linked to a political economy and ways that these linkages can transform in response to major shifts in economic and political governance. All industrialized democracies faced challenges during this period and yet not all governments took on a project to encourage citizens to become homeowners or investors.[34] Moreover, two of the main vehicles through which citizens became "investors"—their houses and their retirement accounts— were heavily regulated throughout the New Deal period, only beginning to liberalize in the late 1960s and 1970s.

The ability to tap into housing wealth and the expansion of citizen participation in financial markets were dependent upon legal and regulatory developments in the 1970s and 1980s, which in turn encouraged a shift in marketing practices as well.[35] Part of what made promoting mass investment seem natural in the United States was that there were already institutions in place to achieve this goal, along with a growing, often racialized, disdain for direct government social policies among many voters. Rather than building new institutions wholesale, policymakers repurposed existing institutions that already were imbued with significant cultural meaning and whose attainment helped to signify belonging and full social and economic citizenship—homeownership, employer pensions, higher education, and developed credit markets—but whose links to government policy had always been somewhat submerged from public view.[36] In this way, the

[33] Others have recognized this as well. Adkins, Cooper, and Koonings similarly argue that the contemporary economy is "dominated by the logic of assets," in their rendering, meaning that future (speculative) value drives people's economic behavior, in contrast with an earlier period where behavior was driven by the logic of commodification and exchange value. While they also point to housing as being an important driver of this shift, they say less about the political and institutional rebuilding that it entailed, and how those in turn also shaped mass political culture. Lisa Adkins, Melinda Kooper, and Martijn Koonings, *The Asset Economy* (Hoboken, NJ: Wiley 2020), 12.

[34] On home ownership as a store of wealth versus a means to wealth, see Herman Mark Schwartz and Leonard Seabrooke, eds., *The Politics of Housing Booms and Busts* (New York: Springer, 2009).

[35] Neil Filgstein and Adam Goldstein, "The Emergence of a Finance Culture in American Households, 1989–2007," *Socio-Economic Review* 13 (3): (2015): 575–601.

[36] Suzanne Mettler, *The Submerged State: How Invisible Government Policies Undermine American Democracy* (Chicago: University of Chicago Press, 2011).

embrace of investment opportunities built on the normative citizenship model underlying the wage-oriented consumer's republic, not fully displacing it but creatively repurposing it to new ends. Conversion and layering involved not only new or shifting regulations and policies but also shifting the culture around asset building. Enabled by new policies and regulations on financial products and their marketing, lenders and financial institutions changed the way they talked about these new products. These changes were often well-received by citizens eager to capitalize on increasing house values and a booming stock market of the mid-1990s.[37] Finally, though leaders of both political parties may have had distinctive motives and parties' specific programs may have varied to a great degree, there emerged by the mid-1990s a basic consensus around the idea of ownership and asset building through expanded participation in financial markets as described below.

The Institutional Repurposing of Housing

"When it comes to owning a home, few people in the world pursue the dream with as much vigor, desire or penny-pinching thrift as Americans," a *New York Times* article in 1988 marveled. What made this notable was not the rate of homeownership, which stood steady at 64 percent of households, but rather, why Americans were flocking to it.[38] The article continued: "No single reason adequately explains why so many people pursue this goal, but today, probably more than ever before, the essential motivation is an economic one: The housing they live in has become, for most households, a solid investment. Today's buyers are pursuing that goal with the avidity of Wall Street arbitragers, and their houses have become not so much good places to raise families—although that is still important—as the bases from which to raise fortunes."[39]

While widespread homeownership had been a bedrock of postwar American society (and its exclusions a signal of this project's failures), the idea that one's house could be tapped as a source of wealth—and particularly, that this was a source that people actually should seek to tap—was relatively new. As Marc Weiss has pointed out, from the earliest efforts in home installment

[37] Louise Story, "How U.S. Banks Sold Home Equity Loans," *New York Times*, August 15, 2008.

[38] Anthony Depalma, "Why Owning a Home Is the American Dream," *New York Times*, September 11, 1988.

[39] Ibid.

lending in the late 1800s, to its standardization and proliferation during the postwar period, the aim of financial innovation in the mortgage market was generally to enable people to one day pay off their houses and own them outright, not to stretch the repayment indefinitely by continually extracting the equity built up.[40] Second mortgages (and even third and fourth) were in high use in the early twentieth century as a way to help people manage the gap between what they needed to pay for a down payment and what they actually could pay. These loans were extended at usurious rates and lenders engaged in this business considered irreputable. They also posed a source of financial risk to borrowers and lenders and, as the Great Depression showed, generated systemic risk.[41] Indeed, the most vocal proponent of increased federal intervention in the mortgage industry (and the architects of FHA mortgage insurance) was the National Association of Real Estate Boards, who had for at least a decade pushed for an alternative to the need to take out second and third mortgages.

There is a brief prehistory of the federal government's promotion of homeownership, seen in its boosterism in the Commerce Department under Hoover, which launched the Own Your Own Home campaign and housed the Better Homes for America movement, which served essentially as a government propaganda arm for several decades. But the important institutional transformation occurred during the Great Depression and New Deal: the creation of the Federal Home Loan Bank Board (1932) which would regulate buildings and loans, the introduction of government insurance for private mortgages through the Federal Housing Administration (1934) and the similar provisions of the GI Bill (1944), and the creation of a secondary market through the Federal National Mortgage Association, or Fannie Mae (1938). These helped to bring about widespread access to low-down-payment self-amortizing mortgages with fixed interest rates repaid over decades.[42] At the local level, zoning and land use policy would also contribute to the political dynamics of postwar housing policy and local politics, as would the introduction of the Interstate Highway System (1956).[43]

---

[40] Marc A. Weiss, "Marketing and Financing Home Ownership: Mortgage Lending and Public Policy in the United States, 1918–1989." *Business and Economic History* 18, no. 2 (1989) 109-118.

[41] Ibid.

[42] Thurston, *At the Boundaries of Homeownership,* Chap 2; Kenneth T. Jackson, *Crabgrass Frontier: The Suburbanization of the United States* (New York: Oxford University Press, 1985).

[43] Jessica Trounstine, *Segregation by Design: Local Politics and Inequality in American Cities* (New York: Cambridge University Press, 2018).

An ideology of homeownership grew alongside the proliferation of home-owners. Whether the state was hidden from view or simply suppressed from people's attention, and despite substantial government involvement in promoting affordable homeownership, it became a symbol of rugged individualism, thrift, and individual achievement. The democratization of mortgage access also generated anxieties for the tens of millions of middle-class homeowners who now had a large long-term obligation, amplifying preexisting practices and patterns of race and class exclusion in largely white suburbs as a way to protect one's "investment."[44] Calls for the removal of ear-lier racial and class barriers—partially met by the Fair Housing Act (1968) and several new lower-income homeownership programs of the 1960s and early 1970s—were also based on the desirability of ownership and invest-ment. Yet the idea of housing as an investment had an underlying dimension of ownership and stability—price stability, with modest rises over time, con-tributing to stable communities—rather than as a speculative asset with large gains in value, into whose wealth one could tap.

Mounting social, economic, and fiscal pressures lead to some of the earli-est shifts towards financialization and away from government having a more direct (yet still indirect) role in housing markets. For decades the mortgage finance system operated as a "special circuit," segmented from other finan-cial markets and not especially profitable, though stable. As with many forms of credit in the early postwar, it served a marketing and budgeting function, allowing people to stretch the payment for an expensive good over decades, making it accessible. The aim was to make it possible to eventually own the house outright while minimizing risk and providing some degree of pre-dictable profit to the lender. Beginning in the 1960s but picking up in the 1970s and 1980s, the mortgage market became more integrated with global financial markets.[45]

These changes did not, on their own, transform housing into an invest-ment asset. On the consumer side, these new affordability tools were still aimed at helping citizens own an asset they could eventually pay off fully. Nor did they render housing liquid for consumers. Even if a homeowner was fortunate enough to see the price of their house increase, it was technically challenging and culturally difficult to tap into that wealth. Second-mortgage

---

[44] David M.P. Freund, *Colored Property: State Policy & White Racial Politics in Suburban America* (Chicago: University of Chicago Press, 2007).
[45] Douglas B. Diamond, Jr., and Michael J. Lea. "The Decline of Special Circuits in Developed Country Housing Finance." *Housing Policy Debate* 3 (3): (1992): 747–777.

lending was also restricted, generally only available through private loan companies or non-bank institutions, and it was considered a last resort after having been vanquished by New Deal mortgage market innovations.

Changes to federal laws in 1980 opened the door for mainstream banks to offer second loans to their customers. Customers soon discovered they could borrow against the increasing value of their homes, a practice that gained even more popularity after the passage of the Tax Reform Act of 1986, which eliminated the deductibility for all non-mortgage debt while retaining the deduction for home mortgage interest.[46] Suddenly, it became relatively more appealing from a tax perspective to use one's home as collateral for credit. Housing also provided more attractive interest rates than other forms of credit, further supporting the increased use of equity. Throughout the 1990s and into the 2000s, regulations shifted to permit banks to offer interest-only, adjustable-rate mortgages; piggyback mortgages; and other novel features.

In summary, the shift toward viewing houses as investment assets (a means to wealth rather than merely a store of wealth) was built upon a stable foundation of postwar homeownership and suburbanization, where jurisdictional control of resources and competition for residents and tax dollars could be leveraged to increase housing prices. However, this shift required new policies and regulatory changes to realign housing financial tools in ways that would enable individuals to continually draw from their equity, which accrued not only through paying down the loan but also due to rising house values.

The Cultural Repurposing of Homeownership into Home Equity

It was not just that institutional changes to activate investment built on already existing *institutions*. The appeal of tapping into home equity also shifted within popular culture. Regulatory changes, evolving marketing practices, and consumer enthusiasm all contributed to the new acceptance of products that were, for various reasons, previously unthinkable. Recall that one of the aims of the New Deal home lending regulations and programs was to reduce citizens' reliance on second mortgages. These regulations made it more challenging for mainstream lenders to offer such products, which were

[46] Glenn Canner, Thomas Durkin, and Charles Luckett, "Recent Developments in Home Equity Lending," *Federal Reserve Bulletin* April 1998, 242.

generally unnecessary in a new context where households need only take on a single loan with a low down payment, repayable over decades, and also carried a stigma. As a result, throughout the 1970s, second mortgages were stigmatized and viewed as a last resort option.

As second mortgages by mainstream lenders became legalized beginning in 1980, they also experienced a rebranding: They became home equity loans. A *New York Times* article in 2008 described the transformation: "Marketing executives knew that 'second mortgage' had an unappealing ring. So they seized on the idea of 'home equity,' with connotations of ownership and fairness."[47] Helping along this new view of lending was the banking industry, whose new advertising campaigns beginning in the 1980s touted the benefits of borrowing against a home's equity. "Now, when the value of your home goes up, you can take credit for it," a Citibank ad from the mid-1980s proclaimed. In advertisements, homes were now likened to credit cards.[48]

By the 2000s citizens were inundated with advertisements for home equity products. From 1999 to 2006, Citibank launched a $1 billion, award-winning "Live Richly" ad campaign. "There's got to be at least $25,000 hidden in your house."—read one of their ads, "We can help you find it."[49] A Fleet Bank ad from 2002 read: "The Smartest Place to Borrow? Your Place."[50] A 2006 PNC ad promised home equity products as the "easiest way to haul money out of your house."[51] As a marketing executive for one of the banks explained to the *Times*, "The second mortgage category, then as probably now, suffered from a pretty bad reputation. . . . It generally tended to be a credit facility of last resort, and it was done by people in dire straits. That was not the audience we were after."[52]

The use of these products rose, too. In 1977, 5 percent of homeowners held home equity debt. This grew to 13 percent in 1993–1994, just a few years after the tax reforms.[53] By 2010, 25 percent of owner-occupied houses had a second mortgage, falling to 12 percent by 2021.[54] Home equity products

[47] Story, "How U.S. Banks Sold Home Equity Loans."
[48] Ibid.
[49] Ibid.
[50] Ibid.
[51] Ibid.
[52] Ibid.
[53] Glenn Canner, Thomas Durkin, and Charles Luckett, "Recent Developments in Home Equity Lending," *Federal Reserve Bulletin* April 1998, 242,
[54] Andrew De Pietro, "How Many Homes Have a Second Mortgage in the US?" *Forbes* July 31, 2023 at https://www.forbes.com/sites/andrewdepietro/2023/07/31/how-many-homes-have-a-second-mortgage-in-the-us/?sh=445957ba7fba Census.

turned out to be big business, yielding returns of 25 to 50 percent over consumer loans by 2008.[55] Home equity loans outstanding rose to a peak of almost $650 billion in 2009 [Figure 2.1]. Ideas about debt also shifted within the financial industry, yet many continued to view houses as fundamentally safe; house prices typically rose, and homeowners were unlikely to overextend themselves if their actual homes were at stake. In summary, the banking industry contributed to the evolution of debt culture, though it could not achieve this alone. It was influenced by the culture of homeownership, regulatory changes, and the gradual shift in priorities over time from wage-oriented consumption to investment.

The Institutional Repurposing of Financial Market Participation

Participation in financial markets also transformed. In 2005, Bush marveled at the evolving language, culture, and mindset surrounding investment that he observed at the time—and he hoped it would continue:

> I like a guy who says, my grandkids are capable of owning and managing something. It's a different mind-set. The 401(k)s, for example, have changed the attitude toward investment, hasn't it? I mean, a 401(k), when you were coming up, Leo, was just three numbers and a letter in the alphabet. [Laughter]. And now it's an idea, where people manage their own retirement, and they own something, they see it, it's visible. It's an important part of our society today and it seems like to me, as we modernize the system of Social Security, we incorporate a portion of that new system into the concept of somebody owning something.[56]

The shift toward promoting individual participation in financial markets was new, but built on a New Deal–era infrastructure. To some extent the rise of investor citizenship had been set in motion even earlier in the twentieth century, first with the World War I bond drives and War Savings Programs which instructed Americans to "invest in victory," and then the rise of a "New Proprietorship" ideology after the war which stressed the idea that democratizing ownership of stocks would give more Americans

---

[55] Story, "How U.S. Banks Sold Home Equity Loans."
[56] President Discusses Strengthening Social Security in Montana, Montana ExpoPark, Great Falls, MT, February 3, 2005.

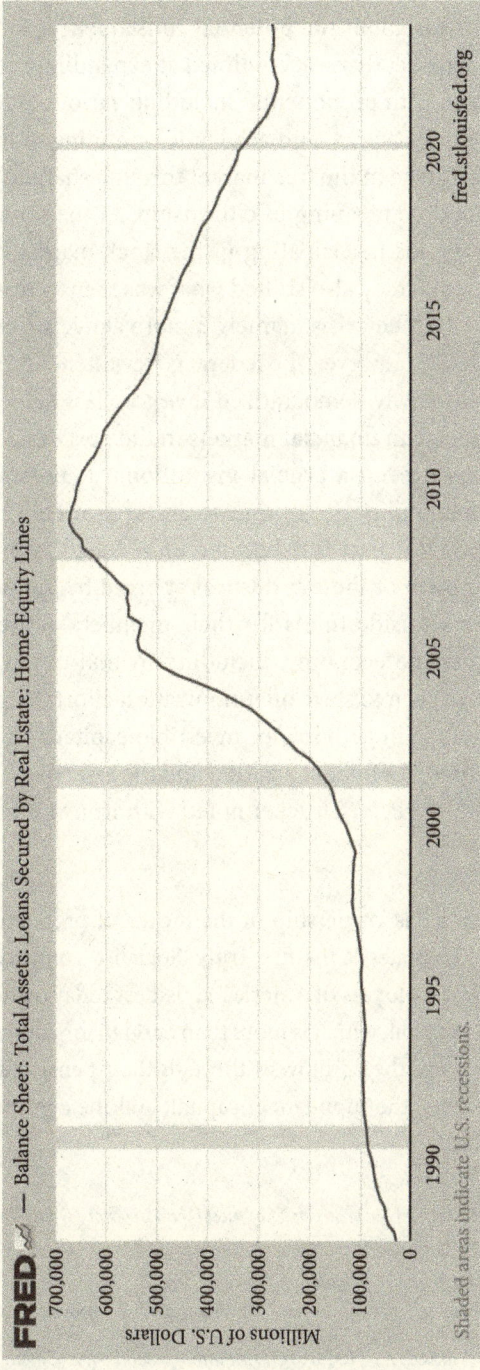

Figure 2.1 Total Value of Loans Secured by Real Estate (Home Equity), Not Seasonally Adjusted

a stake in the free market.[57] The first mutual fund was introduced in 1924. As Julia Ott shows, ideas about the potential consequences for citizenship and democracy animated early projects aimed at expanding citizens' access to investment markets, with proponents (including various federal government, financial, corporate actors, and academic), pointing to the virtues of giving more citizens a stake in the free market through shareholder democracy and transforming the meaning of citizenship. At the same time, with one quarter of households participating in the stock market by 1929, the rise of shareholder democracy also shifted what was seen as reasonable and appropriate responses to the crisis, namely a more active government role in securities regulation.[58] However, the federal government's responsiveness to the demands of this newly democratized investor class helped limit how citizens might participate in financial markets in the postwar decades.

Employer pensions proved a crucial institutional foundation for converting a wage-oriented political economy to an asset-oriented one. These, too, had a pre–New Deal past but became entrenched with the rise of labor. Initially, the growth of these funds was spurred by unions' demands that their employers set aside funds for their members' retirements. The practice spread across the economy, including in non-union workplaces whose employers were keen to stave off unionization efforts by offering new benefits. This generated "huge pools of investible capital,"[59] which would ultimately fuel the growth of financialization and the asset manager sector.[60]

Management professor Peter Drucker noted with irony in the mid-1970s that:

> If 'socialism' is defined as 'ownership of the means of production by the workers'. . .the United States is the first truly 'Socialist' country. Through their pension funds, employees of American business today own at least 25 percent of its equity capital, which is more than enough for control....Only in the United States are the employees through their pension funds also becoming legal owners, the suppliers of capital, and the controlling force in the capital market.[61]

---

[57] Julia Ott, *When Wall Street Met Main Street: The Quest for an Investor's Democracy* (Cambridge, MA: Harvard University Press).

[58] Ibid.

[59] Gerstle, *The Rise and Fall of the Neoliberal Order,* 174–175

[60] Benjamin Braun, "Fueling Financialization: The Economic Consequences of Funded Pensions." *New Labor Forum* 31(1): (2022): 70–79.

[61] Drucker, quoted in Michael A. McCarthy, *Dismantling Solidarity: Capitalist Politics and American Pensions Since the New Deal* (Ithaca, NY: Cornell University Press, 2017) (emphasis McCarthy's).

Yet while the funds may have then owned roughly a quarter of the nation's corporate equities, as Michael McCarthy points out, ownership was not tantamount to control. Control of these funds remained in the hands of "institutional fiduciaries hired by employer-dominated trustee boards" who shifted investment from the safe government bond market to more risky common stocks over time.[62] But the existence of these large pools of capital was particularly attractive to commercial and investment banks, who lobbied for financial deregulation to get in on this action.[63] Financial firms themselves would become important actors pushing for reforms and actively shaping demand for new financial products by attempting to create a middle-class investment culture.[64]

Policy developments during the 1970s and 1980s helped to clear the way for these banks to become more involved. The Employee Retirement Income Security Act of 1974 provided new rules around vesting, funding, and eligibility and created fiduciary standards. McCarthy argues that this paved the way for the financialization of pensions by making financial objectives the overarching determination of investments and diminishing the role of non-financial objectives to factor into such decisions.[65]

In addition, a novel interpretation of Section 401(k) of the Revenue Act of 1978 would lead to the massive expansion of individual defined contribution retirement accounts. The new section had been intended to clarify the rules surrounding tax-deferred profit-sharing plans that had been popular forms of executive compensation but were not widely available to other workers. Soon after its introduction, however, a retirement benefits consultant named Ted Benna realized that 401(k)s could serve as a deferred compensation vehicle to limit executives' tax bills in a period of still high marginal tax rates. The catch was that the plans would need to be available throughout a company and not just to top earners.[66]

Ultimately, the Treasury and the IRS accepted the reinterpretation of the 401(k). By 1982, half of the country's large employers would offer 401(k)s.[67] The 401(k) plans' popularity (and the lobbying that grew around them) also

[62] McCarthy, *Dismantling Solidarity*, p. 77.

[63] Gerstle, *The Rise and Fall of the Neoliberal Order*, 175.

[64] Neil Fligstein and Adam Goldstein, "The Emergence of a Financial Culture in American Households, 1989–2007" *Socio-Economic Review* 13, no, 3 (2015): 575–601.

[65] McCarthy, *Dismantling Solidarity*, p. 105.

[66] Michael Steinberger, "Was the 401(k) a Mistake?" *New York Times* May 8, 2024.

[67] Chandler Friedman, "Evolution of the 401(k)," *Guideline* September 13, 2021. https://www.guideline.com/blog/evolution-of-401k/.

enabled them to survive the Reagan tax reforms of 1986, even as the Reagan Administration was keen to regain the forgone tax revenues.[68] Instead, the 1986 reforms further entrenched the program and even introduced a similar retirement vehicle for government workers.[69] These plans were further entrenched in the Clinton era with the Small Business Job Protection Act of 1996, which simplified the process of employer-matching for businesses with fewer than one hundred employees, and during the second Bush presidency, when the Economic Growth and Tax Relief Reconciliation Act of 2001 introduced the Roth 401(k), a non-tax deferred alternative to the standard 401(k).[70]

Converting "spenders into savers" in Benna's words also generated new anxieties about the complexity of investment decisions.[71] The mutual fund industry grew to fill this gap and was in other ways more favorably situated for this moment than were other types of collective funds (it also bears mentioning that mutual funds had lobbied extensively for these regulatory changes, and according to Michael Fink, an industry insider at the time, had received most of their wish list).[72] For one thing, the mutual fund industry had been granted an exemption from the fiduciary standards set up by ERISA; for another, Department of Labor Regulations surrounding ERISA clarified that employers who allowed their employees to choose among a range of investment options "will not be responsible for their employees' decisions," again loosening the fiduciary responsibilities that ERISA had otherwise put in place.[73] These incentivized employers to switch to defined contribution accounts and along with that the popularity of mutual funds. As Blackrock CEO Larry Fink describes:

> Obviously, we were ambitious entrepreneurs, and we wanted to build a big, successful company. But we also wanted to help people retire like my parents did. That's why we started an asset manager—a company that helps people invest in the capital markets—because we believed participating in those markets was going to be crucial for people who wanted to retire comfortably and financially secure.[74]

[68] Steinberger, "Was the 401(k) a Mistake?"
[69] Friedman, "Evolution of the 401(k)."
[70] Ibid.
[71] Steinberger, "Was the 401(k) a Mistake?"
[72] Michael Fink, *The Rise of Mutual Funds* (New York: Oxford University Press, 2010), chapter 6
[73] Ibid., 130.
[74] Larry Fink, "2024 Annual Chairman's Letter to Investors," https://www.blackrock.com/corporate/investor-relations/larry-fink-annual-chairmans-letter.

We also believed the capital markets would become a bigger and bigger part of the global economy. If more people could invest in the capital markets, it would create a virtuous economic cycle, fueling growth for companies and countries, which would, in turn, generate wealth for millions more people.[75]

By 1990, retirement assets comprised about 20 percent of total mutual fund assets; their share more than doubled over the 2010s.[76]

The Cultural Repurposing of Investment

As with housing, the push to increase participation in financial markets was accompanied by a change in the marketing of financial products. By the 2010s, the mutual fund industry was allocating .2 percent of net assets to marketing, an unusually high proportion due to regulations on this type of financial industry advertising. While the SEC usually prevented companies from paying for marketing costs out of their corporate assets, mutual funds developed ways to engage in this process "indirectly," and the SEC allowed it.[77]

Edward McQuarrie and Meir Statman explore the significant changes in mutual fund industry marketing by analyzing fifty years of magazine advertisements. Previously, mutual funds faced stringent regulations, with the SEC banning all forms of advertising until the 1970s. Prior to 1980, any mutual fund that engaged in advertising was required to adhere to the legal prospectus standards, limiting their capacity to promise high future returns to potential investors. Following 1980, these restrictions were lifted.[78]

Advertising practices of the mutual fund industry over time correspond to these regulations. In the 1960s and 1970s ads might have contained a list of directors and the advisory board, along with a rundown of assets and liabilities in a balance sheet.[79] Following the relaxation of advertising regulations

---

[75] Ibid.

[76] Benjamin Braun, "Asset Manager Capitalism as a Corporate Governance Regime," in Jacob Hacker, Alexander Hertel-Fernandez, Paul Pierson, and Kathleen Thelen eds., *The American Political Economy: Politics, Markets, and Power* (New York: Cambridge University Press, 2021), 270–294.

[77] John P. Freeman, "The Use of Mutual Fund Assets to Pay Marketing Costs." *Loyola University Chicago Law Journal* 9 (3): (1978): 533.

[78] Edward McQuarrie and Meir Statmen, "How Investors Became Consumers." *Journal of Macromarketing* 36 (3) (2016): 1–29.

[79] Ibid.

by the SEC, advertisements very slowly moved from "just the facts" to seize on the new opportunities presented by the liberalization of IRA plans and the shift toward defined benefit plans, which promised a large influx of new individual investors.[80] The growth and maturing of this new "mass market for investment products" along with the increasing legal freedom around advertising led ads to become more expressive and sentimental, featuring photos and profiles of (fictional) people to help sell the idea.[81]

This transformation occurred slowly in the 1980s but grew rapidly during the 1990s, the second half of which was characterized by a booming stock market. As the S&P began to see 20 percent annual returns and the NASDAQ an 86 percent rise in 1999 alone, mutual fund advertisers moved much more from rational appeals to emotional ones, using images and photographs, and not necessarily including much actual financial information.[82] One ad from

> American Century funds, a two-page spread, consumes the entire left page with a picture of the show and pants leg of a man flat on his back. Only when the first line of the body copy is read does the picture's meaning become clear: 'Help me, I'm working and I can't get up.'). The ad puns on a pop culture reference from that era (i.e., 'help me, I've fallen and can't get up'). The copy explains the importance of retirement investing for ordinary working people seeking to get ahead.[83]

After the 2000 crash, advertisements began to emphasize risk and responsibility. McQuarrie and Statmen describe how, during this period, "An almost moralistic tone crops up in ads from this period. The ethos is that of a responsible friend addressing the investor as if he were a drunk sobering up from a bender."[84]

The rise of this type of advertising poses a challenge to traditional theories about financial marketing, according to McQuarrie and Statman. The user of these products has typically been theorized as a recipient of investment information for making rational decisions—yet the products were being marketed to appeal to consumers' emotions, to actively shape their expectations of how they might use these products (and how they might feel about their decisions), and to differentiate them through branding.

[80] Ibid.
[81] Ibid.
[82] Ibid.
[83] Ibid., 16.
[84] Ibid, 19.

Indeed, Vanguard openly attempted (though largely failed) to turn the word Vanguard into a verb, much like "googling."[85]

Political Transformations

Politicians on both sides of the aisle also participated to varying degrees in promoting and expanding mass investment. As the political challenges of the 1960s and 1970s became apparent and linked to the excesses of the New Deal order, the "solution" increasingly became one of untethering the market to benefit consumers better. This began as early as the 1960s, when Johnson started to lift credit controls and enable a vast new experiment with mortgage securitization by 1968, and continued into the 1970s when Ford and Carter started to move more toward deregulation and privatization as part of the bipartisan revolt against big government by the mid-1970s.[86] Reagan may have been a chief architect of neoliberalism through his administration's active involvement in deregulating the financial sector; still, elites from both parties could take credit for reforms and initiatives, both large and small, that helped to promote investment over these decades. It was under Clinton, after all, that Glass-Steagall was dismantled. Democratic Representatives from New York, once at the forefront of New Deal–style policy experimentation during FDR's time in the governor's office, now advocated for the dismantling of the regulations that had been set in place during the New Deal: "Neoliberalism appeared to be a force too powerful for anyone to stop. The decision by Clinton, Schumer, and others to deregulate finance further wrapped the Democrats in the embrace of elites that were driving the new economy."[87]

Moreover, Republicans and Democrats came to support policies to encourage access to homeownership down the income scale, just as new tools for tapping into a house's equity became ever more popular. During George H.W. Bush's administration, the government-sponsored housing enterprises Fannie Mae and Freddie Mac were instructed to increase their support for low- and moderate-income underwriting. Lending was further liberalized during the Clinton era, with the reduction of the 20 percent down payment, which was even further liberalized during George W. Bush's time

[85] Stuart Elliot, "The Verb Treatment for an Investment House." *New York Times*, March 14, 2010.
[86] Cohen, *A Consumers' Republic*, loc. 7138.
[87] Gerstle, *The Rise and Fall of the Neoliberal Order*, 178.

in office, with the passage of the American Dream Zero Downpayment Act
of 2003. This period saw homeownership rates reach their highest ever, with
69 percent of households owning their home. More dramatic was the rise in
minority homeownership: 25 percent for Black homeowners between the
mid-1990s and mid-2000s, and 60 percent for Latino households.[88]

For a time, even presidents of both parties were supportive of some form
of Social Security privatization, a step further towards embracing neoliberal
ideals past the shift towards defined contribution plans. Facing a budget surplus, the Clinton Administration indicated it might entertain allowing some
portion of the Social Security trust fund to be invested by Wall Street (which
Republicans were against) and the idea of creating some form of individual
accounts (which Republicans supported). Nelson Lichtenstein and Judith
Stein write that in October 1997

> Gingrich agreed to a scenario under which the Republicans would hold
> off pushing for a large tax cut in exchange for incorporating private invest-
> ment accounts into Social Security. Clinton was not adverse to the idea.
> Private accounts evoked the opportunity and responsibility the president
> had touted during his campaign for welfare reform. Because the idea was
> so toxic to so many Democrats, however, another set of secret White
> House meetings to work out the complicated privatization details were
> given the code name 'Special Purpose Meetings.' Chaired by Gene Sperling
> and Larry Summers, they continued for several months in late 1997 and
> early 1998. Sperling and Summers thought individual accounts would be
> an effective means of 'neutralizing Republican tax cut proposals' because
> the administration could portray them as a payroll tax rebate. The logic
> of the proposal, they argued, 'is that we could be at a disadvantage if
> we only supported the Social Security Trust Fund, while the opposition
> was "addressing" Social Security through accounts that produce a higher
> return.'[89]

Clinton unveiled a plan during his 1999 State of the Union Address that
would allocate two-thirds of the budget surplus to Social Security, with 20
percent invested in the stock market. The measure was intended to appeal
to liberals who viewed this as a "collective wager on the equities market,

---

[88] Gerstle, *The Rise and Fall of the Neoliberal Order*, 214.
[89] Nelson Lichtenstein and Judith Stein, *A Fabulous Failure: The Clinton Presidency and the Transformation of American Capitalism* (Princeton, NJ: Princeton University Press, 2023), 320–321.

similar to the way many cities, states, and corporations handled defined-benefit pension plans."[90] Another 10 percent of the surplus would be set aside to provide tax credits for a new program of 401(k)-like savings accounts for Americans making less than $100,000. It would leave Social Security untouched.[91] This never materialized, and by the time George W. Bush introduced his plan to partially privatize Social Security, there was scant support from Democrats who saw support for Social Security as a winning issue.

Dueling Political Logics for Promoting Asset Building

That both parties coalesced to some degree around mass investment does not mean that they came to it for the same reasons. Republicans had hoped to bring more people into the "wealth stream," solidifying political support around a limited welfare state and making them more market-oriented. This was part of a deliberate strategy to scale back the welfare state by reducing public spending and helping to contrast deserving thrifty owner/investors from undeserving citizens receiving direct public support. George W. Bush made homeownership and Social Security privatization central planks of his "ownership society," which promised to provide Americans with greater freedom and control over their lives. He was also aware that working-class prospective first-time homebuyers were a largely minority population who had long been excluded from access. This became a way to "pursue racial equality that sidestepped the policies [Republicans] despised: federal jobs programs, raising the minimum wage, building public housing, and strengthening labor unions to give workers more leverage in bargaining for higher wages."[92] Homeownership would support the values they idealized, including "independence, self-reliance, enterprising zeal."[93]

For Democrats, embracing investment was one way to shift the party to the center. The Republicans' sustained electoral strength conveyed a message to Clinton's advisors: "In the Age of Reagan, the party had no choice but to move toward the political center. Clinton argued for more market freedom and less government regulation than what New Deal Democrats had traditionally embraced."[94] Losses in the 1994 midterms (and the failure of

[90] Ibid., 323–334.
[91] Ibid.
[92] Gerstle, *The Rise and Fall of the Neoliberal Order*, 211.
[93] Ibid.
[94] Ibid., 155.

Clinton health reform) further established the need to "appropriate Republican ideas and rework them into Democratic proposals," a process the consultant Dick Morris called 'triangulation.'[95]

Another rationale for the shift was concern over the indirect political consequences of spending, which could be inferred from the relationship between the Clinton administration and the Federal Reserve under Greenspan. The Clinton administration had grown increasingly worried about budget deficits, fearing they might prompt the Fed to raise interest rates, potentially resulting in a repeat of the 1970s economy with similar political repercussions. The response was to curb the welfare state and social spending to prioritize balanced budgets. Promoting asset building among individuals emerged as the favored approach, facilitated by new homeownership initiatives and increased student lending, seemingly with minimal budgetary impact.

There also appeared to be a genuine belief in the safety and utility of new products to help solve the political and social problems that persisted into the 1990s and had not been fully ameliorated by earlier efforts. This was especially true among those excluded or marginalized. And this was a vision of uplift that could sidestep discussions of welfare that had become racialized and conflictual. Democrats may have rejected the Bush plan to partially privatize Social Security, but theirs was not a wholesale rejection of promoting mass investment—they offered a different vision of the 'Investors' Republic.'

4. Taking Stock of the Investors' Republic

Linking citizens to the political economy through expanded asset-ownership was believed to be able to achieve several (sometimes conflicting) goals: fostering savings and asset growth, stimulating the economy by boosting demand, creating stakeholders in both the stock market and local communities, changing individual habits, and possibly influencing public political needs. Were these objectives accomplished? If so, to what degree?

As anticipated, investment participation rose, though unevenly across various sectors and potentially reversible. Homeownership rates reached their highest point just before the financial crisis but have not returned to those pre-crisis levels. Recent years have seen an increase in employees

[95] Ibid., 156.

contributing to their workplace retirement accounts, albeit slowly. However, despite high participation in defined contribution accounts, the reality is that most individuals have contributed minimal amounts, rendering these accounts inadequate alternatives to substantial publicly funded retirement benefits.

The drive for investment has largely reinforced or even exacerbated existing racial disparities in wealth and economic stability, albeit through different pathways and programs. Homeowners of color faced heightened risks of foreclosure during the financial crisis, resulting in the Black-white homeownership gap reverting to levels seen in the 1970s after 2008. Research indicates that the returns on an individual's home investment often depend on the racial makeup of their neighborhood and are influenced by how appraisers determine property comparisons, as well as the homeowner's personal background irrespective of their financial situation.[96] While there is less evidence linking retirement investment returns to participants' racial backgrounds, large and persistent racial disparities exist in access, take-up, investment volume, and rates of early withdrawal due to underlying sources of racialized disadvantage.[97]

After decades of policies promoting wealth accumulation, the bottom 50 percent of the wealth distribution collectively holds a minimal portion of the nation's wealth—just under $4 trillion out of over $150 trillion total.[98] Moreover, the lofty language surrounding democratizing access to finance and ownership obscures the significance of the type of asset ownership and the class disparities in ownership. The bottom 50 percent primarily holds their asset wealth in their homes, followed by durable goods, which include cars, considered a depreciating asset. On the eve of the financial crisis, this group concentrated nearly 60 percent of its wealth in housing, while those in the 50th–90th percentile of wealth held about 40 percent in housing. In the decades leading up to 2007, increases in housing wealth helped mitigate the concentration of top-end wealth that surged in the 1970s.[99] The foreclosure

[96] Junia Howell and Elizabeth Korver-Glenn, "Neighborhoods, Race, and the Twenty-First-Century Housing Appraisal Industry," *Sociology of Race and Ethnicity* 4, no. 4 (2018): 473–490.

[97] Chloe Thurston, "Racial Inequality, Market Inequality, and the American Political Economy" in Hacker, Hertel-Fernandez, Pierson, and Thelen, *The American Political Economy*, 133–57.

[98] Board of Governors of the Federal Reserve System, "Distribution of Household Wealth in the U.S. Since 1989," at https://www.federalreserve.gov/releases/z1/dataviz/dfa/distribute/chart/.

[99] Moritz Kuhn, Moritz Schularick, and Ulrike I. Steins, "Income and Wealth Inequality in America, 1949–2016." *Journal of Political Economy* 128 (9): (2020): 3469–3519.

and financial crisis eliminated a significant portion of many citizens' housing wealth, along with their retirement and investment assets.

In contrast, the top 10 percent of the wealth distribution holds a larger share of their investments in equities and bonds compared to housing; this applies both before and after the crisis. After the global financial crisis, the stock market bounced back quickly, whereas house prices took considerably longer to recover.[100] These different types of investments have produced starkly different returns, which help to account for the unprecedented rise in wealth inequality between the top 10 percent and the bottom 90 percent between 1946 and 2016.

It is also important to highlight the new distribution of debt that has emerged. Since the 1970s, households have increasingly turned to credit (and debt) to compensate for financial shortfalls and to pay for their investment goods like housing and higher education.[101] Increased access to credit and debt served as a salve during a prolonged period of wage stagnation, allowing families to uphold their standards of living and alleviating some political tensions.[102] Credit and debt also grew increasingly important during a period of social policy retrenchment, enabling citizens to self-finance higher education in the wake of state and federal cutbacks in direct aid and to self-insure during times of economic hardship.[103] Although debt has become commonplace for nearly all households except the wealthiest, the top 1 percent of Americans have seen a significant surge in savings over the past forty years. This has resulted in the swift accumulation of financial assets. An estimated two thirds "of the rise in financial asset accumulation of the top 1 percent of the wealth distribution since the 1980s has been a rise in the accumulation of claims on U.S. government and household debt."[104] Between 1980 and 2016, the top 1 percent in the US financed half of the increase in household and government debt.[105] In short, the assets of the wealthy are liabilities for the poor and middle class, as well as the government. This raises questions about the concentration of political and

[100] Federal Reserve System, "Fed Listens: Perspectives from the Public," June 2020, at https://www.federalreserve.gov/publications/files/fedlistens-report-20200612.pdf.

[101] Barry Z. Cynamon and Steven M. Fazzari, "Rising Inequality and Stagnation in the US Economy." *European Journal of Economics and Economic Policies* 12 (2): (2015): 170–182.

[102] Raghuram G. Rajan, *Fault Lines: How Hidden Fractures Still Threaten the World Economy* (Princeton, NJ: Princeton University Press, 2010).

[103] Andreas Wiedemann, "How Credit Markets Substitute for Welfare States and Influence Social Policy Preferences: Evidence from US States," *British Journal of Political Science* 52 (2): (2022): 829–849.

[104] Atif Mian, Ludwig Straub, and Amir Sufi, "The Saving Glut of the Rich." Feb 2021, p. 1, NBER. https://scholar.harvard.edu/files/straub/files/mss_richsavingglut.pdf.

[105] Ibid.

economic power and its relationship to household economic fortunes, as well as the limitations faced by governments.

There are also second-order consequences of the increasing reliance on mass investment. This relates to the rise of financialization and asset manager capitalism, both of which have been empirically shown to contribute to wage and wealth inequality through the rise of shareholder value as the metric.[106] Less directly, the push by pension funds and private equity firms into real estate has been linked to rising rents and increased evictions, raising concerns about whether this system encourages risk-taking and rent-seeking over innovation in more beneficial practices.[107]

A second set of questions pertains to whether the significant rise in the adoption of financial products across the income distribution, along with the growing tendency to view non-financial products like houses as assets, has altered public orientations and behaviors. Fligstein and Goldstein find little evidence that the increased utilization of financial services has changed how individuals at the bottom of the income distribution perceive risk and debt, although they depend on it much more than in the past to bridge the gap between their household income and their daily needs. To the extent Fligstein and Goldsetin detected "a deepening culture of risk-taking and strategic deployment of assets" they found it among middle- and upper-class households, who became more likely to take on debt and "adopt a more thoroughly financial mindset" in order to better compete for positional goods including housing and schools.[108]

Apart from households' new yet varying appetites for risk-taking and strategic asset deployment, citizens' reorientation toward financial markets, along with their growing inclination to view homes as investments, has altered some of their expectations of elected officials. Some advocates of the ownership society believed that providing more citizens with a stake in the market would garner greater support for market-friendly policies. In the aftermath of the financial crisis and other looming crises, instead, we have witnessed heightened political demands for government intervention (including bailouts in the housing and financial sectors) to help safeguard the assets of concerned citizens. This situation has made it riskier for incumbents and has created intergenerational cleavages between financially secure older adults and financially anxious young adults. These cleavages have refracted through political systems based on institutional features,

---

[106] Braun, "Fueling Financialization."

[107] Ibid.

[108] Fligstein and Goldstein, "The Emergence of a Finance Culture in American Households," 578.

particularly veto power points.[109] There are also signs of new political divisions between renters and homeowners regarding local housing supply and production politics, along with concerns about affordability. Initially, this phenomenon mainly affected "superstar" cities, but it has increasingly spread to traditionally lower-cost areas.

The final dimension concerns the shifting locus of policymaking and the increasingly hidden nature of financial regulations, which has altered accountability and governance. In the 1980s and 1990s, banking regulators and Congress were responsible for key changes that transformed investment. By the 1990s, the Federal Reserve also came to play a role in both limiting the scope and costs of the federal government as well as in implicitly backstopping the stock market. In the wake of the global financial crisis the Federal Reserve has played an outsize role in governing the investors republic. Between 2007 and 2009 the Fed introduced a new set of programs that went outside of the scope of its traditional scope of activities, expanding credit, providing liquidity to financial institutions by working with Treasury to create a loan facility (TALF) that can "ease credit conditions for households and businesses by extending credit to US holders of high-quality asset-backed securities."[110] In 2008 the FOMC began purchasing assets at an unprecedented scale through a program known as LSAP, otherwise known as quantitative easing. It presided for over a decade of low interest rates and set public expectations for these to continue. In short, the Federal Reserve had become a sort of social policymaker of last resort.[111] That quantitative easing was not the preferred approach for the European Central Bank points to the prominence of the United States' consumption and credit-based growth model, which traveled through housing.[112]

From the creation of the Consumer Financial Protection Bureau to the years-long efforts by the Treasury during Democratic administrations to require retirement investors to adhere to fiduciary standards, as well as the

---

[109] J.M. Chwieroth and A. Walter, *The Wealth Effect: How the Great Expectations of the Middle Class Have Changed the Politics of Banking Crises* (New York: Cambridge University Press, 2019).

[110] Federal Reserve Bank of St. Louis, "The Great Recession and Its Aftermath," November 22, 2013 at https://www.federalreservehistory.org/essays/great-recession-and-its-aftermath#:~:text =The%20Fed's%20support%20to%20specific,of%20financial%20institutions%20and%20markets.

[111] Larry Jacobs and Desmond King, *Fed Power: How Finance Wins* (Oxford, UK: Oxford University Press, 2016).

[112] Alexander Reisenbichler, "The Politics of Quantitative Easing and Housing Stimulus by the Federal Reserve and European Central Bank, 2008–2018," in Alison Johnston and Paulette Kurzer, eds., *Bricks in the Wall: The Politics of Housing in Europe*, pp. 190–210 (Routledge, 2021).

role of the courts in overturning student debt forgiveness, the bureaucracy and courts have played an important, albeit fragmented and not always visible, role in these areas. This is particularly noted by SoRelle (in volume) regarding consumer financial protection.

If government agencies are complex and opaque, facing challenges for accountability, so too are the private companies that view and present themselves as social providers. For example, Larry Fink's 2024 letter to investors makes the case for bringing in tens of millions of Americans who remain unserved by the current employer-sponsored retirement system:

> In 2023, BlackRock expanded the types of target date ETFs we offer so people can more easily buy them even if they don't work for employers offering a retirement plan. *There are 57 million people like this in America—farmers, gig workers, restaurant employees, independent contractors—who don't have access to a defined contribution plan.* And while better investment products can help, there are limits to what something like a target date fund can do. Indeed, for most people, the data shows that the hardest part of retirement investment is just getting started.[113]

Delegation to private actors can create opportunities for stakeholders to operate "quietly" at a remove from the public, in highly technical policy areas, with little accountability.[114]

5. Conclusion: The Waning of the Investors' Republic?

Recent years have seen intense debate over whether the neoliberal order is in decline or has already been supplanted by a new, undefined order. The global financial crisis exposed neoliberalism's vulnerabilities as a governing order, as many households experienced foreclosures, rising unemployment, and fluctuating home and portfolio values, often linked to earlier deregulatory actions. This period also gave rise to new social movements, such as Occupy Wall Street and the Tea Party, highlighting the pronounced inequality that emerged, coupled with the growth of right-wing nativist populism and the eventual Trump-led transformation of the Republican Party.

---

[113] Larry Fink, "2024 Annual Chairman's Letter to Investors", https://www.blackrock.com/corporate/investor-relations/larry-fink-annual-chairmans-letter.

[114] Pepper Culpepper, *Quiet Politics and Business Power: Corporate Control in Europe and Japan* (New York: Cambridge University Press, 2010).

Government policy choices during the COVID-19 pandemic indicated a shift away from the goal of minimizing government involvement in markets. These included actions like rapidly developing and distributing a vaccine, injecting the economy with historic amounts of stimulus, offering unemployment insurance, supporting employers, implementing eviction and mortgage pauses, attempting student debt forgiveness, and significantly cutting child poverty in half through new family support measures. President Biden's embrace of industrial policy through the CHIPs and Science Act and the Inflation Reduction Act suggested that end of neoliberalism as a policy objective; so too have policy actions taken by President Trump in his first few months after retaking office, including an embrace of tariffs and threats of trade wars, but also a dismantling of what had remained of the New Deal administrative state. New cleavages have also emerged around ownership, with an ascendant "yes-in-my-backyard" movement sharing some support for deregulation, indicating an affinity for neoliberalism, but the emphasis on alleviating supply constraints that challenges the investor republic's normative ideals surrounding homeownership and wealth generation. In addition, the resurgence of the Black Lives Matter movement in 2020 renewed criticism about the inadequacies of a market-oriented thin racial liberalism to make any progress on longstanding material racial inequalities.[115] Each of these point to a political economy experiencing flux in basic questions about governance, institutions, economic ideas, and citizenship ideals. As Felicia Wong writes in a 2022 symposium,

> The neoliberalism that many of us knew in the 1980s, 1990s, and 2000s— that unquestioning faith that the way forward in America was to strive for education, college if you could; to get a good job; and get ahead—is gone, never to return. But the post-neoliberalism we are now living through is chaotic and, for many, terrifying. We are at some kind of inflection point, not only because of COVID, but also because the ideas that held sway and governed our sense of right and wrong have lost their explanatory power. We are living through the midst of paradigm change. And we are just as likely to come out on the dark side—a racist, populist economics upheld by an authoritarian regime—as we are to come out looking more

[115] Felicia Wong, "Overview" Post-Neoliberalism at a Crossroads" *Democracy: A Journal of Ideas* no. 64 (Spring 2022), at https://democracyjournal.org/magazine/64/overview-post-neoliberalism-at-a-crossroads/.

like some combination of the New Deal and the Great Society, updated for a multiracial twenty-first century.[116]

This is indeed a moment of flux in the basic commitments and institutions of the American political economy. But it is also useful not to get bogged down in the chaos on the surface if we are to understand what possibilities exist on the horizon. As this examination of the transition of citizenship visions from the New Deal to the neoliberal orders provides any lessons, it is to consider how even seemingly seismic shifts build on the material and ideas of previous orders. Long after the "fall" of a wage-led consumerist order by the 1970s, consumer confidence and spending remain widely accepted indicators of the economy's health, and "customer satisfaction" permeates many discussions about whether government is functioning effectively and how it might serve people better. There is little indication that citizens have rejected investment and asset building. Housing emerged as a major campaign issue in 2024, and student loan debt in 2020. Contemporary housing politics indicate that homeowners still perceive houses as investments and are reluctant to jeopardize the value of that asset, even if it means alleviating pressures on the housing market for renters and potential homeowners. Home equity now represents a median of 45 percent of household net worth. Individual participation in investment has also been rising in recent years particular in the wake of COVID-19.[117] Yet wealth inequality remains prevalent, with the potential for insider-outsider and intergenerational conflicts. These point to the continuing political salience of finance (and central bank policy) for many citizens (Moschella, in this volume) and of economic imaginaries in shaping demands and actions (Pearson in this volume). Legacies of the New Deal consumerist order may be instructive; even as the neoliberal order may be waning, it is more difficult to say that ideas about stakeholding and investment themselves will cease to be important ways that citizens are linked to the political economy and respond to its changes.

---

[116] Ibid.

[117] Rakesh Kochhar and Mohamad Moslimani, "The Assets Households Own and the Debts They Carry" Pew Research, December 4, 2023, at https://www.pewresearch.org/2023/12/04/the-assets-households-own-and-the-debts-they-carry/.

3

(Un)Democratic by Design

The Political Consequences of Decentralized Financial Regulation in the United States

Mallory SoRelle

"The CFPB is here to stay," cheered an exuberant Senator Elizabeth Warren, pumping her fist in the air in front of the iconic neoclassical façade of the U.S. Supreme Court. Her appearance at the Court on May 16, 2024, alongside a group of consumer advocates, was to celebrate a ruling handed down that day upholding the constitutionality of the Consumer Financial Protection Bureau's (CFPB) funding structure. In a 7–2 decision, the Court ruled against a legal challenge to the watchdog agency's very existence that was brought by payday lenders who sought to hobble the CFPB and its efforts to enact more stringent federal regulations of their industry. Established by the 2010 Dodd-Frank Wall Street Reform and Consumer Protection Act in the wake of the 2008 global financial crisis, the CFPB became the first US federal regulatory agency whose sole mission was to protect consumers' finances. In its first decade of operation, the CFPB, which is housed within the Federal Reserve, provided over $14 billion of financial relief to US consumers, handled over three million consumer complaints, provided financial education materials to over seven million consumers, and enacted a bevy of protective regulations across a range of consumer financing.

While advocates like Warren have fiercely defended the agency, lauding the CFPB's vigorous efforts to improve consumer financial well-being through federal regulation, the agency has sparked the considerable ire of Republican lawmakers and many (though not all) within the financial industry. Instead of fighting against individual rules or enforcement actions, however, opponents have engaged in repeated legislative and legal efforts—like the challenge from payday lenders—to dismantle the CFPB altogether. Representative Jeb Hensarling (R-Texas), former chair of the House Financial

Mallory SoRelle, *(Un)Democratic by Design*. In: *Picking Winners*. Edited by: Lawrence R. Jacobs and Desmond King, Oxford University Press. © Oxford University Press (2026). DOI: 10.1093/9780197831823.003.0003

Services Committee, complained that the CFPB was a "rogue agency," and congressional Republicans have proposed bills to weaken or outright eliminate it by contesting its funding, leadership structure, oversight, and data collection efforts. Mick Mulvaney, who served as interim director of the CFPB under the Trump administration, once called the watchdog a "sick, sad joke."

Republican indignation with the agency went so far as to make abolishing the CFPB a prominent piece of the party's 2016 platform. Most recently, President Trump—whose second term has been characterized by a reinvigorated effort to dismantle the federal bureaucracy more broadly—appointed an interim director of the CFPB, Russell Vought, who immediately took steps to halt the agency's work, fire a substantial portion of its staff, and undo many of the rulemaking and enforcement actions the agency was engaged with. Such single-minded focus on destroying the CFPB once prompted Democratic Senator Dick Durbin's quip that Republicans and Wall Street hate the CFPB "like the devil hates holy water."

Despite being one of a handful of federal financial regulators, the watchdog seems to generate uniquely intense investment from both supporters and detractors. What is it about the CFPB that makes proponents so buoyant, and opponents so alarmed, about its role in finance governance—especially as the underlying policy regime the agency is tasked with implementing has remained largely unchanged since the CFPB's creation? As I contend in this chapter, the promise (or threat) of the CFPB exists in its potential to restructure political power in the rulemaking and enforcement process, with consequences for the broader landscape of consumer financial protection regulation.

The story of consumer financial regulation in the United States has historically been one of decentralization, marked by the fragmentation of policymaking authority both within and across levels of government. While the Federal Reserve Board's role as a central bank concentrates oversight of many aspects of the broader financial marketplace, structural features of the US banking system combine with uniquely decentralized political institutions to generate a fragmented landscape for consumer financial protection. First, the United States has a dual banking system in which financial institutions can be chartered at either the state or federal levels. At the federal level, this led to a patchwork financial regulatory infrastructure comprising multiple agencies, each tasked with oversight for specific types of financial charters. Compounding this decentralization is the nation's federated system, in which policymaking authority is distributed across federal, state, and local jurisdictions; thus the responsibility for certain types of consumer financing is delegated to the states, allowing for fifty distinct approaches to financial regulation.

Adding additional complexity to this fragmented system is the fact that neither of these dynamics is completely stable. Financial institutions can reclassify their charters with relative ease, leading federal agencies to compete for jurisdiction. As new financial innovations emerge, agencies must also decide who among existing regulatory bodies has authority for them— or create a new body to oversee the entity. And finally, federal policymakers can make strategic choices about either devolving authority for a given regulatory issue to the states or preempting—and potentially centralizing—state power to oversee specific consumer protections. While much of the literature about finance governance assumes rational, technocratic motives for such choices, the reality is much more political.

As this chapter will argue, these features of US finance governance have collectively created a decentralized and fluid system of consumer protection that generates significant inequalities with respect to who has protections and who does not. By influencing the costs of participation, the visibility of regulatory actors, and the potential for industry interests to engage in venue shopping, the decentralization of consumer financial regulation generates political consequences that shape the degree to which different actors within the financial marketplace can influence the policymaking process, with significant consequences for the stringency of consumer financial protection. In essence, the chapter describes how the institutional design of finance governance matters for picking winners.

Drawing on theories of federalism, *ex ante* bureaucratic design, and policy feedback, this chapter will explore how the fragmentation of US consumer financial protection regulation—both within and across levels of government—shapes who wields political power over US consumer financial protection. It also explores whether the creation of the CFPB reshapes that balance through centralizing authority to a greater degree, generating the conditions for more robust financial protection even in the absence of underlying legislative changes to the system of financial regulation. Ultimately, this chapter demonstrates how the distribution of administrative authority structures the politics of consumer financial regulation in the United States. When regulatory authority is decentralized, it creates opportunities and incentives for private financing to exert greater power over regulatory outcomes at the expense of wage earners or consumers. As Jacobs and King articulated (see Chapter One, this volume) these distributional effects have critical consequences for social citizenship and inequality in the American political economy.

1. The Fragmented System of US Consumer Financial Protection

The United States is an outlier in the degree to which it relies on regulatory agencies as active sites of policymaking across a range of policy arenas (Hilton 2007). Indeed, some estimates suggest that bureaucratic rulemaking now produces 90 percent of all federal laws enacted each year, making it "the most common and instrumental form of lawmaking" in the United States (Kerwin and Furlong 1992: 114). Despite relying so heavily on bureaucratic policymaking, the United States is also unusual among developed democracies for the degree of fragmentation these agencies exhibit. Bureaucratic authority frequently spans multiple agencies with parallel, often overlapping, missions (Carpenter 2001; Hacker et al. 2021; King and Lieberman 2009).

Regulatory agencies began to emerge at both the state and federal levels during the Progressive Era, gradually replacing the courts as the primary arbiters for issues from industrial competition to health and safety (Glaeser and Shleifer 2001). The proliferation of regulatory agencies accelerated even more following the Great Depression, as policymakers looked to technocrats to help remake the American economy (Prasad 2012). In the 1960s and 1970s, these agencies were increasingly tasked with regulation to protect the public interest (rather than the competitive interests of industry actors) across an array of policies from occupational safety to the environment to consumer finance (Derthick and Quirk 1985; Meier 1985). Perhaps no domain reflects this dynamic more than the case of financial regulation.

Agencies dedicated to overseeing the country's financial institutions represent some of the oldest and most significant regulatory commissions in the United States. The Office of the Comptroller of the Currency, created in 1863 as part of the Treasury Department, was one of the earliest regulatory commissions established to govern financial institutions. It was responsible for supervising federally chartered banks. The Federal Reserve System, consisting of twelve regional banks and a Board of Governors (FRB), was established by the Federal Reserve Act in 1913 during the Progressive Era. The Federal Reserve oversees several types of financial institutions, including US branches of foreign banks and state-chartered banks that are members of the reserve system. New Deal policies under President Franklin D. Roosevelt ushered in the next wave of financial regulators. To better support mortgage financing, the Federal Home Loan Bank Board originated in 1932 to oversee building and loan institutions. It was replaced with two separate regulatory agencies in 1989 in the wake of the savings and loan crisis: the Office of Thrift Supervision, which was designed to oversee a variety of federally chartered savings associations, and the Federal Housing Finance Board, which maintained oversight for the Federal Home Loan Bank system. The Federal Deposit Insurance Corporation (FDIC) was another of the New Deal creations designed to stabilize the banking industry. Established as part of the Banking Act of 1933, the FDIC insures bank deposits and oversees the assets of failed banks. Finally, the National Credit Union Administration, which was initially part of the Farm Credit Administration, became an independent agency in 1970 with responsibility for both state and federal credit unions.

Each of these regulatory agencies was established primarily to promote the safety and soundness of financial institutions and markets, making them prudential regulators. In response to a series of financial panics in the nineteenth and early twentieth centuries, policymakers prioritized financial stability as the primary mission of new federal banking regulators created during this period of state development. Their goal was to avoid bank failures and the ensuing financial panics that followed. The lack of consumer-oriented regulatory agencies in finance governance during this time also made sense, as widespread consumer banking did not emerge until after the New Deal and more robustly after World War II, at which point much of the country's financial regulatory structure was already in place (Hyman 2011; SoRelle 2020). With the rise of "consumer citizenship" that Thurston describes in the previous chapter, however, regulators faced the need to protect borrowers—and not just banks—to sustain an economic system increasingly powered by access to consumer credit (SoRelle 2020). This need was only compounded as "investor citizens" became increasingly burdened by debt and its associated risk.

Until the birth of the CFPB in 2010, the Federal Trade Commission (FTC) served as the primary agency tasked with consumer financial protection, but the FTC had a much broader remit than simply protecting borrowers' credit transactions. The FTC was created in 1914 with the dual mission of protecting consumers and promoting competition across a range of industries. Governed by a five-person board with broad authority to identify and regulate unfair and deceptive practices, the FTC comprises both a Bureau of Consumer Protection and a Bureau of Competition. As part of their activities, the FTC collects consumer complaints on a wide swath of products and practices, of which consumer financial products and services represent only a small part.

As a result of the patchwork development of federal financial regulatory agencies, consumer financial protection laws are implemented and enforced not by a single entity but by each relevant authority for a given financial institution. Table 3.1 illustrates the resulting fragmentation of both rulemaking and enforcement authority as designated by every major consumer financial protection law enacted prior to the formation of the CFPB in 2010.[1] The analysis shows that rulemaking and enforcement authority are, indeed, fragmented to a significant degree. In fact, only four policies assign both rulemaking and enforcement authority to the same agency: Title I of the National Housing Act, Title V of the Fair Credit Reporting Act, the Fair Debt Collection Practices Act, and the Credit Repair Organizations Act. By contrast, sixteen policies divide rulemaking and enforcement authority across more than two agencies.

Not only is the administration of consumer credit regulation fragmented within individual policies, but it is also fragmented across policies. The ability to promulgate rules for consumer credit regulations is distributed across multiple agencies, although a small majority of laws (54 percent) designate the job of rulemaking primarily to the Federal Reserve. Enforcement authority is even more fragmented. More than two out of every three policies (67 percent) divide enforcement authority for a single policy among multiple regulatory agencies. In most of these cases, up to seven agencies are implicated in managing compliance for the specified policy, each

---

[1] This analysis is based on an original dataset designed to systematically capture the administrative arrangement for all major federal consumer credit policies requiring regulatory rulemaking in the United States. The degree of regulatory fragmentation is operationalized with a dummy variable that codes whether rulemaking and enforcement authority for a policy is assigned to a single agency (yes equals one). Significant policies were identified in three steps. First, I compiled the list of policies for which each relevant regulatory agency has jurisdiction. I then supplemented this list with any additional policies identified in the prominent historical literature on the evolution of consumer credit in the United States (see Calder 1999; Hyman 2011; Prasad 2012; Trumbull 2014). Finally, I systematically searched both the Congressional Record and the Congressional Quarterly Almanac for the relevant period to identify any other policies or major policy reforms. I have excluded from the dataset policies that primarily provide technical corrections or updates without making substantive policy changes. The result is a dataset consisting of twenty-two consumer credit policies enacted between 1934 and 2010.

Table 3.1 Fragmentation of Federal Consumer Credit Policy Administration, 1934–2010.

Year	Policy	Rulemaking Authority	Enforcement Authority
1934	National Housing Act (Title I)	FHA	FHA
1968	Consumer Credit Protection Act	FRB	Multiple Agencies
1968	Truth in Lending Act	FRB	Multiple Agencies
1970	Fair Credit Reporting Act	Multiple Agencies	FTC
1970	Provisions Relating to Credit Cards (Title V)	FTC	FTC
1974	Equal Credit Opportunity Act	FRB	Multiple Agencies
1974	Fair Credit Billing Act	FRB	Multiple Agencies
1976	Truth in Leasing Act	FRB	Multiple Agencies
1977	Fair Debt Collection Practices Act	FTC	FTC
1978	Electronic Funds Transfers	FRB	Multiple Agencies
1980	Truth in Lending Simplification and Reform Act	FRB	Multiple Agencies
1988	Fair Credit and Charge Cards Disclosure Act	FRB	Multiple Agencies
1988	Home Equity Loan Consumer Protection Act	FRB	Multiple Agencies
1991	Truth in Savings Act	FRB	Multiple Agencies
1996	Omnibus Consolidated Appropriations Act	FRB	Multiple Agencies
1996	Consumer Credit Reporting Reform Act	Multiple Agencies	FTC
1996	Credit Repair Organizations Act	FTC	FTC
2003	Fair and Accurate Credit Transactions Act	FTC/FRB	FTC
2006	Military Lending Act	DOD	Multiple Agencies
2009	Credit Card Accountability Responsibility and Disclosure Act	FRB	Multiple Agencies
2010	Consumer Financial Protection Act of 2010	CFPB	Multiple Agencies
2010	Improving Access to Mainstream Financial Institutions Act	DOT	n/a

FHA- Federal Housing Administration, FRB- Federal Reserve Board, FTC- Federal Trade Commission, DOD- Department of Defense, CFPB- Consumer Financial Protection Bureau, DOT- Department of Treasury
Source: SoRelle 2020

responsible for enforcing regulations for credit originated by the financial institution they oversee. The FTC is given enforcement authority for just under one third of all policies (28 percent).

While federal regulations experience fragmentation, many aspects of consumer financial protection regulation—especially those affecting state-chartered banks, certain types of credit unions, and non-bank entities (e.g., payday lenders)—have historically been subject to state law. This leads to a system in which responsibility for rulemaking and enforcement for financial protections is fragmented both across federal agencies as well as fifty state jurisdictions based on the type of lender in question. So, for example, states can enact different caps on interest charges and fees for credit cards or choose whether to legalize payday lending and whether and how to regulate those practices.

The distribution of financial regulatory power between the federal and state governments has ebbed and flowed over time alongside broader shifts in federalism, but over the last thirty years, the federal government has made increased use of strategic preemption to accomplish partisan goals regarding the degree of government intervention into the market (SoRelle and Walker 2016). Preemption refers to removing or restricting policymaking authority for an issue from a lower level of government. Democratic lawmakers have increasingly turned to floor preemptions, setting a federal minimum standard that all states must meet, while allowing liberal states to introduce further regulation. Republican lawmakers, by contrast, have pushed for increased ceiling preemption, capping the degree of regulation states can implement. For example, in the realm of banking and finance, 62 percent of preemptions enacted under Republican leadership introduced regulatory ceilings compared with only 40 percent enacted under Democratic leadership (SoRelle and Walker 2016). In each of these cases, the push and pull between state and federal regulators creates conditions for decentralized control over consumer financial regulation.

2. The Political Consequences of Fragmented Financial Regulation

What are the consequences of this fragmented yet fluid regulatory arrangement for the ability of different actors to influence consumer financial protection regulations? In particular, how does the fragmentation of finance governance affect the capacity for public interests to meaningfully shape consumer financial protections? What are the consequences for consumers' capacity to gain access to affordable credit while mitigating risk? Scholars have demonstrated how the US financial system is often tilted strongly in favor of business interests (Johnson and Kwak 2010), especially for issues controlled by the Federal Reserve (Jacobs and King 2016). Moreover, analyses of the American political economy identify the fragmented nature of US political and policymaking institutions—and particularly the venue shopping it enables—as a key facilitator of business power broadly construed (e.g., Hacker et al. 2021; Hertel-Fernandez 2019; Robertson 2018). In this chapter, I contend that the broader administrative arrangement for finance governance is emblematic of these twin patterns. I offer a framework for public interest participation in consumer financial regulation that accounts for the costs of participation, visibility of governing actors, and strategic venue shopping that occur within a decentralized system's rulemaking and enforcement.

Specifically, I argue that the administrative arrangement of regulatory rulemaking and enforcement authority for consumer financial protections produce regulatory feedback effects that shape the political behavior of industry and public interest groups as well as citizens around that issue. Scholars have explored how the *ex ante* design of bureaucratic agencies can influence the policy choices agencies adopt, focusing in particular on *ex ante* design as a tool of democratic accountability to legislatures (Moe 1987; Teske 1991, 2004). But these same principles can also be applied to understand how the larger administrative arrangement for a policy area (rather than a single agency's design) can influence democratic accountability among public interest actors.

I draw on the logic of the growing body of policy feedback scholarship, which argues that public policies, particularly those that become durable features of the political landscape, have the capacity to shape future politics in a variety of ways (Lowi 1972; Mettler and SoRelle 2023; Mettler and Soss 2004; Pierson 1993; Skocpol 1992). While policy feedback scholarship initially focused on social rather than regulatory policy, I contend that the specific administrative arrangement for a regulatory issue has the power to shape the landscape of contestation in which groups and individuals engage. Skocpol notes that "Patterns of bureaucratic development influence the orientations of educated middle-class groups as well as the possibilities for all social groups to 'do things' through public authority" (1992: 47). The specific arrangement of bureaucratic authority, therefore, can ease or complicate participation in the ongoing rulemaking process that determines the contours of most forms of protective regulation by shaping the costs of competition, visibility of participatory avenues, and availability of venue shopping actors can engage in the regulatory process. This theory is consistent with the broader contours of power in the American political economy. As Hacker and his colleagues articulate (2021: 20):

> [T]he diversity and multiplicity of venues in America's fragmented system profoundly alters the terrain of political contestation, advantaging organized actors with the resources and reach to venue shop, while creating powerful incentives for individuals and organizations to hoard resources and free-ride on public goods provision.

Figure 3.1 illustrates the specific pathways along which I argue the degree of decentralization for financial regulatory policy can produce feedback effects, thereby shaping the engagement and efficacy of public interest groups and consumers in protective regulatory policymaking.

Three dimensions of decentralization are accounted for. First, regulatory and enforcement authority may be fragmented across agencies within a given jurisdiction. This matters primarily at the federal level, where multiple agencies may be tasked with carrying out consumer financial protection regulations. (Recall the patterns reported in Table 3.1.). Second, the degree to which regulatory authority is devolved to the states can increase or decrease decentralization of authority. Finally, whether federal policymakers engage in preemption (and what types of preemption they adopt) can influence the degree of decentralized regulatory authority. Decentralization for financial regulation can subsequently shape the participation and efficacy of public interest and industry actors through three primary pathways: the cost of navigating the regulatory process, the visibility of appropriate

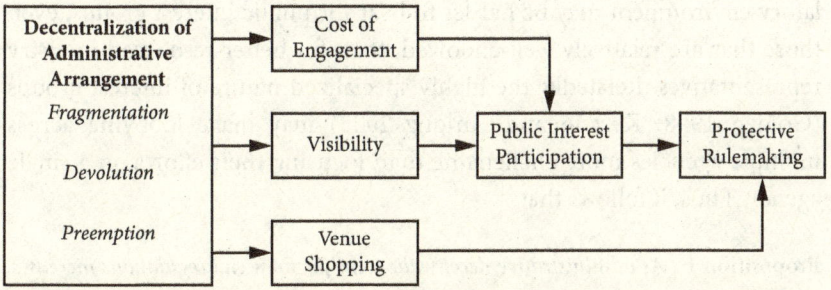

Figure 3.1 Regulatory Feedback Effects of Administrative Decentralization

regulatory actors to engage with, and the ability to venue shop to find receptive regulators.

Costs of Engagement

With respect to the cost of engaging in political contestation, I argue that fragmented, or decentralized, regulatory authority increases the potential resource burden of engagement because it must take place across multiple fronts, while centralized authority reduces that cost. Scholars have demonstrated how individuals and groups incur costs to participate in regulatory rulemaking. For example, they must have knowledge of the rulemaking calendar and modes of participation, and groups must be positioned to organize effectively to exert influence both prior to and during the public comment period (Furlong 1997; Yackee 2006). It is often the perceived cost, and not concerns over the expected return on investment (Kerwin and Furlong 2005; Yackee 2014), that lead public interest groups to limit their engagement in regulatory rulemaking.

When a new issue comes to the fore, the degree of regulatory fragmentation determines how many agencies or states must be lobbied simultaneously. For borrowers, therefore, a fragmented system may significantly raise the costs for people to track proposed rules and navigate the decentralized complaint or comment process to engage on issues of concern. For public interest organizations, rather than investing resources into developing relationships with regulators in a single agency or state, fragmented rulemaking and enforcement authority requires interest groups to establish and maintain connections across as many agencies as have responsibility for either rulemaking or enforcing rules for a given financial regulation. The costs associated with lobbying in a fragmented versus a centralized regulatory environment may be harder to bear for public interest groups, even those that are relatively well-endowed, than for better-resourced industry representatives. Relatedly, the highly specialized nature of interest groups (Golden 1998; Kerwin and Furlong 2005) may make lobbying across multiple agencies more challenging than focusing their efforts on a single agency. Thus, it follows that:

Proposition 1: *As administrative decentralization for financial regulations increases, the costs of participation increase, leading to diminished or narrowed public interest participation in finance governance.*

Visibility of Government Actors

As Figure 3.1 illustrates, the degree of regulatory fragmentation in the administration of a policy may also influence how visible to the average borrower a government agency is in the financial regulatory process. If a single administrative agency is granted oversight for a policy area, people may come to associate that agency with its respective policy jurisdiction. By contrast, when the regulatory oversight for a policy area is dispersed across multiple agencies, it may be far more complicated for citizens to identify the appropriate government body responsible for addressing their concern. Scholars have demonstrated that the ability for a person to identify a clear target for action is a necessary condition of political engagement (Arnold 1990; Gamson 1992; Klandermans 1997). Thus, when government actors are hidden or submerged for a particular issue, citizen engagement on behalf of that issue is diminished (Mettler 2011; SoRelle and Shanks 2024). This has been established in the specific case of consumer financial regulation, wherein the average borrower does not easily perceive government agency involvement in the regulation of financial products and services (SoRelle 2020, 2023).

Devolution and preemption bring a further challenge to visibility beyond that posed by fragmentation within the federal realm. When regulatory oversight is divided across state and federal actors, or preempted from state actors, citizens may not be able to disentangle which level of government is responsible for carrying out consumer financial protection laws (SoRelle and Fullerton 2024). This, once again, may diminish people's capacity to identify and engage with the rulemaking or complaint making for a given issue. Taken together, these issues of visibility suggest that:

Proposition 2: *As administrative decentralization for financial regulations increases, the visibility of relevant government actors decreases, leading to diminished borrower participation in finance governance.*

Venue Shopping

The final pathway along which decentralization can influence financial regulatory outcomes is through the ability to venue shop. As more and more agencies or state jurisdictions are implicated in rulemaking, interest groups have greater capacity to select the venues with which they pursue their desired regulatory outcomes (see Hacker et al. 2021). This dynamic can contribute to what is known as regulatory arbitrage, whereby regulated industries are able to play different agencies against one another in pursuit of the lowest level of regulation (see Carpenter 2014; Levitin 2013). Arbitrage is intensified by two structural elements of the regulatory system: First, at the federal level, many agencies are designed to engage primarily in competitive regulation, meaning they are tasked with ensuring the stability and profitability of the industry under their jurisdiction through pricing and entry policies among others. Consumer protections are a secondary mission. If an agency focused on prudential regulation is given authority over consumer protection rulemaking, bureaucrats may have incentives to defer to the profitability of the industry over the safety of consumers when deciding on the stringency of a regulation.

From the perspective of public interest participation, this phenomenon may affect how receptive bureaucrats are to consumer-oriented concerns. Public interest groups and consumers may think that the chances for successful engagement are higher when dealing with an agency whose mission is to prioritize consumer protection, thus increasing their incentives to engage. By contrast, business interests may be likely to pursue regulation under friendlier terms—namely, with those agencies designed to protect profitability.

The capacity of financial institutions to reclassify to come under the jurisdiction of their preferred agency allows them to leverage these differences in venue mission. Because agencies don't want to "lose" constituents, they have incentives to enact regulations that do not alienate lenders (Carpenter 2014; Levitin 2013). If multiple agencies are responsible for administering or enforcing the same rule to their respective clients, they need to coalesce on the appropriate rule or enforcement strategy. When none of those agencies want to lose clients, this often leads to the lowest common denominator being adopted; thus venue shopping among federal prudential regulators can lead to a regulatory race to the bottom.

A similar dynamic comes from venue shopping at the state level. When decentralization of financial regulation stems from devolution (or the enactment of preemptions that limit or mandate the stringency of state regulations), interest groups may be able to focus their lobbying efforts in states whose partisan or economic environments are most conducive to achieving their results. Business interests may thus be able to concentrate their efforts in achieving deregulation, or lower levels of regulation, in business-friendly states, while public interest groups may focus their efforts in more liberal, consumer protection–friendly states. Because of the relative resource advantage enjoyed by business interests—alongside the lobbying power wielded by conservative, anti-regulatory organizations like the American Legislative Exchange Council (ALEC) (Hertel-Fernandez 2019)—business interests are likely to benefit to a greater degree from this type of state-level regulatory fragmentation. Put simply, they have more resources with which to go shopping. This logic generates the following proposition:

Proposition 3: *As administrative decentralization for financial regulations increases, the ability to venue shop increases, privileging business participation and power in finance governance.*

3. Exploring the Consequences of Fragmented Finance Governance

To explore the potential for decentralization to shape the politics of financial regulation in the United States in accordance with each of the three propositions above, the following section considers three cases, each addressing a different source of fragmentation outlined in Figure 3.1. The first case considers federal fragmentation of credit regulation before and after the creation of the CFPB, focusing particularly on the feedback consequences for public interest participation. The second case considers the 1978 preemption of state usury caps, focusing on how business groups leveraged that preemption to capitalize on venue shopping in the states. The final case looks to the emerging issue of fintech regulation, exploring how decentralization is unfolding in the degree of devolution for addressing earned wage advance apps—a digital alternative to payday loans. This case considers how both business and public interest groups are influenced by the interplay between federal and state regulators for an emerging regulatory issue. For each case, one or more of the feedback mechanisms from Figure 3.1 are explored, drawing both from secondary literature and original archival, interview, and administrative data analysis.[2]

---

[2] Archival research was conducted between 2014 and 2016 at the Franklin Delano Roosevelt and Lyndon Baines Johnson presidential archives and the Consumer Movements archives. Interviews, which focus primarily on the CFPB, were conducted in 2014 and 2015 with leaders from several national consumer advocacy groups.

Federal Fragmentation of Credit Regulation

The growing volume of federal consumer credit protection legislation that began to emerge in the late 1960s meant that policymakers had to decide who would have rulemaking and enforcement authority for the new protective regulations. By the time the first significant regulation of consumer credit, the Truth in Lending Act (TILA), was enacted in 1968, multiple regulatory agencies described previously in the chapter already existed to oversee different types of financial institutions and lenders. Policymakers, therefore, simply assigned authority for the myriad new credit regulations passed in the following decades to whichever of the seven preexisting agencies held responsibility for overseeing the financial institution that provided the regulated type of credit.

But the existing regulatory infrastructure was primarily tasked with prudential regulation—the specific form of competitive regulation that privileges financial institution's profitability and stability, and not the protection of consumers. Regulators thus often lacked the expertise and resources to manage new consumer protection mandates, something they freely admitted to during hearings for the new regulations being considered. James L. Robertson, then-Vice Chairman of the FRB, expressed his concerns with TILA's proposed administrative arrangement despite the agency's overall support for the Act. Robertson explained that the Board was not prepared to create rules for the new law, though he acquiesced that they would be willing to take up the job for what he hoped would be a short period:

> Formulating regulations under this bill would involve the Board in time-consuming consideration of trade practices about which we have very little knowledge ... we will do our best to carry out the assignment, but we hope that in time ... administration of Federal disclosure requirements will be reassigned to an agency better suited to perform the function.
>
> (U.S. House 1967: 668)

But Robertson was even more explicit in his objection to assigning enforcement authority for the new provisions to the Federal Reserve:

> The task of implementing this proposed law will be complicated not only by our lack of knowledge in this field, but also by the fact that the Board has no trained investigative staff. . . . Consequently, we would hope that our only

function under this legislation would be to prescribe regulations. . . . We also hope that Congress will express its desire that all Federal agencies endeavor to secure compliance with the law by lenders and sellers subject to their jurisdiction.

(U.S. House 1967: 668)

The bill eventually adopted Robertson's solution. The authority to propose rules to implement TILA was assigned to the Federal Reserve, despite their lack of expertise in the area, while the power to enforce compliance with the law was fragmented among the existing agencies responsible for overseeing different types of financial institutions. But these other financial regulators were similarly ill-suited to the task. Like the Federal Reserve, their primary missions were to protect the safety and soundness of financial institutions, not to protect consumers. They had neither the expertise nor the incentive to put consumer protection at the fore of their activities. The result is that consumer credit regulations were administered through a fragmented regulatory arrangement in which protecting consumers took a back seat to protecting the profits of financial institutions. This widespread regulatory fragmentation—both across and within policies—presented several problems for public interest participation that are consistent with the theory developed in this chapter.

Costs of Participation

Lobbying financial regulators requires resources, but even the relatively well-endowed national public interest consumer groups struggle with resource constraints. When compared with other policy domains, like environmental protection, consumer groups have less to spend. As one advocate explained:

> If you look across different sectors, the grassroots infrastructure, resources, and capabilities of consumer groups, compared to say, comparable groups elsewhere—environmental groups, health and safety groups, etc.—far more limited and it's always our major weakness. . . . Money, it's very simple. (Interview 0312151)

Exploring the budgets of major national consumer advocacy groups bears this out. While some of the larger national advocacy organizations like the National Consumer Law Center and the Center for Responsible Lending each had annual budgets exceeding eight million dollars in the immediate aftermath of the financial crisis, when lobbying around financial regulation was especially salient (Mayer 2012), much of that money takes the form of restricted funds. For example, according to the Consumer Federation of America's annual reports, the agency had between $1.5 and $2.5 million in unrestricted funds between 2010 and 2014, and that money had to cover all areas of their work, not just consumer credit regulation (CFA 1975–2014). Other national agencies had budgets ranging from only about $500,000 to $2 million.

And the available funding sources could be both limited and unpredictable. As one advocate described of the problem facing consumer groups relative to other public interest causes, "[other groups have] more private donor and foundation and, to some extent industry, aligned industry money as well. Industry money in the consumer financial area is almost all conflicted as well" (Interview 0312151). Foundation support was, in the words of one organization's strategic plan "impossible right now. . . . Some of the commitments we counted on have disappeared because of the economy" (AFFIL 2008). Moreover, some existing organizations perceived that foundations would be less willing to support them because they were not "brand new so can't entice funders as a start up." Another critical source of funding for several organizations came from *cy pres awards*—allocated by judges to nonprofit organizations from unclaimed legal settlement funds. But these windfalls are arbitrary and increasingly under scrutiny (e.g., CFA 1975–2014).

Did the fragmentation of rulemaking and enforcement authority—which required building and maintaining relationships across multiple fronts—exacerbate these resource constraints and inhibit public interest lobbying before the creation of the CFPB? The evidence from advocates suggest it did, at least to a degree. A senior staff member from one national advocacy organization agreed with this assessment, explaining that, "The biggest limit for us is resources and how much we can do" (Interview 1119141). Citing the fragmented environment, another advocate acknowledged, "For the most part, these groups had limited resources, so it's not like they're going to three or four agencies" (Interview 0312151). A third advocate heavily involved in regulatory lobbying suggested that, when an issue was assigned primarily to one organization—in this case, the Federal Reserve—resources were not a severe problem during the rulemaking stage (Interview 0313151). These comments suggest that when regulatory authority was fragmented, costs of lobbying were, indeed, harder for public interest groups to afford.

By contrast, centralization meant lower costs of participation, allowing public interest groups to engage with these specific credit issues more as a result.

Visibility

While costs of lobbying constrain public interest groups' capacity to pursue protective financial regulations, agency visibility is key for individual borrowers who wish to engage in the politics of financial regulation. Scholars have demonstrated how US financial protections hide the role of government actors in the regulatory process, reducing borrowers' political engagement to combat predatory lending (SoRelle 2020, 2023).[3] But how does this relate to the regulatory context? One of the primary ways for consumers to have their voices heard in the rulemaking process is to file complaints that can help agencies detect and address problems. A consequence of regulatory fragmentation prior to the creation of the CFPB, however, was the lack of a unified complaint system for consumers to turn to when they sought redress. Complaint-handling institutions in the realm of consumer finance have long been found by consumers to be either inadequate or obscured (Best 1981). Representative Dennis Moore (D-KS) noted this problem during congressional hearings on consumer financial protection, reporting, "I looked at some of the websites, and it is very, very confusing and takes several clicks sometimes to get to a complaint form or a toll-free number" (U.S. House 2007: 25). Agency representatives acknowledged his assessment, responding that it was a difficult challenge to overcome in the existing regulatory environment.

One of the most significant changes introduced by the CFPB was a central and highly visible consumer complaint system.[4] As one veteran of the consumer movement explained:

> [O]ne of the huge changes is the CFPB complaint database. It's so much more accessible, I think, to consumers. It's responsive, gives them an incentive because it requires a response from the [company] . . . supposedly they do respond, so that's a whole new level of power for consumers. (Interview 1120141)

---

[3] Though see Thurston 2018 for examples of submerged financial governance being highly visible to racially marginalized constituents who lack its protection.

[4] Perhaps another indicator of the complaint database's significance is the degree to which it is reviled by conservatives and businesses, having been a focus of specific legislation to eliminate it. As Mick Mulvaney commented to a room of bankers, he didn't think the CFPB should be running "Yelp for financial services, sponsored by the federal government."

The complaint process was initiated in 2011. It began with credit card complaints, and the CFPB has added new complaint categories over time: mortgages in December 2011; bank accounts and services, private student loans, and other consumer loans in March 2012; credit reporting in October 2012; money transfers in April 2013; debt collection in July 2013; payday loans in November 2013; prepaid cards, credit repair, debt settlement, pawn and title loans in July 2014; and virtual currency in August 2014. As of 2023, the CFPB had taken in over four million consumer credit complaints. The CFPB accepts complaints directly from consumers online or via telephone, mail, email, or fax. Once submitted, the complaint is routed to the appropriate lender or company after staff review. Company responses are provided to consumers. This ability to instigate company action is one of the strong suits of the new system. As one advocate marveled:

> [T]here was a newspaper article talking about somebody [who] complained about overdraft fees with their bank [and] sent a complaint to the CFPB. After complaining and complaining to the bank that they were being mistreated, [they] did not get any response until they filed a [CFPB] complaint, then got a call the next day from somebody at the level of the bank that they could make a change, and they made a change. I suspect that doesn't happen at every bank, but it happens at some, and that's an incredible difference. (Interview 1120141)

Of the complaints handled in 2022, two-thirds were forwarded to companies for a response. About five percent of all complaints submitted to the CFPB fell under the jurisdiction of another agency and were forwarded to the appropriate regulator. Notably, this number of misdirected complaints has fallen sharply from the CFPB's inception. For example, in 2015, nearly one in five complaints were forwarded to different agencies. This suggests that consumers may be much better able to identify the agency for the appropriate type of complaint making as it has become more established—consistent with propositions about visibility. The remaining 30 percent were deemed not actionable. Companies responded to an astounding 96 percent of the complaints sent to them via the CFPB in 2022. Of those cases, just under two thirds (61 percent) were closed with an explanation from the company. The remaining third were closed with some form of monetary or nonmonetary relief—a substantively large rate of remediation.

If centralizing the complaint process in the hands of an agency actively promoting consumer financial protection increases visibility, we should observe growth in consumer complaint making to the CFPB, especially relative to both existing governmental agencies and nonprofit or popular trade associations like the Better Business Bureau (BBB). Indeed, studies have shown in the context of consumer financial protection that making a regulatory agency's complaint process visible to the public increases the likelihood that people report their willingness to engage with the company through complaint making and other forms of contact (SoRelle 2023).

Figure 3.2 reports the percent of all fraud and other consumer complaints submitted to three major organizations—the FTC, the BBB, and the CFPB—since the CFPB first began submitting to the system in 2011.[5] It is important to note in this data that the FTC and the BBB numbers represent complaints for a much larger array of non-finance issues (e.g., consumer software, health care, and sweepstakes); thus we should expect them to comprise a much larger portion of overall complaints. By comparison, the data for the CFPB only includes select consumer financial concerns.

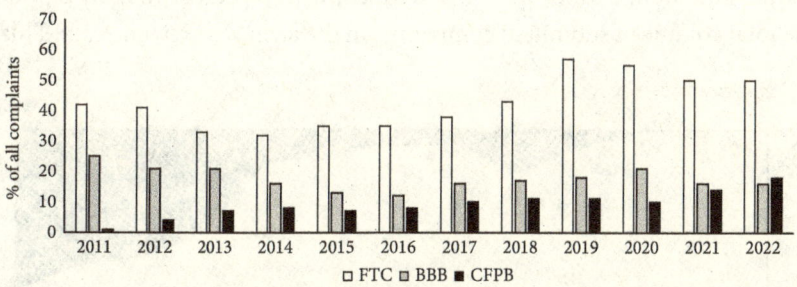

Figure 3.2 Percent of Consumer Complaints by Organization, 2011–2022

Source: Calculated from Consumer Sentinel Annual Reports, 2011–2022.

---

[5] Complaint data was collected by Consumer Sentinel between 2008 and 2022. Consumer Sentinel, established in 1997 for the benefit of law enforcement officials, is a database of consumer complaints that is managed by the FTC. The agency aggregates consumer complaints across all products and services in its jurisdiction, including complaints made to participating federal and state government agencies and private market organizations. Descriptive metrics have been made available to the public every year since 2006. The reports began to incorporate CFPB complaints in 2011, allowing me to analyze patterns of complaint making both before and after the emergence of the CFPB.

As expected, CFPB complaints represent a growing percent of the total complaint volume over this period. In 2011, only one percent of all complaints were submitted through the CFPB. By 2022, almost one in five complaints (18 percent) were submitted through the CFPB, outstripping the total complaint volume for all issues submitted to the BBB. This is a particularly striking change because, while the CFPB is only collecting consumer credit complaints—and a narrower subset than those collected by the other agencies—the measures for both other organizations include a wide variety of non-finance complaints.

Perhaps a better way of examining the potential effect of a more centralized and visible government agency—the CFPB—compared with its predecessors is to look at how much the CFPB contributes to a specific subset of complaints. Since the CFPB has been handling debt collection complaints for a longer period than for some other types of products, Figure 3.3 shows what percent of the total volume of debt collection complaints reported to Consumer Sentinel come from the CFPB versus all other participating organizations.

Once again, the other organizations include both government and market groups that contribute to the database.[6] As the graph shows, debt collection complaints submitted to the CFPB have come to represent roughly half of the total volume of submitted complaints in the agency's first ten years. This

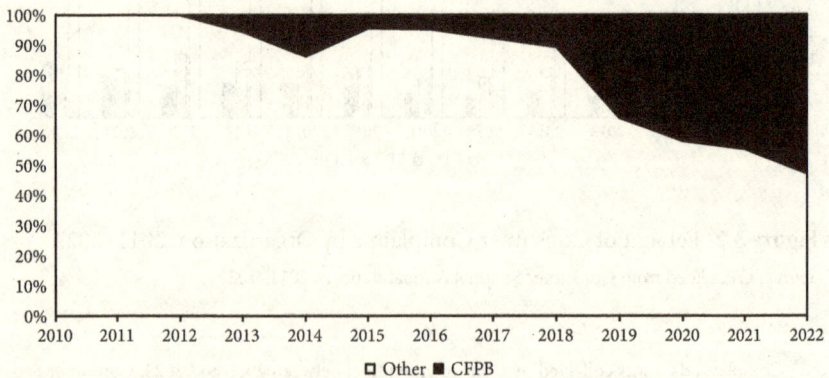

Figure 3.3 Debt Collection Complaints by Organization, 2011–2022

Source: Calculated from CFPB Complaint Database & Consumer Sentinel Annual Reports, 2010–2022

[6] While Consumer Sentinel does not break out its data by reporting agency and product, this number could be calculated using the CFPB's publicly available complaint data for each category.

trend suggests that people are increasingly likely to turn to the CFPB with their credit concerns. Perhaps the increased centralization of authority in a single consumer protection agency has made it easier for citizens to identify a relevant political actor to turn to, thus lowering the costs of engagement. Such a scenario may have been amplified by the extensive and proactive outreach to consumers conducted by the new bureau. Former CFPB Director Richard Cordray elaborated on this point in a 2014 address to the American Bar Association:

> We are the first federal agency ever created with the sole purpose of protecting consumers and seeing that they are treated fairly in the financial marketplace....[I]t means an agency that prides itself on using technology and other new tools to achieve broad outreach to communities across the country and to the individual consumers we were created to serve.

Venue Shopping

Beyond costs and visibility shaping public interest participation, to what extent does fragmentation lead to venue shopping at the federal level? Does the capacity for industry groups to venue shop lead to regulatory arbitrage? During June 2007 hearings about the financial crisis held before the House Financial Services Committee, Sheila Bair, the Republican-appointed Chairperson of the FDIC, explained to lawmakers, "The greatest weakness in today's financial marketplace is the absence of clear consumer protection standards applied uniformly to all participants in the market" (U.S. House 2007: 16). She specifically referenced the problems created by dividing rulemaking and enforcement authority across different agencies with respect to unfair and deceptive acts and practices (UDAP) regulations:

> Well, we enforce UDAP, but we don't have the ability to write rules. And so, because there are no rules, we are finding out we have to use case-by-case determinations and consult a great deal with the Fed and the FTC about what is unfair or deceptive because we don't have the ability to define these terms.
>
> (U.S. House 2007: 27)

The strategy implemented by Congress of fragmenting regulatory authority for credit policies across agencies whose primary missions were promoting prudential regulation should create conditions for regulatory arbitrage. And because lenders have some flexibility to change their charters to come under the authority of the friendliest regulator, financial regulatory agencies have incentives to protect their turf by minimizing regulations, and thus reducing industry backlash. Even those bureaucrats who are inclined toward greater consumer protection are constrained by this competition. The following exchange between Chairperson Bair and Representative Barney Frank illustrates the problem of regulatory arbitrage in stark terms:

BAIR: [S]ince we only have 15 percent of the credit card market, even if we could find authority under safety and soundness to write a rule, we would be imposing that rule only on FDIC-supervised credit card issuers . . .
FRANK: And you would pretty soon have 1.5 percent of the market and not 15 percent if you had a rule and [the other agencies] did not.

(U.S. House 2007: 28)

Frank's response alludes to the possibility that credit card companies would seek to reclassify to avoid FDIC regulations if they were perceived to be too stringent compared with other regulators. Comptroller John Dugan, from the Office of the Comptroller of the Currency, echoed this line of thinking:

I would just add that I agree with that. For many years it was not clear that banking agencies could even take enforcement action under [UDAP]. . . . We do think it would be helpful to have rule-writing authority. . . . Our concern is that if one agency adopts a rule, people could use other charters to do the same activity. . .

(U.S. House 2007: 28)

The result of this scheme for administering credit regulations was that agencies whose primary focus was on bank profitability passed relatively weak consumer protection rules that were then enforced by other agencies with incentives not to unduly anger their constituent banks. Instead of strong rules with active enforcement, consumer protection issues, when dealt with at all, were addressed "informally and confidentially" during other investigatory processes (Carpenter 2014).

It ultimately took fifty years after the enactment of TILA and a massive financial crisis before Vice Chairman Robertson's plea to relocate authority for consumer credit protection rulemaking to an agency designed specifically for that purpose was realized. The Financial Crisis Inquiry Report concluded that, "widespread failures in financial regulation and supervision proved devastating to the stability of the nation's financial markets"

(Financial Crisis Inquiry Commission 2011: xviii). After a difficult fight, the CFPB was ultimately created in 2010 in an attempt to combine much of the rulemaking and enforcement authority for credit regulations under a single agency dedicated to protecting consumers. However, the new agency was not empowered to engage in substantively novel areas of regulation, meaning that outside of the administrative reorganization that the CFPB engendered, other related factors were held constant.

The shift in 2010 toward a more centralized administrative arrangement in the hands of an agency designed to prioritize consumer protection had the potential to change the venue-shopping dynamics that seemed to privilege the interests of banks over borrowers. To what extent did advocates perceive this shift, and how did they view the effects on the efficacy of consumer financial protections? Advocates agreed that prior to the CFPB receptivity was a serious obstacle to effective lobbying. And they attributed the problem explicitly to the fragmentation of the administrative environment amongst agencies designed to promote bank interests. One advocate explained how the lack of focus on consumer protection affected agency behavior from the outset, inhibiting the identification of products and services that needed to be addressed through rulemaking:

> [The structure] meant that it was often hard to identify problems because there was nobody whose job it was, whose primary function it was, it was on them, to look at business practices in consumer welfare. It was a secondary issue behind safety and soundness for virtually all of the banking lenders. (Interview 0312151)

Even after a problem had been identified, the agencies' safety and soundness missions inhibited their ability to enact necessary consumer protections. As another advocate explained:

> For the most part, what the other agencies had was a secondary focus on the issues we're concerned with. Their primary focus was not consumer protection, and their primary focus was the health of the industry that they're regulating, and that often can be articulated in a way that there are contrary interests. If you eliminate this bad product, of course it has an effect on financial welfare of the industry. That's a structural difference that's really important. (Interview 1119141)

Representatives of consumer interest groups agreed that these conditions produced arbitrage, which made it incredibly challenging to get regulators to be receptive to proposals for more stringent reform. One advocate described how arbitrage shaped the process of lobbying for stronger consumer credit protections:

> [T]he structure here, in main part, tended to make it harder for the agencies to mobilize on that problem even when they wanted to address it. . .[I]t took years for all the regulatory agencies [to] align behind an approach, and then the least common denominator situation meant that when they did mobilize behind it, it was pretty weak. (Interview 0312151)

Another expanded on the problem of arbitrage:

> The agencies would compete for members, whether you're a bank, you're a state bank or a federal bank. You can switch, so it was very difficult to get uniform. First, they weren't inclined to be aggressive, and second, they couldn't be consistent. And even if they wanted to act together, it's like getting five agencies together—that's very difficult to do. (Interview 1119141)

The experiences of consumer advocates provide strong evidence to support the argument that the administrative environment for consumer credit policies allowed for industry venue shopping that inhibited the efficacy of public interest lobbying efforts. That argument is made even stronger when contrasting these accounts with advocates' descriptions of their participation in the rulemaking process after the creation of the CFPB, which centralized a significant amount of the rulemaking and enforcement authority for consumer lending in the capable hands of an organization dedicated to protecting consumers. One advocate, who had been busy completing comments in response to several hundred pages of new regulations prior to our meeting, confirmed that working with the new agency was a whole different ballgame (Interview 0313151).

Reducing the incentive for regulatory arbitrage was a key factor in opening the doors to more receptive regulators. As one advocate concluded:

> For us, the most important was the [CFPB's] broad rulemaking authority, and its broad enforcement authority. . . . All that was the key. . . . That's very different than what the other agencies had. . . . It is true that having

this blanket ability to deal with the issues in their area is unique, because before, one agency could act but the other agencies wouldn't, and you'd have inconsistent rules. Now, it's all in one. (Interview 1119141)

Another agreed, summing up the difference succinctly: "Primary focus and market-wide coverage. So, no gaps. No potential for regulatory arbitrage" (Interview 0312151).

Not only did the new administrative arrangement eliminate many of the incentives to engage in arbitrage, but the CFPB also expanded oversight beyond the scope of the lenders overseen by existing financial regulators. One advocate described the expansion of regulatory reach as "totally new, totally fresh, and rather eye-popping" (Interview 1119141). This advocate went on to underscore the ultimate result for public interest lobbyists: "In terms of the history of the [organization], I think this is the most influential we've ever been, since the 70s. I think it's halcyon days for our staff in that regard. They feel they're really accomplishing things."

Federalism and State Usury Cap Preemption

While the previous case explores how fragmentation within a single level of government influences the politics of financial regulation, the dynamics of federalism introduce additional pathways for decentralization. This section explores how the devolution and preemption of regulatory authority shapes the capacity of business interests to influence consumer financial protections. Usury laws—restrictions on the legal interest that can be charged to consumers for a loan—date back to colonial America. By the late 1970s, all but four states had a usury statute in place, although several types of financing had been exempted from those laws (Ackerman 1981). Many states also had additional regulations on the types of fees lenders could charge on top of regular interest rates. In an effort to push for expanded access to consumer credit, federal policymakers saw stringent usury caps as an obstacle. Rather than setting a national interest rate cap, thereby centralizing regulatory authority with a single federal entity, federal policymakers chose instead to implement a unique preemption that incentivized venue shopping to lower the regulatory burdens facing lenders.

In 1978, the Supreme Court ruled in *Marquette National Bank v. First of Omaha Service Corporation* that national-chartered banks were no longer subject to usury laws in the state in which a borrower lived. Instead, banks would be bound only by the regulations for the state in which they were headquartered. This judicial preemption of state consumer protections allowed national-chartered banks to relocate their headquarters to states with virtually no consumer financial protections and "export" higher interest rates and fees across the nation, even to borrowers who lived in states with more stringent caps. The Court's ruling applied the supremacy clause to the National Bank Act of 1864, which established a dual banking system of state- and national-chartered banks (Furletti 2004). In the case of national-chartered banks, it was reasoned, states should not be able to restrict the practices of a lender that was not housed within their jurisdiction.

Emboldened by the Court's decision, Congress enacted a series of legislative measures to further expand a similar preemption of state consumer financial protections. Section 521 of the Depository Institutions Deregulation and Monetary Control Act of 1980 (P.L. 96-221) extended the ability to export interest rates and fees for consumer credit to state-chartered banks that make interstate loans. The Riegle-Neal Interstate Banking and Branching Efficiency Act of 1994 (P.L. 103-328) and §731 of the Gramm-Leach-Bliley Financial Modernization Act of 1999 (P.L. 106-102) further expanded the population of banks that could export most favorable national rates for credit contracts. These choices essentially set states up to win bank business in a competition to see who could be the highest—or, in this case, lowest—bidder for regulatory restrictions.

What followed were conditions amenable to venue shopping. State policymakers had new resource incentives to act to protect or improve their fiscal resources either by keeping existing financial institutions or luring new financial institutions to headquarter within their boundaries. To entice lenders either to stay in state, or to relocate to their state, many state legislatures engaged in a regulatory race-to-the-bottom to reduce usury statutes. In the first five years after enactment of the DIDMCA, fifteen states eliminated usury ceilings with many more raising legal lending limits. As a result, six states came to account for three-quarters of the nation's credit card loan originations despite representing only four percent of the population (Furletti 2004).

Perhaps nowhere was this strategy more successful than in South Dakota and Delaware. The South Dakota legislature raised its state usury ceiling as part of a campaign to boost their local banking industry while enticing Citibank's credit card operations to relocate from New York (Vanatta 2016). Following a similar approach, Delaware entirely repealed its existing usury restrictions to lure MBNA and other mid-Atlantic lenders to make the state their home (Furletti 2004). The result was a stunning increase in state revenues, which fundamentally reshaped state budgets and policymaking capacity. South Dakota's tax income from commercial banks grew from about three million dollars in 1980 to more than 27 million dollars in 1987, while Delaware's commercial bank tax revenue grew an even more astounding amount, from about two million dollars to 40 million dollars (Staten and Johnson 1995: 22). Moreover, by the early 2000s, bank employees represented roughly eight percent of Delaware's adult workforce, generating more than 12 percent of their personal income tax dollars (Furletti 2004).

As other states followed suit with financial deregulation, South Dakota needed to remain an attractive location for Citibank to preserve the state's resource gains. To prevent the lender from doing to South Dakota what it did to New York, the legislature enacted a law that would provide generous tax breaks on bank income exceeding half a billion dollars—a trigger that could only feasibly apply to Citibank (Vanatta 2016). The lending giant has remained, and in 2006 the Citibank CEO attended a 25-year anniversary celebration of the company's move to the Mount Rushmore state, noting it was a partnership that "was good for South Dakota ... [and] saved Citibank" (Vanatta 2016: 78).

The decisions by these states did not happen in a vacuum. They were proactively pursued by industry lenders who saw the shift in decentralized regulatory power as an opportunity to exploit. Companies began to look strategically at the state policy landscape, identifying where they might find legislatures amenable to raising or eliminating interest rate caps. Prior to their move, for example, Citibank determined they would explore relocating to states with usury statutes above 22 percent and legislatures that were in session and open to lobbying. The result was a list of two: South Dakota and Missouri (Vanatta 2016). The impressive returns produced by industry's ability to venue shop were recognized by trade associations as well as public interest group. In the aftermath of the 2008 financial crisis, bank trade associations prioritized preserving preemption in the ensuing Congressional debate over new financial regulations. As U.S. Bancorp executive and chair of the Financial Services Roundtable, Richard Davis, expressed about the unfolding reforms, "If we had one thing to fight for, it would be to protect [federal] preemption [of state law]" (Serres 2010).

Public interest groups had neither the resources nor the leverage to effectively lobby fifty separate state governments. Eliminating usury preemption and fighting for a federal interest rate cap thus became a primary focus of public interest group efforts in recognition of their inability to compete with business in a fifty-state venue shopping game. For example, in the Consumer Federation of America's 1983 annual report, which followed on the heels of both the *Marquette* decision and the passage of DIDMCA, the advocacy group singled out "helping defeat usury preemption" as one of their primary goals—a position that would be reflected in several subsequent reports (CFA 1975–2014). Similarly, preemption was a regular topic in the CFA's newsletter. For example, a 1982 article warns of a savings and loan rescue bill being debated in Congress, "Those words should send a shiver down the spines of all potential consumer borrowers, because where the words banking deregulation are chanted, the words usury preemption cannot be far behind" (CFA 1982).

While the regime set in place by *Marquette* largely remains, the introduction of the CFPB—and the centralization of regulatory authority it established—has smoothed the path for public interest groups to advocate for more federal standards on fees and finance charges. For example, as part of a larger campaign to combat "junk fees" across multiple policy domains, the CFPB has introduced late fee and overdraft fee safe harbor rules that would introduce nationwide caps on charges levied by large banks. These rules would create a new floor preemption requiring states to comply with a minimum standard, thus limiting the capacity of industry groups to venue shop in pursuit of less strenuous regulation. The use of preemption in this case to centralize rulemaking in the CFPB rather than fragment it across states, as the previous section describes, lowers the resource constraints for public interest groups. Instead of lobbying fifty separate state legislatures— an insurmountable cost for most public interest advocates—they can focus their resources on one federal regulator.

Devolution and Earned Wage Advance Apps

While each of the previous two cases revolves around long-standing credit practices and products, the final case explores an emerging issue of financial regulation: fintech. In recent years, financial technologies (fintech)—from cryptocurrency to digital payments—have dramatically reshaped the financial marketplace (Allen et al. 2021). For example, in 2010, fintech lenders originated only three percent of all personal unsecured loans, but by 2018 they accounted for nearly one-third (30 percent) of the market (Jagtiani and Lemieux 2018). One of the most rapidly growing types of fintech are earned wage advance (or access) programs, abbreviated as EWAs. These platforms are part of a growing ecosystem of fintech innovations marketed specifically as less predatory choices for people who struggle with short-term cash flow and otherwise might rely on traditional banking products like payday loans.

EWAs offer cash advances to workers for a small subscription fee or "tip." Many EWA companies operate directly through employers, recouping the cash advance automatically from worker paychecks before the remaining balance is distributed to the employee. Others operate as standalone programs that connect to workers' bank accounts. In this model, the company automatically charges the amount of the advance from a checking account on the designated payday. United States workers made 56 million EWA withdrawals totaling $9.5 billion in 2020 alone, with the industry experiencing major year-over-year growth (Murillo et al. 2022). A proliferation of large companies, like Walmart, Wendy's, and Uber are making EWAs available to their employees, further expanding the market (Collins et al. 2022; Hawkins 2021).

Because of their novelty, EWAs are currently underregulated at both the federal and state levels. EWA companies—echoing the logic of the nascent payday loan industry of the 1980s—argue that their products are not consumer credit to dodge much of the existing financial regulatory infrastructure (Nehf 2022). Under the Trump administration, the CFPB provided EWAs a small victory, issuing an advisory opinion that essentially devolved regulatory authority to the states for these programs. As a result, states can choose whether to regulate EWAs as a form of loan or a type of money-transmission service. Legal scholars have argued that this devolution has created "detrimental regulatory blind spots [that] enable regulatory arbitrage by blurring the lines between once-distinct financial services: money-transmission services and loan services" (Cuttino 2020).

Consumer advocates argue that EWAs are a form of credit, noting that the deferred repayment model they employ has traditionally been associated with a consumer loan. Indeed, payday lenders eventually came under consumer lending regulations for this exact reason. Advocates have expressed a strong preference that EWAs not only be regulated as a form of consumer credit, but that regulations are handled at the federal level. By contrast, EWA providers themselves have pushed states to treat the product as a money-transmission service, hoping for the lowest regulatory bars (Cuttino 2020).

The CFPB's initial choice to devolve authority to the states created strong incentives for venue shopping. With their resource and organizational advantage, industry groups have so far been winning the venue shopping battle. Backing the interests of EWA providers, ALEC has proposed model legislation that would exempt EWAs from state lending regulations, treating the cash advance as a non-credit product and weakening consumer protections. Multiple states are considering or have passed similar bills. By comparison, only a small number, including California, Connecticut, and Massachusetts, are considering provisions to regulate EWAs as credit. The current decentralization of the EWA regulatory infrastructure provides clear advantages to industry actors, whose resources make venue shopping more accessible than consumer groups and borrowers themselves.

4. Importance of Institutional Design for Picking Winners

The concept of a central bank implies, by its very nature, the concentration of regulatory authority for the financial sector. But in a context like the United States, the landscape of finance governance—especially for consumer lending—is instead marked by a historically decentralized approach despite the presence of the Federal Reserve. This chapter demonstrates how the administrative arrangement for finance governance, and in particular the degree of fragmentation it produces, has profound implications for who can wield political influence over that system, with consequence for democratic engagement in regulatory policymaking.

Decentralizing authority for making and implementing rules, both within and across levels of government, has implications for the cost of lobbying, the visibility of government actors involved in the process, and the ability for groups to venue shop to secure their preferred regulatory outcomes. Generally speaking, the cases explored here suggest that financial industry interests benefit from greater fragmentation, while public interests have more opportunities to influence centralized systems. Of course, centralized regulatory institutions can still be prone to industry capture (Bernstein 1955; Huntington 1952; Peltzman 1976; Stigler 1971), but the playing field is more conducive for both public interest groups and citizens to engage meaningfully in the regulatory process. As a result, reforms that restructure the administrative arrangement for financial regulation—like creating the CFPB and investing it with more centralized rulemaking and enforcement authority—can meaningfully change the balance of political power within a system.

It is worth briefly considering, however, the degree to which the centralization of regulatory authority can provide benefits to industry actors as well. Discussions of protective regulatory politics typically pit "consumers" against "businesses," but the financial industry is not a monolith. For some segments of industry, the effort to centralize consumer financial protection in the CFPB generates positive externalities. Take, for example, smaller banks and non-bank entities that are regulated primarily at the state level and come under the jurisdiction of state attorneys general. The presence of the CFPB, with its primary oversight of large bank and non-bank entities, helps to level the playing field from the perspective of state-regulated industries. In the absence of the CFPB, with its centralized—and thus more proactive—approach to consumer financial protection, larger banks may be subject to much less regulatory pressure than their smaller counterparts. This has consequences for how competitive these smaller entities can be.

In cases where financial companies do not benefit from preemption, there may also be increased costs of a fragmented market. In the absence of a centralized agency, these companies face tremendous regulatory compliance costs if they must conform to fifty distinct state regulatory regimes. They face the tradeoff of either bearing the costs of fifty differently tailored products or they can choose to follow the most stringent set of state guidelines for all of their offerings, which may be more burdensome than what the CFPB would require. Of course, industry is generally sufficiently well-resourced to be able to manage these compliance costs (or focus their lobbying in strategic states to lower them), but for emerging or smaller market finance companies, fragmented regulation may be especially burdensome relative to a more centralized approach.

Another consequence of the reality of US finance governance, one that is reflected in the other chapters in this volume, is that the design of financial regulatory institutions is itself inherently political. As the introduction of this chapter illuminates, the very existence of an agency like the CFPB has become a political battle because its design is more conducive to enacting consumer protections. Indeed, the agency's actions since its inception bear that out, with significant strides being made to adopt more robust consumer protections covering overdraft fees, late fees, and payday loans to name a few.

Not only have the agency's rulemaking and enforcement actions returned billions in financial relief to borrowers, but scholars have also shown that the CFPB consumer complaint database reduces racial inequality in the mortgage market, saving over 100 million dollars for minority borrowers (Li 2023).

Of course, centralizing regulatory authority is not a panacea, nor is it the only element of design that can be leveraged to achieve political goals. For example, one of the primary limitations to the capacity of administrative centralization in an agency like the CFPB to improve public interest participation and representation in financial regulation also stems from its design: the investiture of power in a single director. The sway that political appointees hold over the direction of individual agencies—especially when power is vested in a single director rather than a bipartisan board—means that changing presidential administrations may dramatically shape the orientation of rulemaking activity.

Consumer advocates, who were deeply involved in debates over the CFPB's structure from the outset, recognized early on that a pro-consumer director would mean proactive consumer protection, while more bank-friendly leadership could slow that progress. As one advocate acquiesced, "The truth is that consumer financial agencies have their good years and their bad years with a single director. . . . [I]f we get a Republican president . . . you'll see a very sharp shift. Live by the sword, die by the sword" (Interview 0312151). This prognostication was born out in the efforts of President Trump's interim appointees in both his first and second terms. Control over the director position remains a critical lever that presidents—both supporters and opponents of the agency—have at their disposal to exert significant control over the regulatory and enforcement activities of US consumer financial protection.

This presents a catch-22 for a president who opposes stronger consumer protections: On the one hand, weakening the CFPB—or pursuing its elimination through legislative or legal means—would presumably return a greater degree of regulatory power to the patchwork of other federal regulators as well as the states. As this chapter argues, such a move would likely tilt political power back in favor of industry interests over consumers. But such a move could also empower pro-consumer states, for example California, to enact even more stringent financial regulations that companies would be required to comply with. And it would remove a much more direct lever of control over finance governance—the power to appoint a single director (instead of making appointments to bi-partisan boards as in the case of most other federal agencies)—from the president's toolkit.

Despite the ability of partisan administrations to influence the trajectory of a centralized financial regulator, an agency like the CFPB still possesses the power to facilitate more meaningful public interest participation and subsequently enshrine stronger consumer financial protections. Its success in pursuing protective regulations in the absence of major underlying changes to US consumer financial protection legislation exemplifies the role that reducing the relative degree of fragmentation plays in shaping consumer financial protection. And the continued efforts by its detractors to eliminate the CFPB indicate how much it has reshuffled the landscape of political power in finance governance for this particular set of issues. While this chapter explores the relationship between fragmentation and political power in US finance governance, the implications for the political consequences of institutional design in finance governance transcend geographic borders, as subsequent chapters delineate.

References

0312151, [Senior Director] March 12, 2015, Personal Interview.
0313151, [Managing Director] March 13, 2015, Personal Interview.
1119141, [Executive Director] November 19, 2014, Personal Interview.
1120141, [Deputy Director] November 20, 2014, Personal Interview.
1120142, [Campaign Manager] November 20, 2014, Personal Interview.
Ackerman, James M. 1981. "Interest Rates and the Law: A History of Usury." *Arizona State Law Journal* 1: 61–110.
Allen, Franklin, Xian Gu, and Julapa Jagtiani. 2021. "A Survey of Fintech Research and Policy Discussion." *Review of Corporate Finance* 1: 259–339.
Americans for Fairness in Lending (AFFIL). 2008. "Board and Staff Retreat Notes." AFFIL Box 1, Folder 15, Consumer Movement Archives, Manhattan, KS.
Arnold, R. Douglas. 1990. *The Logic of Congressional Action.* New Haven: Yale University Press.
Bernstein, Marver H. 1955. *Regulating Business by Independent Commission.* Princeton: Princeton University Press.
Best, Arthur. 1981. *When Consumers Complain.* New York: Columbia University Press.
Calder, Lendol Glen. 1999. *Financing the American Dream: A Cultural History of Consumer Credit.* Princeton: Princeton University Press.
Carpenter, Daniel. 2001. *The Forging of Bureaucratic Autonomy: Reputations, Networks, and Policy Innovation in Executive Agencies, 1862–1928.* Princeton: Princeton University Press.
Carpenter, David H. 2014. "The Consumer Financial Protection Bureau: A Legal Analysis." Congressional Research Service. Retrieved from https://www.everycrsreport.com/reports/R42572.html.
Collins, J. Michael, Sarah Halpern-Meekin, Melody Harvey, and Jill Hoiting. 2022. "'I Don't Like All Those Fees': Pragmatism About Financial Services Among Low-Income Parents." *Journal of Family and Economic Issues* 44(4): 1–14.

Consumer Federation of America. 1975–2014. "Annual Reports." Consumer Federation of America, unprocessed, Consumer Movement Archives, Manhattan, KS.

Consumer Sentinel. 2008–2015. "Network Reports." Federal Trade Commission. Retrieved from https://www.ftc.gov/enforcement/consumer-sentinel-network/reports.

Cordray, Richard. April 3, 2014. "Prepared Remarks of CFPB Director Richard Cordray." American Bar Association. https://www.consumerfinance.gov/about-us/newsroom/prepared-remarks-of-cfpb-director-richard-cordray-at-the-american-bar-association/.

Cuttino, Nakita Q. 2020. "The Rise of 'Fringetech': Regulatory Risks in Earned-Wage Access." *Northwestern University Law Review* 115: 1505.

Derthick, Martha, and Paul Quirk. 1985. *The Politics of Deregulation.* Washington, DC.: Brookings Institution.

Financial Crisis Inquiry Commission. 2011. *Financial Crisis Inquiry Report.* Washington DC.: Government Printing Office.

Furletti, Mark. 2004. "The Debate over the National Bank Act and the Preemption of State Efforts to Regulate Credit Cards." *Temp. L. Rev.* 77: 425.

Furlong, Scott. 1997. "Interest Group Influence on Rule Making." *Administration & Society* 29(3): 325–347.

Gamson, William. 1992. "The Social Psychology of Collective Action." In *Frontiers in Social Movement Theory*, edited by Aldon Morris and Carol McClurg Mueller, pp. 53–76. New Haven: Yale University Press.

Glaeser, Edward L., and Andrei Shleifer. 2001. *The Rise of the Regulatory State.* Cambridge, MA: National Bureau of Economic Research.

Golden, Marissa. 1998. "Interest Groups in the Rule-Making Process: Who Participates? Whose Voices Get Heard?" *Journal of Public Administration Research and Theory* 8: 245–270.

Hacker, Jacob S., Alexander Hertel-Fernandez, Paul Pierson, and Kathleen Thelen. 2021. "The American Political Economy: A Framework and Agenda for Research." In *The American Political Economy: Politics, Markets, and Power*, edited by Jacob S. Hacker, Alexander Hertel-Fernandez, Paul Pierson, and Kathleen Thelen, pp. 1–48. Cambridge, UK: Cambridge University Press.

Hawkins, Jim. 2021. "Earned Wage Access and the End of Payday Lending." *BUL Rev.* 101: 705.

Hertel-Fernandez, Alexander. 2019. *State Capture: How Conservative Activists, Big Businesses, and Wealthy Donors Reshaped the American States—and the Nation.* Oxford: Oxford University Press.

Hilton, Matthew. 2007. "Consumers and the State since the Second World War." The Annals of the American Academy of Political and Social Science. *The Politics of Consumption/The Consumption of Politics* 611(1): 66–81.

Huntington, Samuel P. 1952. "The Marasmus of the ICC: The Commission, the Railroads, and the Public Interest." *Yale Law Journal* 61: 467–509.

Hyman, Louis. 2011. *Debtor Nation: The History of America in Red Ink.* Princeton: Princeton University Press.

Jacobs, Lawrence, and Desmond King. 2016. *Fed Power: How Finance Wins.* Oxford: Oxford University Press.

Jagtiani, Julapa, and Catharine Lemieux. 2018. "Do Fintech Lenders Penetrate Areas That Are Underserved by Traditional Banks?" *Journal of Economics and Business* 100: 43–54.

Johnson, Simon, and James Kwak. 2010. *13 Bankers: The Wall Street Takeover and the Next Financial Meltdown.* New York: Pantheon Books.

Kerwin, Cornelius M., and Scott R. Furlong. 1992. "Time and Rulemaking: An Empirical Test of Theory." *Journal of Public Administration Research and Theory* 2: 113–138.

Kerwin, Cornelius M., and Scott R. Furlong. 2005. "Interest Group Participation in Rulemaking: A Decade of Change." *Journal of Public Administration Research and Theory* 15: 353–370.

King, Desmond, and Robert C Lieberman. 2009. "Review: Ironies of State Building: A Comparative Perspective on the American State." *World Politics* 61(3): 547–588.

Klandermans, Bert. 1997. *The Social Psychology of Protest*. Oxford: Blackwell Publishers.

Levitin, Adam J. 2013. "The Consumer Financial Protection Bureau: An Introduction." *Review of Banking and Financial Law* 32(2): 321–369.

Li, Xiang. 2023. "Does the Disclosure of Consumer Complaints Reduce Racial Disparities in the Mortgage Lending Market?" Available at *SSRN 4741819* https://papers.ssrn.com/sol3/papers.cfm?abstract_id=4741819.

Lowi, Theodore. 1972. "Four Systems of Policy, Politics, and Choice." *Public Administration Review* 32(4): 298–310.

Mayer, Robert N. 2012. "The US Consumer Movement: A New Era Amid Old Challenges." *Journal of Consumer Affairs* 46(2): 171–189.

Meier, Kenneth J. 1985. *Regulation: Politics, Bureaucracy, and Economics*. New York: St. Martin's Press.

Mettler, Suzanne. 2011. *The Submerged State: How Invisible Government Policies Undermine American Democracy*. Chicago: Chicago University Press.

Mettler, Suzanne, and Mallory SoRelle. 2023. "Policy Feedback Theory." In *Theories of the Policy Process*, edited by Christopher Weible and Samuel Workman. 5th ed. Boulder, CO: Westview Press.

Mettler, Suzanne, and Joe Soss. 2004. "The Consequences of Public Policy for Democratic Citizenship: Bridging Policy Studies and Mass Politics." *Perspectives on Politics* 2(1): 55–73.

Moe, Terry M. 1987. "Interests, Institutions, and Positive Theory: The Politics of the NLRB." *Studies in American Political Development* 2: 236–299.

Murillo, Jose, Boris Vallee, and Dolly Yu. 2022. "Fintech to the (Worker) Rescue: Earned Wage Access and Employee Retention." Available at *SSRN 4067701*.

Nehf, James P. 2022. "Fintech, Payday Loans and the Changing Landscape of Cash-Advance Consumer Credit in the United States." *International Journal on Consumer Law and Practice* 10: 1–21.

Peltzman, Sam. 1976. "Toward a More General Theory of Regulation." *Journal of Law and Economics* 19: 211–240.

Pierson, Paul. 1993. "When Effect Becomes Cause: Policy Feedback and Political Change." *World Politics* 45(4): 595–628.

Prasad, Monica. 2012. *The Land of Too Much: American Abundance and the Paradox of Poverty*. Cambridge, MA: Harvard University Press

Robertson, David B. 2018. *Federalism and the Making of America*. New York: Routledge Press.

Serres, Chris. 2010. "Bill Has Banks Fearing Power of the States." *Star Tribune*. Retrieved from https://www.startribune.com/bill-has-banks-fearing-power-of-the-states/87956447.

Skocpol, Theda. 1992. *Protecting Soldiers and Mothers: The Political Origins of Social Policy in the United States*. Cambridge, MA: Belknap Press of Harvard University Press.

SoRelle, Mallory E. 2020. *Democracy Declined: The Failed Politics of Consumer Financial Protection*. Chicago: University of Chicago Press.

SoRelle, Mallory E. 2023. "Privatizing Financial Protection: Regulatory Feedback and the Politics of Financial Reform." *American Political Science Review* 117(3): 985–1003.

SoRelle, Mallory E., and Allegra H. Fullerton. 2024. "The Policy Feedback Effects of Preemption." *Policy Studies Journal* 52(2): 235–255.

SoRelle, Mallory E., and Delphia Shanks. 2024. "The Policy Acknowledgement Gap: Explaining (Mis) Perceptions of Government Social Program Use." *Policy Studies Journal* 52(1): 47–71.

SoRelle, Mallory E. and Alexis N. Walker. 2016. "Partisan Preemption: The Strategic Use of Federal Preemption Legislation." *Publius: The Journal of Federalism* 46(4): 486–509.

Staten, Michael, and Robert W. Johnson. 1995. "The Case for Deregulating Interest Rates on Consumer Credit." Monograph 31, Credit Research Center, Purdue University.

Stigler, George J. 1971. "The Theory of Economic Regulation." *Bell Journal of Economics and Management Science* 2: 3–21.

Teske, Paul. 1991. "Interests and Institutions in State Regulation." *American Journal of Political Science* 35(1): 139–154.

Teske, Paul. 2004. *Regulation in the States*. Washington, DC: The Brookings Institution.

Trumbull, Gunnar. 2014. *Consumer Lending in France and America: Credit and Welfare*. New York: Cambridge University Press.

U.S. House. Committee on Banking and Currency. 1967. *Consumer Credit Protection Act: Report (to accompany H.R. 11601)*. 90th Congress. December 13, 1967. H. Rep. 90–1040.

U.S. House. Committee on Financial Services. 2007. *Improving Federal Consumer Protection in Financial Services: Hearing before the Committee on Financial Services*. 110th Congress, June 13, 2007.

Vanatta, Sean H. 2016. "Citibank, Credit Cards, and the Local Politics of National Consumer Finance, 1968–1991." *Business History Review* 90(1): 57–80.

Yackee, Susan Webb. 2006. "Sweet-talking the Fourth Branch: The Influence of Interest Group Comments on Federal Agency Rulemaking." *Journal of Public Administration Research and Theory* 16(1): 103–124.

Yackee, Susan Webb. 2014. "Participant Voice in the Bureaucratic Policymaking Process." *Journal of Public Administration Research and Theory* 25: 427–449.

4

Policy and Politics of Payment Systems

Brian Libgober

In the social science literature, central banks are usually described as exercising a few key functions: providing basic financial services for the government, serving as lender of last resort, and executing monetary policy (e.g., Goodman 1991). To the extent that social scientists consider the role politics plays in how a central bank carries out its responsibilities, they have most typically done so by focusing on how such institutions manage the fraught distributive issues around interest rates and the money supply (Rogoff 1985; Christopher Adolph 2013; Binder and Spindel 2018; Adolph 2018). And yet, much of the harshest criticism that the Federal Reserve and other central banks faced in the wake of the 2008 financial crisis focused not so much on their *monetary policies*, but rather their disastrously lax approach to *supervising* financial institutions (e.g., Jacobs and King 2016, 2018). Regulation, supervision, and enforcement are core functions that the Federal Reserve and many other central banks do perform, and that others have done in the past or could again in the future. Certain conceptual models of what central banks are or what they might do seem to have little room for regulation ensuring the safety and soundness of banks, protecting consumers, and advancing broader distributive and economic goals. To be sure, not all central banks stray so far as the Federal Reserve does from the supposed "macroeconomic core" of central bank activity (Wymeersch 2007). Indeed, some countries (notably the United Kingdom) that may have given the central bank important prudential or consumer regulatory functions in the past have been refocused more purely on macroeconomics and steered them away from the messy details of financial regulation (Freytag and Masciandaro 2005). Yet others have doubled down on central banks as financial regulators, including the United States and also others (Jackson 2009). It would be a mistake, therefore, to think of the teleological endpoint of central banks as the exclusively monetary-policy-focused organizational actor

Brian Libgober, *Policy and Politics of Payment Systems*. In: *Picking Winners*. Edited by: Lawrence R. Jacobs and Desmond King, Oxford University Press. © Oxford University Press (2026).
DOI: 10.1093/9780197831823.003.0004

as described in classic models of Kydland and Prescott (1977) or Barro and Gordon (1983). Indeed, as Jacobs and King argue in this volume, the ways that countries organize financial governance are highly path-dependent, with attempts to move off-path facing resistance due to cultural expectations and interest group demands. The role of central banks as financial regulatory authorities is therefore sticky and hardly an (American) aberration. As we consider how to build a social scientific literature around the politics of central banks, we must give a central place to the crucial regulatory role that these kinds of institutions can and do play in financial markets.

A key challenge facing financial regulatory politics, however, is that many such policies land closer to Wall Street than to Main Street. Most financial regulatory policies directly influence the patterns and practices of financial institutions. Only much more indirectly do they tend to affect small businesses, consumers or financial market "civilians." The esoteric subject matter of finance creates difficulties for developing compelling and digestible research on the topic, despite its importance. Audiences rarely have trouble accepting the notion that *someone* should pay attention to what is happening with financial regulation. Some may, however, find themselves wondering whether and why it might not be *someone else* that does so. Finding topics that hit close to home, such as Chloe Thurston's work on housing or Malorie SoRelle's work on consumer finance, and also work that demystifies and concretizes the work of financial governance, such as Alice Pearson's chapter in this volume, are exactly the sort of contributions necessary to entice audiences to grapple with the highly consequential and highly political quality of these institutions' decision-making.

In addition to these and other excellently chosen cases in this volume, Jacobs and King have richly demonstrated across a number of books and articles that cross-national comparisons can illuminate the stakes and the politics behind systems that have a depressing tendency to be naturalized and regarded as inevitable (e.g. Jacobs and King 2016, 2018, 2024). While Jacobs and King's model building is certainly very necessary and much appreciated by those tilling in the same orchards, their focus on national financial systems leaves room for considering how the broader explanations rooted in political economy play out with respect to the particular policies those national systems adopt. In turn, consideration of specific policy cases can be expected to challenge or nuance their broader perspective on national financial system governance. Indeed, in order to crystallize the differences between financial governance models, it is crucial to have examples of how countries with differing models of financial governance reach different outcomes for nearly identical problems arising at roughly the same time. Such examples would also do much to highlight the necessity for thinking about the politics of financial regulation as an important part of comparative political economy, and also convey what the larger model of financial regulatory governance might be missing.

Given such considerations, plastic payment card regulation represents an ideal case, with Australia and the United States offering a particularly strong contrast. Let me first introduce the topic of plastic payment cards and motivate the topic of its regulation, before turning to explain the work of this chapter (Vanatta 2024). In regard to plastic payment cards, the first thing to know is that there are two major varieties: credit cards and debit cards. When a consumer pays for a product via debit, their bank account is decreased by the cost of the transaction. The bank account of the merchant is increased by the same amount, less a transaction fee or "discount." With payment via credit, the transaction is similar, except the consumer's bank increases a revolving loan balance instead of debiting their account. Because credit card purchases are essentially loans, they involve more risk to the bank, and so the merchant discount rate is typically higher than with debit transactions in order to compensate the consumer's bank for taking the risk. The companies that facilitate the transaction between the merchant bank and the consumer bank are called "payment networks."

Payment networks are a "platform" businesses in much the same way that Uber, Amazon, or Meta are platform business (Thelen 2018; Culpepper and Thelen 2020). The "market failure" that regulation might aim to correct is very much an outcome that these firms design (Rilinger 2024), and from which they profit. The two largest payment platforms in most countries are Visa and Mastercard. Both Visa and Mastercard are members of the S&P 100, a rare club for the most well-established and valuable public companies in the world. They each earn over 10 billion dollars a year while processing approximately 10 trillion dollars worth of transactions. In plastic card schemes, the payment networks set the discount rate that determine the size of the "tax" or "toll" on transactions passing over their network. To compete with one another, these networks kick back part of the transaction tax to consumer-facing banks. In turn, these banks entice customers to sign up for their card offerings with valuable inducements such as cash bonuses, airline miles, lounge access, and even more eclectic club goods such as "Sculpted Yoga™ at the Guggenheim . . . an exclusive evening of yoga, mindfulness, and art at the Guggenheim Museum, hosted by Equinox."[1] The fees that card-issuing banks earn off their cards, and which pay for these customer benefits, are known as "interchange fees." Interchange fee offerings differ by network and by card, with the high-rewards card favored by high-income earners often leading to higher interchange fees. Merchants accept these higher fees because they want to appeal to high-income consumers, and in general they accept interchange fees because customers want to use these technologies to make a sale. Merchants are able to offset the costs of receiving payment by raising prices, but network rules often require merchants to give all consumers the same price regardless of payment method. In this way, plastic payment networks facilitate the upward redistribution of wealth from lower income to higher income consumers, from those who cannot afford "premium" cards to those who can.

If this complex web of kickbacks, upward wealth redistribution, and taxes on retail transaction seems to be an activity crying out for government intervention, it will come as little surprise that plastic card markets are often regulated. Indeed, because of their tight connection with and expertise in the intricacies of payment systems, *central banks* are frequently the ones entrusted with the task of addressing the gravitational tendency of plastic payment systems toward market failure. Central banks in the United States, Australia, Brazil, China, and numerous other countries today regulate plastic payment cards, the dominant non-cash payment mechanism for retail transactions.[2] Moreover, the effectiveness of these regulatory regimes is highly varied. While data on pricing of card services is scarce (and intentionally kept so by the card companies), one commonly used measure of the network's extractive capacity is the size of its interchange fees. The interchange fee, it bears repeating, is the kickback accruing to banks that issue plastic cards from the network, the "transfer" in the tax-and-transfer scheme. Depending on the particular network or even the *particular card* involved in the retail transaction, one may see deeper or more superficial "haircuts" for merchants off their sales, greater or lower interchange fee revenue to banks, more generous or less generous incentives for card holders, and more or less extensive upward wealth redistribution associated with this Rube

---

[1] https://perma.cc/8YGC-AFST.

[2] The Kansas City Fed tracks public authority involvement in plastic card markets worldwide, and as of August 2023 finds that forty-seven countries have sought to regulate these markets. Twenty of these involve central bank regulation, usually in the form of price-ceilings. Other public authorities most typically implicated include competition authorities and courts (Hayashi et al, 2023).

Goldberg machine. Figure 4.1 shows the cost of a typical transaction using credit and debit in five countries according to data from the Reserve Bank of Australia. In the United States, the interchange fee on a $50 credit card purchase would be roughly 90 cents (or 2 percent). In Australia, the interchange fee on the same transaction would be less than $0.11 (or 0.2 percent). Debit cards have lower transaction costs in both contexts, but still the US debit card transaction costs six times as much as it would in Australia. A "risky" credit transaction in Australia has almost a third the interchange fee of a "safe" debit transaction in the United States.

What explains the exorbitantly higher costs of these financial services in the United States than in other jurisdictions? I argue that such questions should be regarded as being at the very heart of the politics of central banking, as central banks so often are the ones called upon to regulate these markets. National comparative analysis has a unique ability to reveal paths not taken and available alternatives not considered. Following their lead, this chapter will explore the strongly contrasting regulatory paths that two countries have taken, and also evaluate some potential explanations for why they have done so. In particular, it turns out that the regulatory regime for plastic cards developed by the US Federal Reserve is very weak as compared with the regime developed by the Reserve Bank of Australia. In part, the US

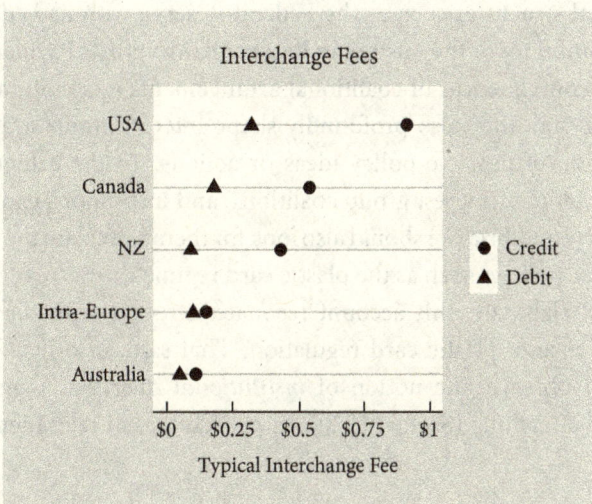

Figure 4.1 Typical Costs of a $50 Transaction across Four-Party Schemes in Five Countries

Source: Reserve Bank of Australia, Review of Retail Payments Regulation, October 2021.

regulatory regime is weak by Congressional design. Yet it has emerged far frailer than what its Congressional authors had hoped or might have reasonably expected, or even what the Federal Reserve initially proposed to do. By contrast, the Reserve Bank of Australia is notable for having developed a very robust set of payment system regulations. Indeed, the regime that Australia developed within the first few years of regulating these products was already much more robust than the US regime only started thanks to the Dodd-Frank Act enacted almost a decade later. The United States was later and frailer to the plastic payment regulation game than Australia, despite the fact that these technologies originated in the United States.

Momentarily taking for granted that the regulatory regimes are as described, I wish to press toward the essay's deeper focus on causes. Jacobs and King's theoretical framework in this volume represents a strong starting point for answering this question. They describe national financial governance regimes as falling into either neoliberal or social rights equilibria.[3] Although I do not read Jacobs and King to be asserting that neoliberalism is an endpoint of no return, their framework presents these regimes as "sticky" for several reasons. In particular, their account explains the stickiness of financial governance equilibria through three factors: interest coalitions, cultural expectations or "toolkits" (Swidler 1986), and institutional arrangements. These explanations are distinguishable, but hard to fully separate. Institutional structures such as the Federal Reserve with its Federal Open Market Committee or the Australian Reserve Bank with its Payment Systems Board are consequences of coalitional arrangements and cultural expectations. That said, they also profoundly shape interest group strategies and the reception of possible policy ideas or actions. To the extent that cultural expectations, interest group coalitions, and institutions explain broad *system-level* equilibria, we should also look for them to explain the resolution of particular policies such as the plastic card regime.

As I will elaborate, this account resonates strongly with the comparative experience of plastic card regulation. That said, in order for it to fit the story I observe, the notion of *institutional structures* requires some conceptual stretching (Sartori 1970). In particular, as I read them, the sort

---

[3] Jacobs and King use the term "model," which for most purposes is certainly appropriate. To distinguish more clearly between the outcomes and explanations for politics, however, I will use the term *equilibrium* to describe a prevailing state of affairs and *model* to describe a set of causal processes that create this outcome. Doing so will help avoid the redundancy inherent in discussing explanatory models for national models of financial governance.

of institutional structures that Jacobs and King most emphasize are the set of policymaking organizations, their internal configuration, and the relationships of these entities with one another. Without denying the causal importance of institutional structures so conceived, one may still trace the process by which the US regulator "watered down" its debit card regulations and conclude that the Federal Reserve could have produced a better outcome for the public. To explain why the US central bank failed to regulate as effectively as it might have in this case, one needs something more. Indeed, I argue that the institutional mechanisms for engaging stakeholders were a pivotal explanation for why the resulting financial regulation was so weak in the United States. If the structures for engaging stakeholders were altered, it might (or even likely would) have resulted in different outcomes. Put differently, despite the admittedly balkanized structure of financial regulatory policymaking in the United States, the Federal Reserve might have developed a far stronger regulatory regime, but a stronger regime was not considered as strongly as it might have been due to the lopsided pattern of interest group participation in the rule development process. In short, the Federal Reserve's *laissez faire* approach to stakeholder governance, in many ways typical of US regulators, produced a considerably more finance-friendly regulatory regime than the far more intentional approach the Australian regulator has used. Institutions for channeling or diverting information from financial system stakeholder are a key aspect of the politics of central banking, and very much an important explanation for why systems develop strong regulatory frameworks or ones that allow the finance sector to win at the expense of other groups.

1. Plastic Card Markets: Competitive Solutions and Regulatory Perimeters

A core premise of this chapter is that the Australian and US cases have dramatically different regulatory regimes for these financial products. Before reaching this point, however, I wish to address a more naive question about whether regulation is desirable at all and if the market failure paradigm makes any sense. Can an efficient, high-performance plastic card regime exist with dramatically lower profitability for card companies? Figure 4.1 certainly suggests so, but such charts may hide important qualitative differences. Consideration of the question offers an opportunity to cover the market mechanism and sharpen the policy questions at stake in regulation. I will argue that indeed a dramatically lower cost solution is not only theoretically possible, but it actually exists—not in an obviously very different national economic and policy context, but in Canada. Surprisingly, service costs in this third market are not subject to specific economic regulation as they are in the United States or Australia. Indeed, despite the lack of regulation, the pricing of debit card transactions in the Canadian marketplace are roughly half what they are than the United States. The fact that prices in Canada for this financial product were so much lower was undoubtedly an important causal factor in the development of US regulation. Many retailers that pushed for regulating these products did business on both sides of the border and so were quite aware that the fees had to be priced far above, and argued this point before the regulator as a key fact supporting the notion of market failure in the United States.[4]

The major explanation for why debit card prices are so much lower in Canada is the market power of a homegrown debit card network, Interac. Interac was founded in 1984 by a collection of Canadian banks. Their goal was to allow customers to use ATMs across institutions. Eventually, they grew the network into a point-of-sale system that spread widely to retailers and businesses across the Canadian provinces. Although in the 1980s there was competition between Interac and other similar domestic networks, as well as between Interac and its fast-growing American competitors, all the major Canadian banks eventually unified to support the domestic payment system. Given the concentration of the Canadian banking sector, the support of the largest banks in Canada was enough to ensure they covered the vast majority of consumers. Importantly, a key feature of the Interac collaboration that differed from Mastercard and Visa was its financing and pricing strategy. As a 1996 consent decree with the Canadian competition authorities makes clear (Competition Tribunal (Canada), 1995), Interac was a nonprofit venture that financed capital investments primarily through membership dues from participating banks. It charged member banks its cost of providing service. This bears repeating: In Canada's debit card market, the fees that Interac charged initially, and indeed still charges, are *zero*. Interac does not need to induce banks to join its platform, because they all own the platform already. Interac carries a very large volume of transactions, although

---

[4] Meeting Between Federal Reserve Staff and Merchant Payments Coalition, Nov 2, 2010. https://www.federalreserve.gov/newsevents/rr-commpublic/merchants_payment_coalition_meeting_20101102.pdf.

it is not the only network that provides debit cards in Canada. Even so, the pricing structure it uses has implied that other entrants into the marketplace, such as Visa and Mastercard, have needed to price their services "dramatically lower than [their pricing] in any other market in the world," (O'Connell 2009) as the CEO of the Interac network testified before the Canadian Parliament.

That Visa and Mastercard would mark up the same service by 200 percent depending on which side of the border they happen to be on is startling, in some ways even more startling than the now familiar differences in the cost of medical care and prescription drugs between the United States and Canada. The profits accruing to pharmaceutical companies are part of the bargain to getting these valuable medicines developed. As far as other differences in the cost of medical care, these are complicated by differences in quality that are hard to measure. By contrast, it is not immediately obvious what "quality" of debit card payment might mean. Academics affiliated with the International Center for Law and Economics have published widely on the benefits of payment platforms and the downsides of regulation. In one typical article, the authors claim that debit cards are less useful internationally and on the internet than US-equivalent cards (Lee et al. 2013). They also claim that Canadians pay more for basic banking services, with free checking accounts relatively rarer, for example, because there is a smaller subsidy via debit card interchange for the creation of accounts. Of course, it could also be argued that these are relatively trifling inconveniences or even advantages. Indeed, some would say it is *a good thing* that the Canadian system makes the cost of banking services visible, as consumers will move their business to lower-cost providers and encourage market efficiency. The largely hidden implicit costs of banking services to US consumers arguably make inefficiency (and profits) rampant. The most persuasive argument that Lee et al. (2013) offers is that the limited profitability of the debit card system in Canada has encouraged the expansion of alternative plastic payment systems with potentially more worrisome features for consumers (e.g., credit cards). Indeed, Figure 4.1 does reveal that Canadian interchange fees on credit cards are high by international standards, although not as high as the costs of plastic cards in the United States. While low-cost debit card services probably do something to constrain the cost of a substitute good (i.e., credit card payments) it appears that Canada has not fully escaped the issues in the plastic payment marketplace because its "competitive" solution is not comprehensive. The risk of regulatory arbitrage and flight to other market segments or payment technologies is ubiquitous in finance but especially here.

As a way of provoking consideration of the possible directions of regulatory arbitrage, Figure 4.2 distinguishes three possible models of plastic card payment. In addition to debit and credit, which have already been described, it adds a third: prepaid plastic cards. In a prepaid card scheme, which are increasingly commonly used for welfare and other governmental benefits, an account tied to the card is loaded with value and the card otherwise typically processes much like a debit transaction. Prepaid cards raise concerns about know-your-customer laws, organized crime, and other unsavory issues that are much less worrisome when cash is tied to accounts held in banks. While I am unaware of "premium prepaid" cards which offer high interchange fees and generous kickbacks to consumers, one could imagine that incautious regulation might encourage their development.

Another and perhaps even likelier direction of regulatory arbitrage is less on the dimension of payment timing, and more on the level of network structure. Figure 4.2 presents a "four-party" payment system, which is the one used by the dominant networks Visa and Mastercard as well as other smaller providers such as Interac. The four-party model assumes that the network, the issuer, and the acquirer are all different entities. But not all networks are structured with such separation. Particular merchants often conspire with their banks to issue cards to their customers directly, capitalizing on their direct relationships with consumers and cutting out consumer

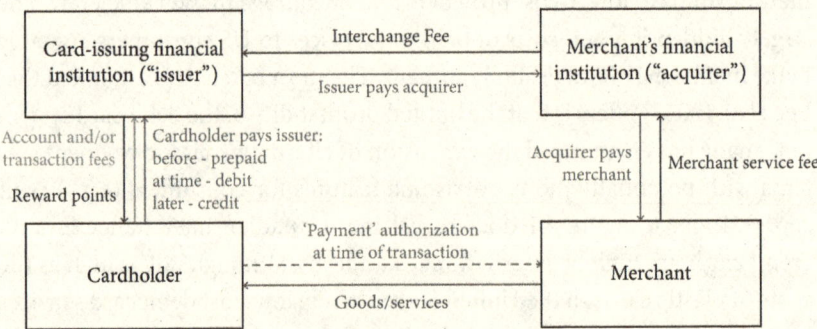

Figure 4.2 Stylized Flows in Plastic Card Transactions

Source: Reserve Bank of Australia. Review of Retail Payments Regulation: Issues Paper. November 2019. https://www.rba.gov.au/payments-and-infrastructure/review-of-retail-payments-regulation/pdf/review-of-retail-payments-regulation-issues-paper-nov-2019.pdf.

bank middlemen to reduce costs. In such a "closed loop" system, the merchant's bank plays a role akin to the issuer and network, but for a limited set of transactions, although one can imagine a number of retailers gathering together on a shared closed loop. Fintechs such as Paypal or Venmo are attempting an analogous and opposite strategy, and claiming an increasingly large share of payment transactions through their so-called "three-party" architecture. In a three-party system, the network internalizes the role of issuer and acquirer, so that the customer and the merchant have direct banking relationships with the network. By integrating the role of other banks in the transaction, the three-party network is often able to realize efficiencies, but also potentially more pricing power. Some of the first payment plastic systems, notably Diner's Club and American Express, both continue to operate three-party payment models. The challenge for such networks is acquiring customers so that merchants will want to take payment using the system. An open network can go to a bank and, if it convinces the bank to adopt the system, acquire a large number of customers quickly. Historically, the three-party network does not have this luxury.

Having said that, payment practices in China have evolved in interesting ways over the last decade and they may give an indication of where things are headed. In China, Alibaba and WeChat exploited their relationship with consumers as internet stores and messaging apps, respectively, in rolling out three-party payment networks that now each have over a billion users. Instead of paying with a plastic card, it is possible to scan a QR code with a phone (see Figure 4.3). Flight from plastic cards to similar-functioning, but different enough platform payment mechanisms is also a possibility from overly stringent regulation. If the Chinese experience is any indication, then large platform tech companies such as Apple, Facebook, and Amazon are

(a) A card imprinter   (b) A payment terminal   (c) QR codes

Figure 4.3 The evolution of retail payment mechanisms
Source: Wikimedia.

reasonably likely successors for payment processing if plastic card networks were regulated to extinction. Such a turn of events would not obviously be better for consumers, merchants, or anyone outside of these large technology platforms, and policymakers who consider regulating such markets are reasonably wary about provoking a transformation in the marketplace toward that kind of "integrated" payment platform.

2. Regulatory Regimes Compared: The United States and Australia

Plastic card regulation is multifaceted; however its primary mechanisms in both the Australian and US case are the reduction of interchange fees via direct price (fee) limits and other measures that more indirectly seek to stoke competition. Table 4.1 compares some salient aspects of the Australian and United States plastic payment regulation regimes. Of particular interest are the fee limits and their application. Australia has a ten-cent interchange limit if pricing of debit card transactions works off a fixed fee, or 0.2 percent of transaction value if priced depending on size of transaction (Reserve Bank of Australia 2016b, [4.1]). If a transaction costs less than $500, and the vast majority of such transactions are relatively small, then the ten-cent limit is the binding constraint. By contrast, the United States limits debit card interchange transactions to 21 cents plus 0.05 percent of the value of the transaction, which is more than double.[5] Australia has a 0.8 percent of transaction cost limit on credit transactions (Reserve Bank of Australia 2016a, 4.1). The United States does not comprehensively regulate plastic cards and, in particular, does not regulate credit card interchange fees or related network rules.[6]

Besides hard price-caps, the Australian regime encourages price reductions through market mechanisms by ensuring that the transaction costs associated with plastic payment are visible to consumers and retailers. These efforts have no equivalent in US regulation. In Australia, merchants have

[5] Board of Governors of the Federal Reserve System. 2011. "Federal Reserve Issues a Final Rule Establishing Standards for Debit Card Interchange Fees and Prohibiting Network Exclusivity Arrangements and Routing Restrictions." June 29, 2011. https://www.federalreserve.gov/newsevents/pressreleases/bcreg20110629a.htm.

[6] There is a long-running antitrust case about network rules in the United States, however the competition laws implicated are not specific to plastic cards and are therefore beyond the scope of this essay.

Table 4.1 Comparing Key Features of the Regimes for Regulating Plastic Payments in Australia and the United States.

	Australia		United States	
Regime Coverage	Comprehensive		Debit Only	
Regime Features	Interchange Fee Limits		Interchange Fee Limits	
	Credit	0.8%	Credit	None
	Debit	10 cents for fixed price; 0.2% for variable price	Debit	21 cents + 0.05% transaction value
	Merchant Surcharging	Merchant's choice	Merchant Surcharging	Network's choice
	Cash Discounts	Merchant's choice	Cash Discounts	Merchant's choice
	Honor-all-cards	Merchant's choice	Honor-all-cards	Network's choice
	Clearly Distinguishable Cards	Required	Clearly Distinguishable Cards	Not required
	Network exclusivity	No, but subject to preclear-ance	Network exclusivity	Two networks minimum
	Routing restrictions	Prohibited	Routing restrictions.	Prohibited
Regulations	Interchange Fee Limits All Networks	2003	Interchange Fee and Rules Prohibitions	2011
	Update and Prohibitions on Rules	2006	Fraud-Prevention Limit Adjustments	2012
	Update and Prohibitions on Rules	2007	Network Exclusivity Update	2022
	EFTOPs Interchange Fee Limits Revised	2010	NPRM: Interchange Fee Limit Reduction	2023
	Interchange Fee Limits Reduced	2016		
	Interchange Fee Limits Reduced and Sub-benchmarks	2021		

a right to offer different prices to customers presenting different cards, including the right to decline some cards offered by one network but not others. Australia requires cards have clearly distinguishable markings that allow merchants to develop nuanced pricing strategies for the kinds of cards presented. By contrast, the United States only protects the right of merchants to offer discounts for cash. Networks are free to prevent merchants from surcharging. Visa, Mastercard, and other networks in the United States insist on honor-all-cards rules that require merchants to accept all co-branded cards on their network if they want to be on the network at all. In particular, the honor-all-cards rule forces merchants to accept the premium cards that exacerbate upward redistribution, even if they have no particular interest in accommodating high-end consumers, who may have more than one alternative card on hand that simply does not offer equal kickbacks. The honor-all-cards rule can also serve to protect less efficient banking providers, for example because it does not allow the merchant to discriminate against those banks who must insist on a higher interchange fee to provide the service at all. The aspect of the rule enabling discrimination against banks would prove important in the US case as many of the least efficient consumer banks are that way because they are smaller and lack economies of scale, so the honor-all-cards rule is a rule that protects the least profitable banks from discrimination by savvy merchants.

The one and only way that the US regime offers questionably stronger protection to merchants is through its prohibition on network exclusivity. This rule requires that chips on debit cards provide at least two network routes for a transaction, and no restrictions on merchant's choice of how to route a debit transaction. This is a valuable benefit, to be sure. It provides some modicum of competition over the "rails" that connect the consumer and merchant bank. In fact, one major issue with debit card regulation in Australia has been bank issuers defaulting their cards to use the more expensive "international" debit network rather than the less profitable local debit network. The Australian regime does not force cards to be capable of passing the transaction over two or more sets of rails, so in this sense is weaker, however it does subject new cards that are only able to go over a single set of rails to preclearance, meaning that they need specific regulatory approval. Moreover, the vast majority of debit cards carry at least two networks, and the merchants in Australia also have the right to choose their transaction's network route just as they do in the United States. By contrast, testimony from US consumer groups suggests rampant evasion of the prohibition on network exclusivity (Mierzwinski Testimony, Senate Judiciary Hearing May

4, 2022). Not only is the regulatory regime of Australia more robust in every distinguishable dimension, it is also much more dynamic. As the table shows, Australian card regulation has been comprehensively reviewed every five years or so since the early 2000s. The Federal Reserve has only recently proposed its second interchange fee limit reduction some twelve years after its first set of regulations. The Federal Reserve's 2023 updated debit regulation proposal has not received finalization at present writing more than nine months after its initial promulgation. One may reasonably doubt that it will be finalized.

3. Contrasting Legislative Paths to Delegation

The differing qualities of the regulatory regime are partially attributable to differences in their legislative antecedents. At least superficially, the circumstances that caused legislative action in both cases were fairly similar. Considering first the Australian case, it is worth noting that the early 1990s were a difficult time for Australia economically. The country had in those years experienced its worst recession since the Great Depression. Challenging economic conditions led to the collapse of several notable financial institutions, including two government-controlled savings banks. The Labor government became increasingly unpopular as the economy continued to flail, leading eventually to its ouster in March of 1996 by John Howard's center-right coalition. Several months after assuming office, the Liberal-National Treasury Secretary Peter Costello established the Financial System Inquiry, better known as the Wallis Inquiry after its chairman, who also happened to be the President of the Business Council of Australia, a trade association representing the nation's largest corporations. In contrast with the 1981 Campbell Inquiry, undertaken by the prior Liberal-National Coalition government with an explicitly deregulatory focus, the Wallis Inquiry asked to "stocktake" about the deregulatory efforts. It was also asked to make recommendations about regulatory responsive that would balance economic efficiency and growth with concerns about stability and fairness (Wallis 1997, vii).

While the Inquiry made numerous recommendations, important to our purposes is its viewpoint on payment systems, which parliament would soon adopt via the Payment Systems Regulation Bill of 1998. In particular, the Inquiry recommended the creation of a separate "Payments System Board" within Australia's central bank, which would be headed by the Governor of the Reserve Bank of Australia but have a more diverse membership, with an outright majority of members appointed by the Treasurer for five-year terms. The PSB would be the primary regulator of payment systems, and the Wallis Inquiry adopted a clear view that access to payment systems needed to be open "and not controlled by industry organizations" as for example Bankcard was at the time. The Inquiry also recommended the establishment of performance benchmarks (Wallis, 1997, 54), the disbanding of the ASPC, and explicitly granted PSB a role in assessing whether pricing of interchange was "appropriate." The Payment Systems Regulation Bill empowered the PSB to achieve these ends with broad powers

(1) The Reserve Bank is given the power to designate payment systems. . .
(2) The Reserve Bank has the following power to designate payment systems: (a) it may impose an access regime on the participants in the payment system. . .(b) it may make standards to be complied with by participants in the payment system. . .c) and it may arbitrate disputes relating to the payment system. . .(d) it may give directions to participants in the payment system (PSR Bill of 1998, Part 3)

These powers are later elaborated as implying that the Reserve Bank can designate whatever it wants as a payment system; can setup an access regime that identifies who are participants in that system (and thereby also regulate them); set up whatever standards they desire to promote the public interest as they see it; and also serve as a judge in disputes between participants. It is worth noting that the Reserve Bank's administrative power is quite breathtaking from the US standpoint, although constrained to some degree by the "public interest" standard to which the Bank is held:

In determining, for the purposes of this Act, if particular action is or would be in, or contrary to, the public interest, the Reserve Bank is to have regard to the desirability of payment systems:(a) being (in its [the Reserve Bank's] opinion) (i) financially safe for use by participants; and (ii) efficient; and (iii) competitive; and (b) not (in its opinion) materially causing or contributing to increased risk to the financial system. (Parliament of Australia 1998, p. 5)

These powers were soon put to use. Beginning in 2002, the PSB began to impose a new and comprehensive regulatory regime on plastic payment systems. In particular, it began by applying new disclosure rules on all three major networks simultaneously, and then in 2003 began applying network-level interchange fee caps. Initially, these were based on somewhat complex formulas to account for the differing costs that each network bore, but in 2005 a common limit of 0.5 percent per transaction was imposed on the two major networks (Bullock 2010). On credit cards, this same limit continues to be in force, although the PSB in its most recent review reiterated that it continues to believe "there is no strong justification for significant interchange fee payments in mature card systems." We shall return to dwell on the significance of such statements in considering the organizational culture of the regulators. The PSB's primary reason for holding off on further reductions was concern about advantaging three-party systems, only one of which (American Express) is regulated, and associated concerns of regulatory flight we have previously addressed. Debit and prepaid card interchange fees have followed a similar trajectory, in 2010 they were capped at twelve cents per transaction and are currently at ten cents, with a prevailing average of eight cents per transaction.

While US plastic payment card regulation also emerged from a financial crisis, it did not develop from a comprehensive reform effort led by general business interests. Instead, it emerged as more of a pet project for a key senator and acutely impacted non-finance business groups. The earliest inklings of similar plastic card regulation in the United States were a 2006 Senate Judiciary Committee Hearing (U.S. House Committee on the Judiciary 2006). It is worth noting that these efforts were held some eight years after Australia's Parliament decided to extensively regulate this market. "I was the most junior member of the Judiciary Committee when I first learned about interchange fees,"[7] Senator Durbin would later remark about that hearing, although his comments at the time already find him presenting pretty well-formed opinions. Indeed, he explicitly characterized interchange fees as "a 2 percent tax on grocery purchases and a lot of other purchases." He expressed dismay in that hearing at the power of the credit card companies, recently demonstrated through the success of the 2005 Bankruptcy Abuse

---

[7] Durbin, Richard J. 2024. "Credit Card Competition Act of 2023 (Executive Session)." *Congressional Record* Vol. 170, No. 50 (Senate), March 21, 2024: S2484-S2485. https://www.congress.gov/congressional-record/volume-170/issue-50/senate-section/article/S2484-1.

Prevention Act. The 2006 interchange fee hearing did not bear any immediate fruit in terms of concrete bills or proposals. Indeed, there appears to have been more interest in laws protecting consumers from abusive billing practices, which ultimately culminated in the CARD Act, enacted May 22, 2009.[8] The CARD Act did not address swipe fees, although Durbin would later reveal that he had wanted to propose regulating credit card swipe fees as part of that reform, but he was stymied (by whom he does not say) (Congressional Record, May 12, 2010, S3589). Other reporting suggests that the finance lobby actively and successfully headed off this possible course of action (Mattingly and Schmidt 2011).

In July of 2009, with the ink still wet on the CARD Act, the Retail Industry Leaders Association—a trade group for large big box retailers such as Walmart, Target, and Home Depot—is reported to have met in Washington and decided then to focus on pursuing a proposal that "eventually became the Durbin amendment" (Mattingly and Schmidt 2011). As Mattingly and Schmidt (2011) report, the retailers pursued a sophisticated and multipronged strategy of mobilizing grass roots support of 20 million small-business owners; subsidizing meetings between some owners and their representatives; and the deployment of an all-Republican lobbying firm Fierce, Isakowitz, and Blalock. By contrast, the finance industry was "preoccupied with other threats" in the Dodd-Frank Act. On May 12, 2010, Senator Durbin introduced what would eventually become Section 1075 of the Dodd-Frank Act, and the amendment passed 64 to 33 seemingly without debate the very next day.

While some would later argue the lack of debate on the amendment reflects its status as a sort of ill-conceived or one-man afterthought, contemporary reporting and my own interview-based work confirm that the provision was among the most hotly contested pieces of the Dodd-Frank Act. Senator Durbin contemporaneously explained the reason for the silence about the hotly contested provisions as being that "[i]t is not an easy amendment. . .because we have some competition among friends." What exactly Durbin meant by that remark is not exactly clear. The *New York Times* report about the amendment's passage (printed on page one of that day's issue) described how one Republican Georgia Senator had the uncomfortable task of informing SunTrust, the largest bank in his state, "that this time

---

[8] Around the same time of the hearing there were a number of precursor bills floating around, including Senator Dodd's Credit Card Act of 2005, Senator Menendez's Credit Card Reform Act of 2006, and then Representative Sander's Consumer Credit Card Protection Act of 2005.

he planned to vote against the bank and with Coca-Cola and Home Depot, two other Georgia companies that had lobbied him fiercely" (*NY Times*, May 15, 2010).

While it is possible that Durbin may have had in mind conflict between major lobbying powerhouses, my own view is that foremost in his mind was probably the conflict between interests that a US politician would have substantial reservations about opposing in public—in particular, credit unions and smaller local banks, on the one hand, and small retail businesses on the other. Indeed, Durbin's remarks dwelt much more squarely on the fact that small business was so very much in favor of the bill, for obvious reasons, and he also seemed to want to undermine the *bona fides* of lobbyists for these smaller financial entities. Indeed, Senator Durbin's floor remarks provide an unusually candid view of the coalitions in play and the rationale for the legislative compromise. In particular, Durbin noted that "you would think there would be general support of this across the board, except from the credit card companies and the biggest banks. But it turns out there is opposition to this from the so-called independent community banks and credit unions." To mollify this group, Durbin had initially proposed to exempt banks with less than $1 billion in assets under management, but when that proved insufficient he expanded the exemption to $10 billion. "99 percent of banks would be exempt," Durbin argued, "All but the very largest banks in America . . . All but three credit unions in the United States have less than $10 billion." Durbin went on to call out the trade associations for smaller financial entities as lacking "clean hands in the debate" and lobbying in bad faith. "Why do they still oppose it?" Durbin wondered aloud on the Senate floor, "I have learned why. The Independent Community Bank Association is a major issuer of credit and debit cards. They are one of the top 25 credit card issuers in the United States and are the 23rd largest debit card issuers. They make a lot of money off interchange fees. . . They are not arguing on behalf of small banks. Sadly, they are arguing on behalf of their own trade association credit cards and the fact they receive these generous interchange fees." He described the Congress as simply asking for the Federal Reserve to act as "arbiter" in determining whether interchange fees are reasonable and proportional. Indeed, Durbin repeated several times during the debate "We do not establish a rate. That is left entirely to the Federal Reserve to review" (Durbin 2010, S3704).

And review they did. Section 1075 of the Dodd-Frank Act gave the Federal Reserve nine months from enactment to promulgate rules that standards about what fee was reasonable and proportional. On December 12, 2010, the agency issued a proposed rule that described two potential regulatory approaches. Under the simpler alternative, an interchange fee limit of $0.12 was proposed. Under the more complex alternative, a limit of $0.07 was proposed but the issuer could earn up to $0.12 if they could establish that their variable costs were at least that high. The proposed rule clarifies that these fee limits were arrived at through a survey of covered debit-card issuers (Board of Governors of the Federal Reserve System 2010, 81725), and in particular that $0.07 was the median variable cost for card issuers and $0.12 was the 80th percentile of costs for such issuers. Such fee levels appear to present as a classic exercise in what Posner (2014) calls "norming," a style of financial regulation designed to impose costs only on a minority of weaker firms. Posner criticizes norming as a strategy for avoiding political conflict at the expense of substance, although it is notable that at least in this case the proposed fee levels would have been relatively low in terms of international comparison, at least as low as current Australian regulatory levels and considerably lower than Australian fee limits at the time.

The proposed rules clearly did not create substantial room for profit off debit interchange fees, and more surprisingly created substantial pushback from small and medium-sized financial entities. Although not directly implicated by the regulation, these firms feared that Visa and Mastercard would evolve pricing norms in such a way as to set rates closer to these levels. Although I am not aware of their having specifically threatened to set fees against small entities in this way, one cannot discount the possibility that Visa and Mastercard may have done so. The costs associated with debit cards for smaller firms were likely relatively higher, although the survey instrument did not reach them so it is hard to know. Whatever the case, the agency received a torrent of criticism on its proposal, over 1500 unique comment letters, and extensive questioning on Capitol Hill. On March 29, 2011, Fed Chairman Bernanke informed Congress the rule would not be finalized by its statutory deadline, indeed the agency would miss their deadline by roughly eighty days. As described above, the Federal Reserve's final fee limit was more than three times larger than it might have been. Indeed Senator Durbin would later chide the Federal Reserve that "the intent of the Durbin Amendment was not to allow covered issuers to maintain a sizable profit margin; yet, the Board's final rule did just that." (Durbin Letter to Fed, May 10, 2024). He would also note in that same 2024 letter that the NPRM's proposal to update the regulation every two years had been left far by the wayside, and that their proposal to lower the base fee from 21 cents to 14.4 cents did not close the distance required under his own amendment.

The key question that the comparison of the two cases draws out is why the United States initially appeared on track to develop a price cap that was half of Australia's, at least against the large financial entities covered by the law, but pulled its punches and wound up with one that was more than twice as high. The consequences of this decision were profound. Equity analysts estimated at the time of Durbin's ratification that debit interchange fees represent about 14 percent of Mastercard's total revenue and 30 percent of Visa's revenue (Shutler and Frazer 2011). With annual revenues for each of these firms measured in the tens of billions annually, the Federal Reserve's decision to set a higher fee limit *for the next decade* was an event of huge policy significance, with a net cost to the public likely measuring in the hundreds of billions of dollars.

4. Institutional Differences

With the initial puzzle of Figure 4.1 now sharpened into one of how central banks have allocated their discretion around fee limits especially, I turn to the question of differences between central bank institutions. Table 4.2 highlight the key differences.

Table 4.2 Comparing Key Features of the Institutional Design of Plastic Payment Regulators in Australia and the United States.

	Australia	United States
Enabling Legislation	Payment Systems Regulation Bill (1998)	Durbin Amendment to Dodd Frank Act (2010)
Primary Regulator	Payment Systems Board	Federal Reserve Board
Board Membership	RBA Governor	Seven Governors
	RBA Appointee	
	ARPA Member	
	(Up to) Five Treasury Appointees	
Term Length	5 years for appointees No limits for agency designates	14 years

By far the most obvious difference between the institutions is the fact that the Australian financial reform created a special board within the Reserve Bank of Australia to handle this particular policymaking task, while the Federal Reserve had no such special policymaking body for payment systems. It is notable that the idea of special purpose boards within the central bank is not novel to the Australian case. Indeed, in the United States monetary policy is not set by the Federal Reserve Board but rather by the Federal Open Market Committee (FOMC). The FOMC has all seven members of the Federal Reserve Board, but also the Presidents of five reserve banks. The Federal Reserve Board of Governors, appointed for fourteen-year terms, approves the agency's regulatory policies, such as those involving payment systems. By contrast, in Australia the Reserve Bank Board of Australia makes monetary policy while the Payment Systems Board makes policies related to the agency's major supervisory responsibility over payment systems.

The Payment Systems Board is headed by the Reserve Bank's governor (their CEO, equivalent to the role of Chair). It includes an additional representative of the Reserve Bank, a representative from the Australian Prudential Regulation Authority, and most notably five additional appointments by the Treasurer. The Treasurer, who is a political figure in Australia chosen by the parliamentary majority, appoints their people for relatively short terms (five years). The structure of the committee is such that the Treasurer's direct appointees have an outright majority on the Board. It is worth noting that the RBA Governor serves for a seven-year term and is also appointed by the Treasurer, while the members of the leadership of the Australian Prudential Regulatory Authority are on five-year terms and also appointed by the Treasurer. Clearly, much of the ultimate appointment authority goes to the Treasurer. Although not statutorily required, it is also notable that one of the Treasurer's appointees has been for the last decade the chair of the Australian Competition and Consumer Commission (ACCC). This softer membership norm likely helps to embed a focus on these important dimensions of the plastic payment policy in the central banks' decision making, and also collaboration with competition authorities. It is notable, however, that the earliest and likely most consequential decisions for the agency were made prior to the appointment of the ACCC chair.

While statutory analysis appears to give relatively great influence to the Treasurer and thereby the parliamentary majority, and also creates opportunity to empower the users of payment systems on the board without tipping central bank monetary policy, in practice the appointments do not appear to have worked out that way. The overwhelming number of Board members for the PSB have received their appointment from Liberal Treasurers, for example (see Figure 4.4). In part, this development has occurred because until recently (May 2022), the Labor government has only had control of Treasury for an almost five-year period between December 2007 and September 2013, which was generally insufficient to promote turnover given the typical five-year appointments. Compounding matters, some Liberal appointees were reappointed by the Labor government. From the standpoint of biography, the differences between Labor and Liberal appointees hardly appear obvious. The first appointee by the Labor Treasurer, Brian Wilson, was the Managing Director of investment bank Lazard, for example, while the first three appointees by the Liberal Treasurer were also professionals from the banking industry. Over a dozen of the twenty-seven board members this body have been bankers or from the finance industry. One even spent over twenty years at Visa. A brief skim of their biographies reveal that besides banking and finance, the most common professional backgrounds for board members is (a) banking or finance law and (b) internal hires from the Reserve Bank.

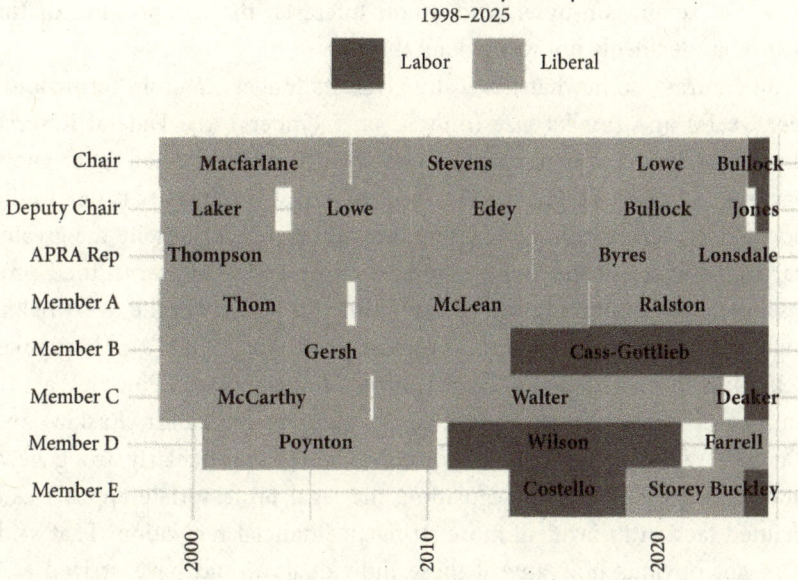

Figure 4.4 Members of the Payments Systems Board by Party of Appointing Treasurer.

To the extent that one identifies the stringency of Australian regulation with a defined bloc or background of board members, one must presume it comes from the viewpoint of these internal promotions. The current governor of the Reserve Bank of Australia, for example, Michelle Bullock, was the chief manager of the bank's Payments Policy Department from 1998–2007 and then head of the department until 2010. She was appointed by the RBA as its own designate in 2016. After reappointment and promotion to the Governorship, Bullock is expected to serve until 2030, making her undoubtedly one of the most important single individuals for Australian Payments Policy. Judging from her comments in various public fora, she presents as a reluctant, but nevertheless insistent regulator. She hardly presents as a Naderite warrior for consumers. Indeed, rather than having any obvious commitment to one set of stakeholders over another, what immediately becomes obvious is her passion and knowledge of the subject matter. In 2023, the then recently installed Chair of the Reserve Bank of Australia began her remarks at the Summit of the Australian Payment Networks, a trade association event funded by large banks and payment networks, by declaring, "Payments—I love payments. And I'm in a room full of like minded people, so I'm ecstatic to be here."[9] To the extent that one would have anticipated an institution setup to deliver for broad, politically powerful retail, consumer, and union interests, the composition of the board has decidedly not worked out that way.

By contrast, somewhat ironically given its longer statutory terms fourteen years) and smaller size (only seven members), the Federal Reserve Board has since the enactment of plastic card regulation had much more partisan balance (see Figure 4.5). In large part, this diversity is due to the norm of Governors not completing their entire terms. Despite the greater partisan balance of the Board members of the Federal Reserve, their professional backgrounds are more monolithic. In particular, the overwhelmingly most common background is as an economics PhD (e.g., Bernanke, Yellen); with a smattering of lawyers turned financiers (e.g. Powell, Warsh); and government-lawyers turned law professors (e.g. Barr, Raskin, and Tarullo). While none of these backgrounds betray a particularly strong viewpoint against plastic card regulation, the legal professoriate appears as a defined faction in favor of more stringent financial regulation. That said, it is not obvious how any of these individuals would have arrived at a hardened viewpoint on the topic of plastic payments, with the possible

---

[9] https://youtu.be/Ue50HSlZnjM?si=BPwBiE_EAGQsR3ro&t=79.

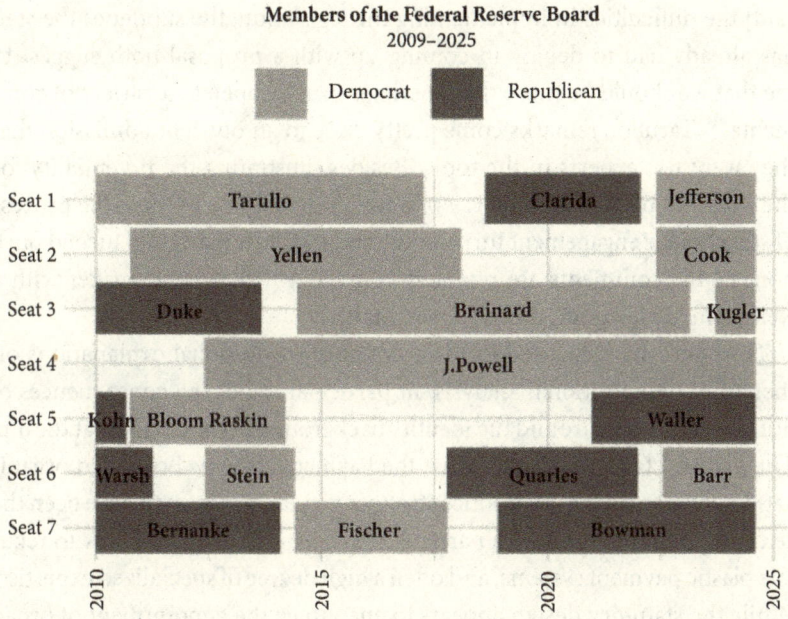

Figure 4.5 Members of the Federal Reserve Board by party of appointing President.

exception of Michael Barr (a Biden appointee) who helped craft the 2009 CARD Act.

The lack of any particular interest in the regulatory subject matter of payments regulation among the Board came through strongly at the first meeting where the Board decided to propose the rule, which has thankfully been recorded for posterity (PSB meetings are not public). After receiving a fifteen-minute presentation by the staff of their proposed policy, Chairman Bernanke asked two questions: first, he asked them to explain "the economics" justifying government intervention in plastic cards utilities and, second, indicated that he knew other countries did regulate these costs but wanted to know how the proposal compared. For better or worse, none of the Board members at the Federal Reserve was constituted like Bullock to self-describe as a payments geek. Indeed, even the clearly pro-regulation Tarullo, while seeming to advance the viewpoint that the Durbin amendment would be best read as requiring something closer to a 4 cent cap and no allowance for bank profits, remarked "I think we need to be particularly open-minded here to comments. I mean, sometimes when we put out a proposed rule we are pretty convinced that we've got it basically right . . . [that said] the difficulties in implementing the legislation, the subtleties the staff has already had to deploy in coming up with a proposal both suggest to me that we should be more than, perhaps usually open to a variety of comments."[10] Tarullo's remarks come pretty close to an outright admission that they were not experts in the topic. Besides illustrating the potentiality for the Board to be pushed one way or another depending on how the process of stakeholder engagement turned out (and indeed already had turned out), none of the comments are remotely consistent with a policymaker with a well-formed viewpoint on its subject matter.

Thus far, I have focused in my account of institutional explanations on themes of organizational analysis, in particular about the consequences of bureaucratic structure and the identity background of the deciders at the top. The primary takeaway is that what the Payment Systems Board did organizationally, if anything, to produce stronger regulation seems to have been the selection of individuals with particular interest in the topic of how to regulate plastic payment systems, and often a high degree of specialized expertise. While the statutory design appears to encourage the appointment of broad interests, in practice the body has been dominated by bankers, albeit not often bankers with a vested interest in plastic payments (with one possible exception in the retired vice-president at Visa). By contrast, despite the Federal Reserve's structural independence, in practice it has represented a more diverse array of partisan interests over the almost fifteen years of plastic card policymaking. That said, the professional backgrounds of the FRB were not conducive to the cultivation of expertise or concern about payment systems in particular, especially given the relatively monolithic background of board members in academic economics.

5. Cultural Expectations

If the previous section has made the case that the most important difference institutionally was that the PSB was set up to care about the issue in a way that the Federal Reserve was not, then the purpose of this section is to consider how that sense of mission or purpose filtered down through the central bank to the staff. Indeed, the record of deliberation at the Federal Reserve Board conveys the clear sense that the staff had presented the

---

[10] https://www.youtube.com/watch?v=IaJqZMfqXNY.

Board with a take-it-or-leave-it offer: a policy that was getting approved late for proposal and headed for a missed deadline is not one that the Board can easily reject. There is less decision-making transparency about the PSB's process than the Federal Reserve's, unfortunately, so it is harder to assess the extent to which staff versus the Board drove the policymaking process in that agency. That said, the PSB members meet once per quarter in Sydney for three-and-a-half hours "and usually conclude with a light lunch."[11] The control mechanisms appear to be such that the staff of the PSB also had plenty of room to move into the driver's seat.

Defining the role of culture in predicting organizational behaviors is difficult, particularly in a rational choice framework (Kreps 1990; Gibbons and Prusak 2020; Acemoglu and Robinson 2024). Much of what organizations do is a result of practice, and as Hannan and Freeman (1984) argue what organizations are primarily good at is doing tomorrow what they did today. The role of cultural expectations is often most visible at periods of rupture or crisis, when the actor has to do something *different* than what it has before, and in this sense the early years are a particularly revealing time to look at an organization to understand its cultural assumptions. At a conference in 2010, then Head of the Payments Policy Department and later governor Michelle Bullock was asked a question about the incentives that industry has to self-regulate and the credibility of the "RBA threat" to impose regulation on the industry:

> I think things have changed dramatically since the payment system board was formed in 1998. At that point in time, there was very much a point of view that the regulator should be very hands off. The payments industry can look after itself. It became quite clear early on that the Payment System Board and the RBA meant business. And the result of that has been that the industry, whether or not they agree, they know that they do have to do something about it.[12]

The cultural shift in the industry that the PSB engineered required an extraordinary commitment to follow through on its regulation, and we have seen that right from the gate the PSB was issuing very strong regulations that forced the industry to heel. A strong viewpoint or agenda on payments

---

[11] https://www.rba.gov.au/about-rba/boards/psb-board.html.
[12] Bullock, "Address to Cards and Payments Australasia 2010" (March 15, 2010) https://www.rba. gov.au/speeches/list.html#bullock.

come from the earliest available staff documents. In September of 1999, the Payments System Board and Australia's Competition and Consumer Commission launched a systematic study into debit and credit cards, with the final report appearing in October of 2000 (Reserve Bank of Australia 2000). As governmental reports go, it was remarkably damning. It noted that concerns about consumers and merchants receiving no benefits due to technological improvements *could already at that time* be found in other governmental reports going back nearly a decade. Page (ii) of the executive summary of the report describes plastic payment cards as an unambiguous case of market failure: "[I]n contrast to most other markets, end-users of card services do not have any direct influence on the price-setting process. This reduction in the normal market discipline has potential implications for efficiency and equity." The report did accept the basic premise that payment networks have substantial value and that interchange fees might prove necessary to ensuring their existence; however it did not find any economic principles for determining how high these fees should be nor in which way these should flow (i.e., perhaps customers or merchants should receive a discount for taking payment in plastic, because such payment is potentially more efficient for the card-issuing bank than alternatives such as cash or check). The report concludes by articulating two broad principles for interchange fees to function efficiently. First, these fees should "not overcompensate financial institutions for the costs they incur," and second the fees should "be subject to regular review as costs and other conditions" change, in particular with the presumption that costs should generally decline with technological improvements. Neither condition was met in Australia at the time, and in the staff's view that implied the need for regulation.

While Bullock's remarks to the Australian Payment industry suggest some possibility of cooption or mission-malaise, in fact even recent documents and reports from Reserve Bank staff reaffirm many of the basic principles of regulation that we shall see are quite at odds with the tenor of comparable discussions in the US context. The 2021 "Conclusions Paper" from their most recent regulatory review asserts, "The Board's long-held view is that interchange fees should generally be as low as possible, especially in mature payments systems." It went on to cite a number of possible benefits associated with lowering fees further, including lower payment costs, less costs for goods and services, and more competition in the market for payment products. In justifying some degree of inaction in lowering fees, the

PSB staff argued that the costs in Australia were already low by international standards, that the standards had been changed only four years prior, and customers were pivoting to debit cards away from credit cards, which the regulator considered a positive development for multiple reasons. It is worth recalling the theoretical concerns about regulatory flight that were raised earlier. The wait-and-see approach the PSB describes in 2021 is not necessarily consistent with cooption, although some degree of that is a possible concern.

By contrast, the staff of the Federal Reserve Board appear to have had far less commitment to the basic premises of regulation. In May of 2009, even before the Durbin amendment was enacted, several economists who would later be involved with the rulemaking published a discussion paper on the topic (Prager et al. 2009). The report highlights many of the policy issues inherent in card regulation discussed above—for example the potential for higher prices and cross-subsidies from lower to higher-income individuals (p. 9). The authors canvas the theoretical literature and conclude that "profit maximization does not, in general, lead the network to set the interchange fee at the level that maximizes social welfare" (p. 21) and moreover "competition between card systems is not a sufficient condition to yield an efficient interchange fee" (p. 23). In looking at the comparative evidence, they note that Australia had generated dramatic reductions in prices of payments (p. 39). At the same time, they also noted with some concern that "the average value of cardholder rewards had declined and average annual cardholder fees have risen."

While one might think that these remarks were building toward an endorsement of Australian-style regulation in the United States, in fact they were headed toward ambivalence and discomfort with the entire regulatory project.

> Some common concerns arise in connection with all of the policy options discussed in this section. First, the possible effects of any intervention are highly uncertain. Although economic models can provide some insights regarding the qualitative effects of a policy intervention, they typically have little to say about the quantitative magnitudes of these effects. Furthermore, the theoretical models tend to be highly stylized, and therefore may fail to capture important real-world features that influence the effect of an intervention. . . . A second concern common to all of the interventions considered here is the possible redistribution of surplus (i.e., the difference

between benefits and costs) across parties. . . . A lower interchange fee, for example, might involve lower surplus for card users and issuing banks and higher surplus for noncard users and merchants. Such concerns do not relate to economic efficiency, but rather involve judgments about equity in the distribution of surplus among different groups in the economy. . . . Finally, much of the debate surrounding the payment card industry has focused on interchange fees in four-party credit card systems. However, issues regarding the structure of fees in a transaction also apply to debit and three-party card systems. . .a narrow intervention that targets interchange fees for credit cards (or even interchange fees for both credit and debit cards) could have effects on competition and pricing throughout the entire retail payments market.

The overall takeaway was "policymakers should proceed with caution, carefully assessing the potential effects of any contemplated intervention upon the payments system as a whole." One wonders how the Federal Reserve could possibly make monetary policy if it held itself to this evidentiary standard, where there are also weak and stylized models with poor predictive power, rampant and complex issues of economic distribution, and unpredictable side-effects with possible downside risks. Indeed, the overall recommendation of the report appears to be policy "F. Do Nothing," which the authors assert "has a number of advantages" in light of the fact that there was "no rigorous empirical evidence" to support the existence of interchange pricing inefficiencies generally predicted by the economic theory they themselves discuss.

The Federal Reserve staff's palpable discomfort with the notion of redistribution is remarkable, especially considering what other actions the agency as a whole was taking at the same time, and surfaced repeatedly in their discussions and decision making. During the finalization of the rule, Bernanke asked the staff about how the rule would affect consumers, which he described as "the ultimate beneficiary—we hope." The staff member who answered, also one of the authors on the 2009 report, gave her proposal the hard sell: "it's very hard to predict how any individual consumer will be affected. . .and we can't really say in advance how those are going to play out."[13] The lingering sense of unease and discomfort among Federal

---

[13] Board of Governors of the Federal Reserve System. 2010. *Open Board Meeting on Proposed Rules Governing Debit Card Interchange Fees and Routing*. December 16, 2010. Video, YouTube. https://www.youtube.com/watch?v=IaJqZMfqXNY.

Reserve policymakers continued to reveal itself throughout the Board's final vote approving the measure. "Whether we ultimately disagree on whether the manifestations of this malfunction merits Congressional intervention," Governor Raskin argued, "it appears to me that we have no choice in this matter but to adhere to Congress's directive." One can count a half-dozen instances of policymakers at the Federal Reserve expressing grave doubts about the project, and the argument that pro-regulation faction members such as Raskin appeared to have landed upon was that the statute requires action, advisable or not. It is worth noting that this same logic did not, ultimately, always carry the day in the Federal Reserve's Dodd-Frank related policymaking. Mandatory regulations relating to executive pay practices, for example, still remain unimplemented at present writing and the last notable action on the topic was a public proposal from the OCC that no other agency signed onto and was not formally published in the Federal Register.

Despite apparently continuing ambivalence in the trajectory of US plastic payment policy, the staff of the Federal Reserve appears as the primary drivers of the recent push toward stronger plastic card regulation. A staff memo from April 30, 2021, three months after the inauguration of President Biden, asks the Board to approve proposed revisions to the network exclusivity rules to include a variety of transactions (for example online transactions) that were not included in the original rulemaking.[14] The memo asserts repeatedly the staff's perspective that the Board's regulations were no longer in compliance with the statute. Even more assertive, in their October 25, 2023 proposal, the staff noted the failure of the Board to regularly update the rules and argued for a proposed rule that would allow them to update, without notice-and-comment (or a Board vote), the interchange fee limits to 3.7 multiplied by the average transaction cost (at the time 3.9 cents), hence a 14.4 cent limit. Indeed, some of the same staff that had proven unable or unwilling to muster a defense of their own proposal in 2010 were arguing before the Board in 2023 in defense of a revised proposal that the anticipated downsides of regulation had not materialized. Meanwhile, new staff economists were much more forceful in the public deliberations about the 2023 proposed rule: "The data that we've collected since 2011

---

[14] Board of Governors of the Federal Reserve System. 2021. "Federal Reserve Board Invites Public Comment on Proposed Changes to Regulation II Regarding Network Availability for Card-Not-Present Debit Card Transactions and Publishes a Biennial Report Containing Summary Information on Debit Card Transactions in 2019." May 7, 2021. https://www.federalreserve.gov/newsevents/pressreleases/bcreg20210507a.htm.

gives us a good idea of what the effect of the proposed revisions would be on various participants in the market." In response to the questioning of Trump-appointee Governor Bowman, who also happened to be an heiress to a Kansas community bank and also staunch opponent of plastic card regulation, the staff remarked "retailing is a very competitive industry. And thus economic theory will predict that merchants should have—the competition should ensure that merchants have low profit margins and thus pass on costs and savings onto consumers." This economic rationale, so important for the Australian PSB in the early 2000s, was also clearly available to the staff of the Federal Reserve in 2010; they simply did not present it as fact or as theory worth acting upon. While acknowledging the empirical circumstances made evaluation "challenging," the economist defending the proposed revision in 2023 cited one study with a compelling methodology that found "clear evidence that merchants pass on the cost of accepting card payments onto consumers." Experience with market regulation, changes in the orientation of academic economists, and new data appear to have brought the staff of the US central bank closer to their Australian equivalents. Still, the difference in initial comfort of the staff with their messily "political" role of assessing risk and reward in allocating costs and benefits in a complex economic ecosystem has a substantial explanatory role in why such different overall outcomes in plastic card regulation prevailed.

6. Interest Group Coalitions

In discussing the legislative origins of US plastic card regulation, the important tension between retail and consumer interests on the one hand, and various categories of financial interests has been developed. These are the key stakeholders that plastic payments implicate and they are largely the same interests involved in Australian regulation as well. Yet the differences between the two political economies result in a very different balances of forces, with very different implications for card regulation.

A key launching point for this discussion is the contrast between the Australian regime that draws all financial entities in and the US regime that excludes smaller banks and financial institutions. Indeed, we have already seen that Durbin determined an exemption for banks with $1 billion in assets under management was insufficient for passage, while a rule that applied only to banks with $10 billion in assets achieved a supermajority in the Senate. Call Reports from 2010 reveal that there were 7094 banks in the United States at the time, of which 90 were subject to the higher threshold, 6531 of whom were exempt even from the lower threshold, and 473 banks that fell in between and would have been subject to fee caps under the Durbin Amendment as originally proposed but not as it was ultimately passed. Every state in the United States has at least one such intermediate bank, while the median state has six. There were 7556 credit unions in the United States at that time. Three were subject to the higher threshold, with 165 credit unions in 37 states that escaped the interchange regulation when the coverage threshold was changed. The key to legislative success in the US Congress was splitting the finance coalition, or at least ensuring that regulation only fell upon the shoulders of the ninety largest banks that are heavily concentrated in a single state, New York. The change in coverage had a dramatic effect in narrowing the number of senators whose constituents had a particular stake in this fight.

While organizations that provide banking services are highly numerous and highly dispersed in the United States, the Australian banking sector has a paltry number of institutions that are highly geographically concentrated. There are only 135 depository institutions in Australia according to the Australian Prudential Regulatory Authority, and only seventy-seven of these are domestic entities.[15] There are four big players in Australian banking that dwarf the rest, two of which are based in Melbourne and two of which are based in Sydney. The geographic reach of finance in the United States, particularly small and medium-sized banks, makes it very politically powerful in an electoral system with plurality voting in compact geographic districts. The Australian legislature is bicameral, with the lower chamber elected via instant-runoff voting from single-member districts, while the upper chamber uses proportional elections, with each state sending a total of twelve members. The geographic concentration of finance in Australia puts the finance coalition at a relative disadvantage in obtaining representation in its House of Representatives, while the proportional representation in the Senate may also undermine the ability of finance to find natural allies in that body; therefore the interaction of financial sector organization and legislative organization was such that the geographic basis for an antiregulatory legislative coalition was much more limited in Australia than in the

[15] Australian Prudential Regulation Authority (APRA). *Register of Authorised Deposit-Taking Institutions*. Accessed September 16, 2025. https://www.apra.gov.au/register-of-authorised-deposit-taking-institutions.

United States. Moreover, the larger financial institutions in Australia were at least in the late 1990s still attempting to develop their own functioning alternative to Visa and Mastercard a la the Canadian Interac. Called the Bankcard, this Australian card scheme had very significant market penetration. As the large Australian banks had such significant market share already, and viewed the major threat as losing market share to foreign entrants, they did not have the curious dependency on interchange fees that led many smaller financial institutions to panic about the possible downstream effects of plastic payment regulation.

The relatively sleepy politics of PSB appointments help illustrate the fact that the interest group politics that enabled or at least did not block plastic payment regulation in Australia have not changed enormously since its creation. By contrast, the difficult coalition politics that characterized passage of the Durbin Amendment also continued to stymie the rulemaking process in the United States. In a letter dated December 9, three days prior to the publication of the proposed plastic card regulation, thirteen Senators (two of whom had even voted for the Durbin amendment) wrote the Federal Reserve a letter complaining that "having the government fix prices in almost any venue is a bad idea."[16] They encouraged the Federal Reserve to "take sufficient time to gather and analyze all of the relevant facts before issuing a proposed rule." These Senators expressed concerns about harm to consumers through checking account fees, the limited evidence of merchants passing through lower prices, and in particular the possibility that the networks would force smaller and less efficient banks to make do with interchange fees below their transaction costs. On December 15, Rep. Barney Frank, Chairman of the House Financial Services Committee and co-sponsor of the Dodd-Frank Act, piled on, complaining about the possible downstream effects on community banks. While Durbin had successfully split the finance coalition, the Federal Reserve was unable to maintain that divide for even a few months.

The agency would go onto receive 11,000 comment letters, many from smaller banks and credit unions that the law had intended to exempt from the amendment's consequences. Indeed, the Federal Reserve did very little to placate these groups. At an appearance before Congress in February of 2011, Bernanke laid out the case for how and why it was unable to guarantee that

[16] Senate (Carper et al.). 2010. *Senate Debit Interchange Comment Letter*. December 9, 2010. Letter to Ben Bernanke, Chairman, Board of Governors of the Federal Reserve System. https://www.federalreserve.gov/newsevents/rr-commpublic/senate_debit_interchange_letter_20101209.pdf.

the regulation would not result in significant damage to these smaller entities. Senator Tester asked FDIC director Sheila Bair what she thought about the likely effect of the Federal Reserve's regulation. She said in no uncertain terms it needs to be delayed and rethought—but Bernanke did not reply to this criticism of his agency's regulatory performance. The finance sector as a whole spent wildly on a lobbying campaign that included subway advertisements, astroturfing efforts, and more conventional administrative and legislative lobbying (Carpenter and Libgober 2023). Although much of this activity escaped measurement (Libgober and Carpenter 2024), Governor Raskin estimated that all told "millions of lobbying dollars have been spent, and hundreds of meetings have occurred."[17] Indeed, the culmination of these efforts was a failed bid by Senators Tester and Corker to delay the implementation of the Durbin amendment pending further study by the Federal Reserve and several other banking regulators of the potential effect on consumers, smaller financial institutions, and credit unions (Carpenter and Libgober 2023). Although Tester-Corker's bill failed on June 9, 2011, it did receive fifty-four votes, a remarkable twenty-one-vote improvement relative to the thirty-three-vote opposition the Durbin amendment had received just over a year before. The Federal Reserve Board did proceed to implement its regulation just weeks after the limiting vote failed, although in a substantially watered-down form relative to its initial plan.

In considering the interest group politics of the US case, the passivity of consumer interest in particular is remarkable. As Bernanke described, consumers were supposed to be the major beneficiary of the law, but as Durbin alluded to earlier the organizational representation of consumer interests was highly conflicted because of the fact that credit unions were an important constituency, and set of financial backers, for many of the most outspoken consumer groups (Carpenter and Libgober 2023). Other general interest groups such as AARP and the NAACP did participate in rulemaking, but against the regulation and on behalf of the financial services industry. According to my interview-based work, consumer advocates who did strongly support the regulation viewed this participation as a result of these nonprofits being "bought off" by large financial interests who simply opposed plastic card regulation as a threat to their profit margins. An intriguing study by economists entitled "The Hall of Mirrors" finds that non-profits

---

[17] Board of Governors of the Federal Reserve System. 2011. *Open Board Meeting Transcript.* June 29, 2011. https://www.federalreserve.gov/mediacenter/files/openboardmeeting20110629.pdf.

receiving grants from corporate philanthropies have a higher propensity to submit comments on regulations that the corporation comments upon, and these comments tends to be more similar to the comments of the donor corporation than other comments (Bertrand et al. 2021).

7. Administrative Process and Institutions Supporting Stakeholder Engagement

As we have already seen, the fact that plastic card regulation emerged in any form in the United States is somewhat miraculous, and likely would not have happened but for the insistence of a few policy entrepreneurs like Durbin and regulation-oriented Governors such as Raskin and Tarullo. Despite the organizational and cultural configurations that put the relevant regulator on an inferior footing in the United States as compared with Australia, the Federal Reserve still actively contemplated a fee-cap regime that was far more "draconian" than Australia's, and governors with an inordinate responsibility for regulation such as Tarullo up until the time of the first proposed rule thought they had struck a relatively moderate position. They seemed willing to go further to the point of interpreting the statute to disallow compensation for profits entirely. The discussion of the prior section certainly suggests that shifting winds on Capitol Hill and the collapse of the enacting coalition had a significant responsibility for these developments. Yet the collapse of the enacting coalition was an event whose seeds were sown in the rule development process, in particular through the approach to stakeholder governance that failed to surface the tensions inherent in the consumer-retail coalition and preserve the key division between big and small financial institutions.

As Carpenter and Libgober (2023) describe, the first meeting between financial institutions and the Federal Reserve happened a mere two days after the Dodd-Frank Act was signed into law, and the pattern of stakeholder engagement that followed was remarkably imbalanced in favor of directly regulated entities, in stark contrast with predictions of the structure-and-process whereby administrative procedures are supposed to "stack-the-deck" in favor of the enacting coalition, in this case clearly including a dominant role for large-scale retailers and manufacturers of consumer goods (McCubbins et al. 1987, 1989). Figure 4.6 shows the pattern of meetings between the rulewriting team and categories of interest groups. It is worth

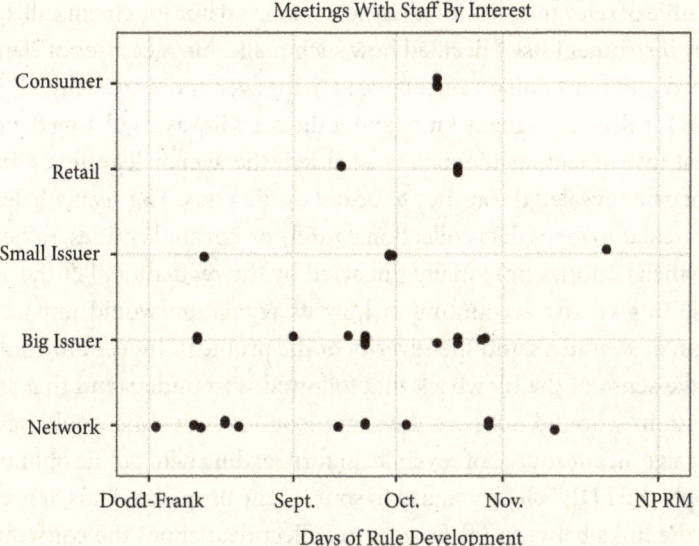

Figure 4.6 Meetings by Category of Stakeholder Over Time. Each Dot Is a Meeting Listed on the Federal Reserve's Website.

noting that due to gaps in US lobbying disclosure laws, none of these meetings would appear in conventional lobbying databases and social scientists focused on the role of money in politics in the United States have almost totally ignored this form of lobbying (Libgober and Carpenter 2024), despite evidence that these contacts produce significant shifts in the market valuations of firms that obtain such under-the-radar access (Libgober 2020a). The inattention to the enacting coalition of merchants and consumer groups is particularly startling, although smaller banks also clearly had very little opportunity to engage policymakers. As Carpenter and Libgober (2023) argue based on a careful analysis of the rulemaking records, a key turning point in the rule development process happened after September 13, 2010, which coincided with the fielding of a survey instrument to estimate issuer's costs. However imbalanced the rule development was overall, Figure 4.6 reveals it was practically a monolith before.

Carpenter and Libgober (2023) attribute substantial significance to the design of the survey instrument for the overall course of rulemaking. One reason that the design of the survey instrument was so crucial is because all subsequent decisions about rates were based on data from that instrument; whether a reasonable and proportional fee was at the 50th or the 80th percentile of relevant costs for all issuers was an ad hoc judgment call, but the survey instrument itself decided how such malleable measures of "fairness" mapped into hard dollars and cents. Perhaps even more crucially, all *justifi-cations* for what the agency knew about the costs it was regulating depended on that instrument, as the data is what lent the agency legitimacy and the lack of data revealed the agency to be out over its skis. The agency's decision in particular to focus data collection entirely on covered entities, rather than all financial entities potentially impacted by the regulation, left the agency unable to give any accounting of how its regulation would impact these groups, or to understand the severity of the problem. Indeed, the only way to make sense of the blowback that followed is to understand that smaller institutions who did not have the same economies of scale would have lost a very significant source of revenue, in turn leading elite public opinion (for example the FDIC chairwoman) to sour on the proposal. Thus, it is easy to trace the links between (a) failures to collect data about the consequences of the proposed policy; (b) the intense reaction of smaller financial institu-tions, a politically very powerful block in Congress, and also credit unions that straddled the consumer-finance coalition; (c) a majority vote in the Sen-ate for a law to delay perhaps indefinitely the policy; and (d) the raising of interchange fee limits to a level that hardly constrained the market for the next fifteen years (and perhaps beyond).

Harder to understand is why the Federal Reserve Board got to the point where it made such a mistake about the likely perception of its proposal. The pattern of stakeholder engagement revealed in Figure is itself a likely and powerful explanation. The rulemaking logs reveal the deputy counsel for the Credit Union National Association had a long call with the head of the Division of Reserve Bank Operations and Payment Systems a mere two weeks after the enactment of Dodd-Frank to explain her concerns that the networks would simply impose the same interchange rate on large and small financial institutions, thereby sweeping these smaller entities into the regulatory regime that was supposed to exclude them (Carpenter and Lib-gober 2023). No further meetings with smaller financial institutions were held until October, after the survey instrument was already in the field. The Federal Reserve staff leaned heavily on Visa and Mastercard in determining how to measure costs, as these networks had experience fielding similar sur-veys to what the Federal Reserve planned to do. Later in the commenting process it would be revealed that Consumer Federation of America also had experience surveying their credit union members about the costs for providing debit services, but this expertise was not considered "relevant" because the Federal Reserve did not learn about it until it was far too late. The process of engaging stakeholders in rule development not only failed to reveal the intensity of preferences or the cleavages in the supporting political coalition, it also deprived the agency of relevant expertise. Further meetings with potentially affected interests would have likely slowed the rulemaking, however, and it is plausible that the staff which did not particularly have an investment in the regulatory task was more concerned about meeting its nine-month statutory deadline (which it did not do because of the ensuing political conflagration).

American institutionalists have made much of the role of administrative procedures in shaping how public opinion is channeled to agencies (McCubbins, Noll, and Weingast 1987; McCubbins and Schwartz 1984). The irony is that the consensus among administrative law scholars (e.g., Elliott 1992), supported as well by recent quantitative evidence from political science (Libgober 2020a), holds that the commenting process is far less policy determinative than the rule development phase that happens earlier. Despite its heavily face-to-face character, the process of ex parte meetings and even more informal conference and interstitial-space interactions is almost entirely unregulated in the United States (Sferra-Bonistalli 2014). Outside a few exceptional agencies (such as the Federal Reserve), the ex parte meeting process also has no transparency—there are no public records available to produce figures similar to Figure 4.6 most agencies, and in the majority of cases there are no *private* records potentially subject to FOIA either. While the commenting process itself is relatively transparent, at least on the input side (Dooling and Potter 2024), it is also remarkably loosely structured in the United States. It relies on interest groups to self-organize to submit feedback if they have sufficient concern. As SoRelle (2020) vividly illustrates, such self-organization does not just happen, and particularly in highly fractured regulatory policymaking like finance the administrative burdens associated with organizing to provide feedback on regulation present an enormous barrier to public input on regulation. As I have argued here and elsewhere, the laissez-faire approach to stakeholder governance is an important explanation for why many agencies, but especially financial agencies, consistently fail to deliver on their statutory mandates and for the broader public. Attempts for more structured processes have a long history in the United States (Schuck 1979), yet thus far these have largely failed to yield much fruit (Langbein and Kerwin 2000).

The administrative process in Australia is in many respects similar to that of the United States, with their rulemakings involving the initial production of a "consultation paper," upon which the regulator receives comments, followed by the issuance of a "standard," which is akin to what the United States would call a final rule. Like most regulatory agencies in the United States, the Payment Systems Board does not publish systematic records about who it meets with and what they discuss during proposal development;[18] therefore our visibility into what actually happens during rule development is far more limited in the Australian than the US case. Yet from analysis of annual and other reports, it is possible to glean much about what takes place there. Additionally, public comments are available, which allows for a much more objective view as to what stakeholder engagement is like.

Figure 4.7 shows the patterns of interest group commenting across four Australian plastic payment rulemakings. Several points are worth mentioning. First, the notice-and-comment process is much quieter than the raucous

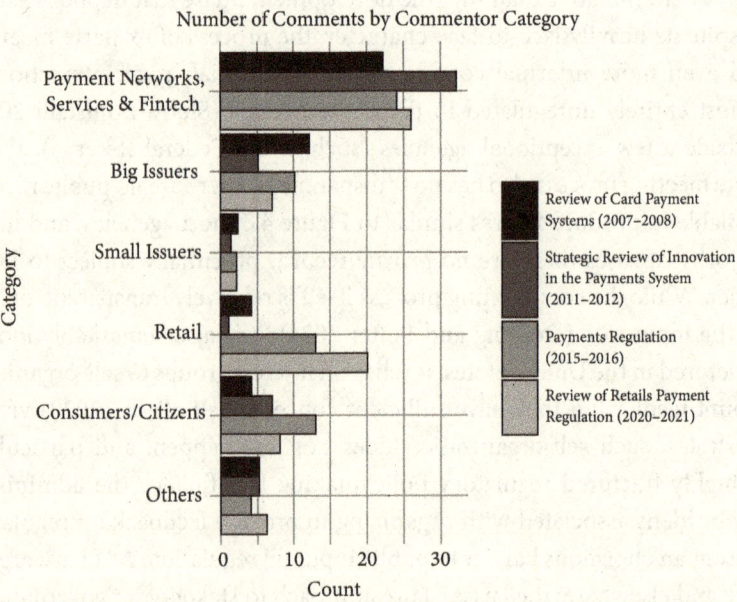

Figure 4.7 Comments by Category of Stakeholder in Four Australian Regulatory Reviews.

[18] Ellis Connolly (Head of Payments Policy, Reserve Bank of Australia), email to the author, July 31, 2024.

11,000-comment event that was the Durbin rulemaking in the United States. The 2007–2008 and 2011–2012 regulatory reviews received around fifty comments, while the other two reviews received sixty-six and sixty-nine comments. The level of commentary that these rules received would not have been out of place in the United States; indeed it would be a pretty typical of commentary for the minority of rules that receive any public feedback whatsoever (Libgober 2020b). Second, to the extent one expected more extensive participation by broader groups, that is also decidedly not the case. Finance, especially the payment networks and fintechs, dominates rulemaking participation at the comment stage, followed in most years by the large issuing banks (although in recent years retail has become more active). The high propensity of directly regulated entities to participate is neither atypical for rulemaking, not is it obviously an indicator of regulatory capture (Libgober 2020b). Still, to the extent one had hope that differences in the notice-and-comment process between the two countries explained the highly variable policy outcomes, even a very brief glance at the evidence suggests that is unlikely.

Far more interesting, it turns out, are the differences in stakeholder engagement during proposal development. While readily available resources for the early years of the PSB are limited, the agency's 2007 annual report describes both formal and informal consultations with a wide range of participants, including the usual suspects in finance, but also merchants and academics. The 2008 annual report describes the agency undertaking "bilateral" consultations with "industry participants, associations, and consumer groups," as well as a 90-person conference in November at an Australian University; six months after that conference there appeared the publication of a preliminary conclusions paper about their 2007 review of regulation. While it is hard to know for sure given the limited transparency, one gleans that consultation with stakeholders in the first decade of Australian payments regulation was deeper and broader than what was witnessed at the Federal Reserve, even if public voice in the United States—at least in the comment process—was louder.

As important as these differences were, the second decade of Australian plastic card regulation has witnessed moves toward corporatism and the constitution of stakeholder groups by the regulator that previously did not exist—or did not exist in a way that was most useful to the regulator. In 2014, the Board was instrumental in creating the Australian Payments Council, a strategic coordination body comprising senior executives from across the payments industry, including card schemes, financial institutions, retail banks, and crucially the Bank itself. Simultaneously, the Board also created the Payments Consultation Group. In the words of Eric Connolly, the current Head of Payments Policy at the Reserve Bank, "the purpose of this group was to provide a structured mechanism for users of the payments system to express their views on payments system issues as an input to our payments policy work." While the membership list of this body is not published, it includes a range of consumer and business groups, as well as large businesses and other governmental agencies—it *does not* include banks or other payment service providers. It appears as no coincidence that the regulatory reviews that followed the constitution of these groups, and especially the latter Consultation groups, witnessed a dramatic increase in retail and consumer participation in the regulatory process. "In instances where we were seeking feedback from stakeholders on a regulatory change," the Head of Payments Policy explained, "we would encourage interested members of the Payments Consultation Group to make a submission as part of our standard consultation process." Clearly the Australian regulator's efforts to stimulate public commentary by constituting its own advisory bodies and quasi-interest groups has born substantial fruit.

Australia and the United States are both common law systems whose administrative processes share great similarities. The formal legal requirements are similar in both cases, with a highly transparent end-stage of public commentary in which a small number of highly engaged stakeholders tend to dominate, particularly directly regulated interests. Both systems also make a black box out of the process of ex parte consultation that sets the agenda for that public end-stage. There are two major justifications for that questionable arrangement. The first is to encourage participant transparency. If all meetings between the Federal Reserve and US consumer groups were videotaped, for example, it is unlikely that many would have been willing to meet for fear of what their credit union constituents and donors would say. The second consideration, which is probably more important as an explanation for why the procedures take the form they do, is that nontransparency allows bureaucrats freedom to go where they need to go to get the evidence to support their decisions. Put differently, the distribution of meetings by interest in Figure is a bad look, and the fear is that agencies will be distracted from the task of information acquisition if they are concerned about appearances.

While the Reserve Bank and the Federal Reserve both operate in a world of high discretion about who they meet with and when, the two agencies have approached the use of that discretion in very different ways. More-over, the Australian regulator has taken a hugely more proactive approach to constituting the very interests implicated by their policies, in so doing cre-ating venues, administrative processes, and governance institutions that are missing in the United States and which do not fit easily in the four corners of the Administrative Procedures Act. The fact that the public author-ity in Australia runs a major deliberative forum where various regulated entities discuss payments policy puts the agency at a dramatic informa-tional advantage relative to the typical world of bilateral negotiations or notice-and-comment. In particular, the opportunities to detect fissures in the industry, which often has a great capacity to present a united front, strengthens the informational hand of the regulator considerably.

To sharpen and better understand the contrast, one might consider why the financial services industry in Australia was not able to thwart the forma-tion of such institutions and resist a move by the Australian bureaucracy against laissez-faire stakeholder governance. It is easy to imagine what a successful stand against coordination could have looked like. If financial stakeholders boycotted the Australian Payments Council, for example, this institution would have collapsed. Yet this resistance did not occur or leave much traces in the record, and it is possible to reasonably guess as to why. Resisting bureaucratic coordination is a collective action problem for an industry. No CEO wants to be the last one in the room or the only one left out. Keeping a regulator who is reaching out at arms distance could also make future cooperation challenging. If such dynamics appear to greatly empower a regulator that strives for coordination, then it also suggests that the Federal Reserve, if it really wanted to do something similar, likely could have succeeded in doing so. Indeed, the Federal Reserve currently has five advisory boards, three of which were created by the Board on its own ini-tiative. The structural puzzle is not so much why the Australian financial services industry was not able to resist a move toward coordination which the US financial services industry was able to block. Rather, the question is why the Australian regulator wanted to move in this direction, while the Federal Reserve did not want to do that. The most logical answer would appeal to notions of bureaucratic culture which have complex structural antecedents. Jacobs and King allude to many of those that I shall return to momentarily, but it is worth noting there are others possibilities and factors as well. In particular, courts plausibly play a much more signifi-cant role in shaping what agencies do in the United States, and "innovative processes" may pose (or seem to pose) risks to agencies in taking policy actions. Another point is that the Australian system is parliamentary while the US system is Presidential. Presidentialism creates possibilities for structural political independence that are much weaker in parliamentary systems. Once given independence, agencies jealously guard it. Experimentation with stakeholder governance may be a poor strategy to the end of being "above politics" and worthy of the gift of independence that can easily be clawed back if the agency appears to be picking winners.

8. Discussion and Conclusion

This chapter has discussed an important distributive policy problem, plastic card swipe fees. I have emphasized that the performance of national financial systems in addressing this particular problem is highly varied, and in many cases that variation is due to differing performance of central banks in their supervisory and regulatory tasks. Using Jacobs and King as a framework, I have explored the differences in two extreme cases, the United States and Australia, and considered the role of institutional organization, cultural toolkits, and interest group coalitions in explaining the differing outcomes. These factors appear important in explaining variation in national financial governance equilibria, and the comparative case analysis also has a good deal of explanatory power with respect to particular policies. Indeed, the creation of a separate policymaking committee within the central bank was surely an important driver of stronger supervision in Australia, which in turn led to a more committed regulatory culture. No less critical, and perhaps a worthy topic for additional and deeper reflection in future work, was the very differing interest group ecology of finance and consumer groups in the two cases. The far-flung, highly varied, and highly numerous financial sector in the United States creates opportunities for consumer groups that often struggle for resources. That very opportunity may hobble them when it comes time to challenge finance-led inequality.

A key claim of this chapter, however, is that even despite the important and cross-cutting factors of culture, interests, and organization, stronger regulation in the United States than Australia was not only possible, it was actively considered. This fact implies that the Jacobs and King factors were on their own important, but not on their own sufficient, to explain the differing paths financial regulation took. Administrative processes for channeling public preferences and sussing out information—or not—were also decisive in explaining why swipe fee regulation went off the rails in the United States, and also plausibly explain why Australia has done so much more to combat finance-led inequality. For too long, political science scholarship has reduced administrative processes such as notice-and-comment, ex parte meetings, rules about judicial review, and so forth, to mere tools for ensuring that legislative principles get what they want out of administrative processes. Indeed, institutional American politics research has largely regarded these as substitutable instruments for ensuring the bureaucratic agent stays faithful. The politics of central banking, whether it concerns monetary or regulatory policy, represents a sharp context for challenging the principal–agent approach to bureaucratic politics. It is both notable and somewhat unsurprising that so many works in this volume target administrative processes that these central banks use. These include the more standard fare of administrative law like notice and comment, which SoRelle's chapter and this chapter address, but also the more unusual but no less important processes and institutions like the listening tours that Alice Pearson studies (Pearson 2024). How the central bank acquires information about public wants and needs is at the core of what the politics of central banking should be about.

Inevitably in such a chapter, a few topics have been left by the wayside for future work. I highlight three. First, this chapter has presented the particular case of swipe fee regulations in a way that is highly independent of other financial governance choices, although they are clearly not. The Canadian case all-to-briefly discussed shows that domestic banks were in some cases capable of preventing the encroachment of a highly extractive payment system run by foreign finance conglomerates. The political causes of this ability to resist, and why these banks did not try to compete, is an interesting puzzle no doubt connected to the constellation of interests, institutions, and culture that Jacobs and King describe, but deserving of greater study. Second, the international trade and competition aspects of both US and Australian policymaking have received relatively little attention in this chapter. In part, this fact is because the administrative source materials do not emphasize it. Even so, the fact that policymakers seem to mention these aspects little is not conclusive, as it would be hard for any of the policymakers to note that Visa and Mastercard are foreign companies in Australia and domestic companies in the United States. While there have been occasional objections in the United States to the notion that the United States is subsidizing foreign transactions and payment infrastructure, it could equally be argued that the profits in the US financial marketplace allow these networks to provide services abroad at lower cost than a domestic supplier would be able to, thereby deterring entry and solidifying the position of US companies as a global financial duopoly. The domestic consequences of this arrangement in the United States require deeper analysis. More work on the international political economy roots of financial regulation is clearly warranted (Broz 2009; Zaring 2019), and swipe fees would no doubt be an interesting case in that context as well. Finally, the chapter has not reckoned as deeply as it might with the notion that Visa and Mastercard are platform companies and that what explains variation in the two cases is differences in the extent of their platform power. The sympathetic mobilization of smaller financial institutions against plastic payment system regulation was not possible in Australia for several reasons, the most important being that there were few such entities and they were not so dependent on the platforms to make their businesses operate. By contrast, the threat that Visa and Mastercard would apply the regulatory caps to nonregulated entities provoked a huge sympathetic reaction on the part of smaller financial institutions, many nominally nonprofit credit unions in the consumer finance coalition, that was very consequential for the shape that rulemaking ultimately took. The structural power of finance as a causal factor merits further reflection in general, but it likely also has an important role in explaining the differing course of swipe fees in the United States and Australia.

Works Cited

Acemoglu, Daron, and James A Robinson. 2024. "Culture, Institutions and Social Equilibria: A Framework." Working Paper. National Bureau of Economic Research.

Adolph, Christopher. 2018. "The Missing Politics of Central Banks." *PS: Political Science & Politics* 51(4): 737–742. https://doi.org/10.1017/S1049096518000847.

Barro, Robert J, and David B. Gordon. 1983. "A Positive Theory of Monetary Policy in a Natural Rate Model." *Journal of Political Economy* 91(4): 589–610.

Bertrand, Marianne, Matilde Bombardini, Raymond Fisman, Brad Hackinen, and Francesco Trebbi. 2021. "Hall of Mirrors: Corporate Philanthropy and Strategic Advocacy." *Quarterly Journal of Economics* 136(4): 2413–2465. https://doi.org/10.1093/qje/qjab023.

Binder, Sarah, and Mark Spindel. 2018. "Why Study Monetary Politics?" *PS: Political Science & Politics* 51(4): 732–736. https://doi.org/10.1017/S1049096518000835.

Broz, J. Lawrence. 2009. *The International Origins of the Federal Reserve System*. 1st paperback ed. Ithaca, NY: Cornell Univ. Press.

Bullock, Michele. 2010. "A Guide to the Card Payments System Reforms." Reserve Bank of Australia Bulletin, September 2010. https://www.rba.gov.au/publications/bulletin/2010/sep/7.html#r0

Carpenter, Daniel P., and Brian Libgober. 2023. "Administrative Politics with Clear Stakes and Venues: Strategic Commenting Upon Federal Reserve Debit Card Regulations." In *Accountability Reconsidered: Voters, Interests, and Information in US Policymaking*, edited by Charles M. Cameron, Brandice Canes-Wrone, Sanford C. Gordon, and Gregory A. Huber. Cambridge University Press. DOI: 10.1017/9781009168311.019.

Christopher, Adolph. 2013. Bankers, Bureaucrats, and Central Bank Politics: The Myth of Neutrality of Cambridge Studies in Comparative Politics. Cambridge: Cambridge University Press. https://www.cambridge.org/core/books/bankers-bureaucrats-and-central-bank-politics/987D5B65EB146DFE95D40AD2647AE1F0.

Competition Tribunal (Canada). 1995. "Interac—Statement of Grounds and Material Facts." Case Documents, file no. CT-1995-002. Filed December 14, 1995. https://decisions.ct-tc.gc.ca/ct-tc/cdo/en/item/464896/index.do

Culpepper, Pepper D., and Kathleen Thelen. 2020. "Are We All Amazon Primed? Consumers and the Politics of Platform Power." *Comparative Political Studies* 53(2): 288–318. https://doi.org/10.1177/0010414019852687.

"Debit and Credit Card Schemes in Australia: A Study of Interchange Fees and Access." 2000. Sydney: Reserve Bank of Australia. https://www.accc.gov.au/about-us/publications/debit-and-credit-card-schemes-in-australia.

Dooling, Bridget C.E., and Rachel Augustine Potter. 2024. "Regulatory Body Shops." Duke Law Journal 73 (8): 1677–1742. https://scholarship.law.duke.edu/dlj/vol73/iss8/2.

Durbin, Richard J. 2010. "Speech." *Congressional Record* 156, no. 72 (Senate), May 13, 2010, S3704. https://www.congress.gov/congressional-record/volume-156/issue-72/senate-section/article/S3684-2

Elliott, E. Donald. 1992. "Re-Inventing Rulemaking." *Duke Law Journal* 41: 1490.

Freytag, Andreas, and Donato Masciandaro. 2005. "Financial Supervision Fragmentation and Central Bank Independence: The Two Sides of the Same Coin?" *SSRN Electronic Journal*. https://www.aeaweb.org/articles?id=10.1257/pandp.20201091.

Gibbons, Robert, and Laurence Prusak. 2020. "Knowledge, Stories, and Culture in Organizations." *AEA Papers and Proceedings* 110 (May): 187–192. https://doi.org/10.1257/pandp.20201091.

Goodman, John B. 1991. "The Politics of Central Bank Independence." *Comparative Politics* 23(3): 329–349.

Groven, Harald. QR codes for mobile pay in China. Photograph, April 23, 2017. Licensed under CC BY-SA 2.0. Wikimedia Commons. https://commons.wikimedia.org/wiki/File:QR_codes_for_mobile_pay_in_China.jpg

Hannan, Michael T., and John Freeman. 1984. "Structural Inertia and Organizational Change." *American Sociological Review* 49 (2): 149–164. https://www.jstor.org/stable/2095567.

Jackson, Howell E. 2009. "Learning from Eddy: A Meditation Upon Organizational Reform of Financial Supervision in Europe." In *Perspectives in Company Law and Financial Regulation*, edited by Michel Tison, Hans De Wulf, Christoph Van Der Elst, and Reinhard Steennot, 523–539. 1st ed. Cambridge University Press. https://doi.org/10.1017/CBO9780511770456.029.

Jacobs, Lawrence R., and Desmond King. 2016. *Fed Power: How Finance Wins*. New York: Oxford University Press. https://www.amazon.com/Fed-Power-How-Finance-Wins-ebook/dp/B01BLYGOT4.

Jacobs, Lawrence R., and Desmond King. 2018. "The Fed's Political Economy." *PS: Political Science & Politics* 51(4): 727–731. https://doi.org/10.1017/S1049096518000884.

Jacobs, Lawrence R., and Desmond King. 2024. "Social Rights and the Politics of Financial Governenace." In this volume.

Kreps, David M. 1990. "Corporate Culture and Economic Theory." In *Perspectives on Positive Political Economy*, edited by James E. Alt and Kenneth A. Shepsle, 90–143. 1st ed. Cambridge University Press. https://doi.org/10.1017/CBO9780511571657.006.

Kydland, Finn E, and Edward C. Prescott. 1977. "Rules Rather Than Discretion: The Inconsistency of Optimal Plans." *Journal of Political Economy* 85(3): 473–492.

Langbein, Laura I., and Cornelius M. Kerwin. 2000. "Regulatory Negotiation Versus Conventional Rulemaking: Claims, Counterclaims, and Empirical Evidence." *Journal of Public Administration Research and Theory* 10(3): 599–632.

Lee, Ian, Geoffrey A Manne, Julian Morris, and Todd J Zywicki. 2013. "How Payment Cards Benefit Canadian Merchants and Consumers, and How Regulation Can Harm Them." George Mason University Law and Economics Research Paper Series 13–58. Macdonald-Laurier Institute.

Libgober, Brian. 2020a. "Meetings, Comments, and the Distributive Politics of Rulemaking." *Quarterly Journal of Political Science* 15(4): 449–481. https://doi.org/10.1561/100.00018135.

Libgober, Brian. 2020b. "Strategic Proposals, Endogenous Comments, and Bias in Rulemaking." *The Journal of Politics* 82(2): 642–656. https://doi.org/10.1086/706891.

Libgober, Brian, and Daniel Carpenter. 2024. "Lawyers as Lobbyists: Regulatory Advocacy in American Finance." *Perspectives on Politics* 22(4), (January), 1045–1064. https://doi.org/10.1017/S1537592723002943.

Mattingly, Phil, and Robert Schmidt. 2011. "How Wal-Mart Swiped JPMorgan in $ 16 Billion." *Bloomberg Technology*, June 28, 2011. https://www.bloomberg.com/news/articles/2011-06-28/how-wal-mart-swiped-jpmorgan-in-16-billion-debit-card-battle.

McCubbins, Mathew D., Roger G. Noll, and Barry R. Weingast. 1987. "Administrative Procedures as Instruments of Political Control." *Journal of Law, Economics, and Organization* 3 (2): 243–277. https://doi.org/10.2307/764829.

McCubbins, Mathew D., Roger G. Noll, and Barry R. Weingast. 1989. "Structure and Process, Politics and Policy: Administrative Arrangements and Political Control of Agencies." *Virgina Law Review* 75: 431.

McCubbins, Mathew D., and Thomas Schwartz. 1984. "Congressional Oversight Overlooked: Police Patrols Versus Fire Alarms." *Political Science* 28(1): 165–179.

Morin, Basile. 2018. Credit card terminal in Laos. Photograph, April 24, 2018. Wikimedia Commons. https://commons.wikimedia.org/wiki/File:Credit_card_terminal_in_Laos.jpg.

Parliament of Australia. 1998. Payment Systems (Regulation) Bill 1998. Introduced 26 March 1998. Federal Register of Legislation, Australia. https://www.legislation.gov.au/bills/C2004B00343

Posner, Eric A. 2014. "How Do Bank Regulators Determine Capital Adequacy Requirements?" *SSRN Electronic Journal*. https://doi.org/10.2139/ssrn.2493968.

Prager, Robin A, Mark D Manuszak, Elizabeth K Kiser, and Ron Borzekowski. 2009. "Interchange Fees and Payment Card Networks: Economics, Industry Developments, and Policy Issues." Finance and Economics Discussion Series 2009–23. Federal Reserve Board. https://www.federalreserve.gov/pubs/feds/2009/200923/200923pap.pdf.

Reserve Bank of Australia. 2000. Debit and Credit Card Schemes in Australia: A Study of Interchange Fees and Access. Reserve Bank of Australia. https://www.rba.gov.au/payments-and-infrastructure/resources/publications/payments-au/interchg-fees-study.pdf

Reserve Bank of Australia. 2016a. Standard No. 1 of 2016: The Setting of Interchange Fees in the Designated Credit Card Schemes and Net Payments to Issuers. May 26, 2016. ¶ 4.1. https://www.rba.gov.au/payments-and-infrastructure/review-of-card-payments-regulation/pdf/standard-no-1-of-2016-credit-card-interchange-2016-05-26.pdf

Reserve Bank of Australia. 2016b. Standard No. 2 of 2016: The Setting of Interchange Fees in the Designated Debit Card and Prepaid Card Systems. May 26, 2016. https://www.rba. gov.au/payments-and-infrastructure/review-of-card-payments-regulation/pdf/standard-no-2-of-2016-debit-and-prepaid-card-interchange-2016-05-26.pdf

Rilinger, Georg. 2024. *Failure by Design*. Chicago: University of Chicago Press.

Rogoff, Kenneth. 1985. "The Optimal Degree of Commitment to an Intermediate Monetary Target." *The Quarterly Journal of Economics* 100(4): 1169. https://doi.org/10.2307/1885679.

Sartori, Giovanni. 1970. "Concept Misformation in Comparative Politics." *American Political Science Review* 64 (4): 1033–1053. https://doi.org/10.2307/1958356.

Schuck, Peter H. 1979. "Litigation, Bargaining, and Regulation." *AEI Journal on Government and Society*, July–August. https://www.aei.org/publication/litigation-bargaining-and-regulation/.

Sferra-Bonistalli, Esa L. 2014. "Ex Parte Communications in Informal Rulemaking Proceedings." Washington, DC: Administrative Conference of the United States.

Shutler, Christopher, and Jeremy Frazer. 2011. "Durbin and Mobile in Focus; Assuming Coverage with Outperform Ratings." Equity Research. William Blair & Company.

SoRelle, Mallory E. 2020. *Democracy Declined: The Failed Politics of Consumer Financial Protection*. Chicago: University of Chicago Press.

Swidler, Ann. 1986. "Culture in Action: Symbols and Strategies." *American Sociological Review* 51 (2): 273. https://doi.org/10.2307/2095521.

Thelen, Kathleen. 2018. "Regulating Uber: The Politics of the Platform Economy in Europe and the United States." *Perspectives on Politics* 16(4): 938–953. https://doi.org/10.1017/S1537592718001081.

U.S. House of Representatives, Committee on the Judiciary. 2006. Credit Card Interchange Fees: Antitrust Concerns? Hearing before the Committee on the Judiciary, 109th Cong., 2nd sess., Serial No. J–109–100, July 19, 2006. Washington, DC: U.S. Government Printing Office.

Vanatta, S. H. 2024. *Plastic Capitalism: Banks, Credit Cards, and the End of Financial Control* (New Haven: Yale University Press).

Wallis, Stanley. 1997. *Financial System Inquiry Final Report*. Canberra: Australian Govt. Pub. Service.

Wymeersch, Eddy O. 2007. "The Structure of Financial Supervision in Europe: About Single Financial Supervisors, Twin Peaks and Multiple Financial Supervisors." *European Business Organization Law Review* 8: 237–306. https://doi.org/10.1017/S1566752907002376.

Zaring, David. 2019. *The Globalized Governance of Finance*. 1st ed. Cambridge University Press. https://doi.org/10.1017/9781108594295.

5

The Unbearable Lightness of the Phillips Curve

Wages and Employment in Inflation Targeting

Alice Pearson

In the week following Christmas 2021, the economist Isabella Weber published an opinion piece in the Guardian. Titled *Could Strategic Price Controls Help Fight Inflation?* (Weber 2021) the article highlighted that economists' models of inflation foreground the role of wages in price stability but overlook another factor: profits. Inflation had recently resurged after ten years of a Consumer Price Index frequently below 2 percent targets and central banks responded by raising interest rates, which cascaded across different categories of debt—from mortgages to student loans. Absent, Weber argued, were profits and their role in inflation. A different conception of the problem led to a different set of potential solutions—namely, returning to price controls as a policy.

Weber's article highlights the occlusion of profits in the pursuit of price stability. Macroeconomic models of inflation assume distinct relations, particularly between "wages" and "prices," which foreground some issues while both eclipsing and exacerbating others. Imaginaries of relations inscribed in the macroeconomic models that guide monetary policymaking have distinct material effects (Braun 2014; Bear 2020; Mann 2013). Specifically, economists have modeled inflation through the Phillips Curve, and associated concerns with preventing wage-price spirals (e.g., Blanchard 1985). These suggest that workers' increases in wages lead to increases in prices, which in turn generate impetus among workers to push for further increases in wages. Wages therefore serve as threat to the price stability that central banks are tasked with targeting. The implication is that targeting inflation entails tempering wages.

Alice Pearson, *The Unbearable Lightness of the Phillips Curve*. In: *Picking Winners*. Edited by: Lawrence R. Jacobs and Desmond King, Oxford University Press. © Oxford University Press (2026).
DOI: 10.1093/9780197831823.003.0005

In the opposite of an open secret, the orientation of central banks towards wages is formally inscribed in the models and practices of policymakers, yet largely neglected in public spheres. Since the 1990s, central banks have increasingly professed transparency (Blinder 2004; Blinder et al. 2024; Moschella & Pinto 2019). However this focus on transparency is obscured by the simultaneous impetus of central banks to use communication as a policy tool, generating speech acts with performative effects based on both carefully crafted communication and strategic silence (Bear 2020; Braun 2016; Braun & Düsterhöft 2022; Holmes 2013, 2018; Moschella & Pinto 2019). Moreover, this focus on transparency has eclipsed the role of (il)legibility in economic institutions, where technocratic practices may be formally transparent but illegible to citizens. The legitimacy of central banks' mandates for inflation targeting may rest partly on a citizenry's lack of awareness of the dynamics this targeting assumes and produces. Less than two months after Weber's article, Bank of England Governor Andrew Bailey astonished journalists by calling for workers not to ask for pay raises in an interview with the BBC. Such a public acknowledgment of the preference of independent central banks for wage stagnation seemed egregious, despite being core to monetary policymakers' concerns in institutions tasked with a primary mandate of price stability.

In a rare instance of journalists holding economists to account for the assumptions underpinning macroeconomic models, talk show host Jon Stewart subsequently highlighted the orthodoxy of economists' neglect of profits in a pointed interview with former Treasury Secretary Larry Summers. Following Covid-19 supply chain disruption and the invasion of Ukraine, in March 2023 Summers diagnosed the causes of inflation as instead emanating from President Biden's fiscal stimulus: "[T]he problem is we had a massive stimulus and an economy that could only produce so much. We had huge levels of demand, and those huge levels of demand kept pushing up prices and pushing up wages. But ultimately, it was too much water in the bathtub, the bathtub overflows. You put too much demand in the economy and you get high and rising prices." Stewart looked skeptically at him, raising eyebrows as he outlined recent analysis that suggested demand was approximately 30 percent to 35 percent of inflation and increasing wage costs approximately 20 percent, with an additional "huge corporate profit aspect...the stock market assets have gone up 150 percent. CEO pay has gone up 1500 percent. Workers' wages haven't gone up at all. I think you're misdiagnosing the sickness." As they debated the appropriate focus for stimulus,

Stewart challenged the distributive implications of price stabilization tools: "The tools that we have though are basically saying to somebody, 'Everyone's paying more for gas and groceries and that's really hard, so here's what we're going to do. We're going to throw 10 million of them out of work, so we all don't have to share that burden'. Why aren't we attacking corporate profit in any way? Because that's been estimated to be 30% of inflation, 40% of inflation."

Summers seemed surprised at this attempt to hold economists to account for monetary policy and tried to disarm Stewart by asking if he thinks that Apple, whose platform the interview would be aired on, should not increase prices were it possible. Stewart responded: "Let me flip that on you. When there's a tightness in the labor market, what you're saying is that the workers shouldn't do the same, that the workers, just following the same capitalistic principles that allow Apple to charge more for their phones, shouldn't charge more because wage inflation is driving inflation." He pressed the mechanism: "[T]he Fed is going to intervene to make that not possible." "No, the Fed is intervening to control the overall level of demand growth," Summers defended. "And what will that do to the labor market?," Stewart asked. Summers, seemingly taken aback, reluctantly conceded: "It will loosen it." By "loosening" the labour market, Summers meant that raising interest rates to tackle inflation would increase unemployment and reduce potential for wage raises. Central bank expertise had largely been uninterrogated by journalists, and this marked a rare acknowledgement in the media of the asymmetry of economists' attempts to conceptualize and address inflation through wages over profits, implying that wage suppression was a potential casualty of price stabilization.

This chapter unpacks how labor remains a core problematic in inflation targeting, with a concomitant placing of 'profit margins' at the margin of concern. I ask why, following public statements such as Bank of England Governor Andrew Bailey's, price stabilization can come to sound synonymous with wage suppression, by showing how economists' models for targeting inflation entail the tempering of wages. The chapter focuses on the period of simultaneous low inflation and low unemployment in the UK between the 2007–2009 financial crisis and Covid-19, centering on 2015–2020. Economists during these years became preoccupied with the "wage puzzle" of why low unemployment did not lead to rising wages. I take the Bank's enduring preoccupation on wages and unemployment as itself a puzzle, given the erosion of worker bargaining power and concurrent low rises in wages, and the prominence of other factors in inflation such as profits. This chapter thus addresses the puzzle of why economists pursuing price stabilization continued to be preoccupied with wages at all.

1. The Imaginaries of Economic Models

The chapter juxtaposes different approaches to capital and labor by central banks and traces their distributive implications. It asks how labor and capital emerge—or are eclipsed—as objects of concern for policymakers. I argue that the problematizations and positionalities of macroeconomic models enmesh with the extractive capacities of contemporary capitalism (Bear 2020; Mann 2013, 2019). Tracing how "wilful blindness," "strategic ignorance" and "unknown knowns" (Best 2022, 2024; McGoey 2012; McGoey & Davies 2012; Pearson 2024) are created, sustained, and negotiated in central banks, I excavate logics that permit and foreground labor as a problem over profits. While orientations towards profits and labor may be subtly shifting in certain corners of economics, the dynamics that the chapter traces both reveal how approaches to inflation were crystallized in the past and how they may retain traction in the present.

Scholars in cultural political economy, sociology, and anthropology have shown how disparate ways of conceiving economic processes have distinct material effects, demonstrating how "economic imaginaries" (Gibson-Graham 1996) both reflect and produce particular relations. Science and Technology Scholars (STS) have argued that economics as a discipline is performative, creating the realities that it purports to describe, through devices that are assembled by economists acting as practitioners in public and private institutions (Callon 1998; Callon & Muniesa 2005; MacKenzie et al. 2007; MacKenzie 2008; Mitchell 2005). These processes are not merely neutral implementations of technical assemblages, but are embedded and mobilized by economists, politicians, and policymakers within political projects (Bear et al. 2015; Braun 2014; Mirowski & Nik-Khah 2007; Muniesa 2021; Ortiz 2021; Pearson 2024), with economic models acting as "conversion devices" for gendered, racialized and classed forms of personhood and relations (Bear et al. 2015). Macroeconomic models are not merely abstract representations, rather mobilizing certain imaginaries of relations has distinct political consequences (Bear 2020; Braun 2014; Mann 2013). Dissecting and destabilizing categories of economic models reveals the ethical and political relations that they encode. Laura Bear has therefore argued for interrogating the "political economy of technologies of imagination" (Bear 2020:2) enacted by economists in technocratic institutions, suggesting that such policymakers engage in speculative practices that are founded on ethical claims and organize extractive relations, generating inequalities. Building on this approach, I unpack inequalities of relations inscribed in economic models, and in turn reveal how these models are set in motion through particular configurations of relations, with the tensions, contradictions, and commitments that animate these practices.

Scholars have thus attended to the politics of economics, by "foreground[ing] the political life of economic knowledge" (Scott 2024:835). Drawing on wider discussions of agnotology in regimes of contemporary governance, they have examined forms of wilful blindness, strategic ignorance and uncomfortable knowledge in economics (Best 2022, 2024; Gross & McGoey 2015; McGoey 2012; McGoey & Davies 2012; Pearson 2024). Jacqueline Best analyzes the strategies that central bankers mobilize to deal with unknown knowns, arguing that "[b]ecause central banks' authority is linked to their expertise, the knowledge that is often most uncomfortable for them is the fact of their own ignorance in the face of an uncertain economy" (Best 2022:560). Best combines "concepts of knowledge controversies and contested failures" (2023:2) to chart how central bankers negotiate and sustain challenges to their expertise. I draw on these approaches to examine how central bankers retained focus on the role of employment and wages in inflation targeting despite the demise of labor power since the 1970's.

Since the 1980's, central banks have increasingly inhabited institutional arrangements of "independence". They have been partitioned from parallel institutions of Treasuries that are considered instead to be governed by politicians, which, it is suggested, solves a time-inconsistency problem by rendering central banks unsusceptible to the sways of election cycles (Barro & Gordon 1983), thus constraining the democratic control of central banks through temporal logics (Downey 2021). While central banks are categorized as independent, this institutional isolationism refers to assembling boundaries with other governmental institutions, though central banks often maintain close relations with financial sectors (Braun 2020; Dietsch et al. 2018; Jacobs & King 20216; Krippner 2012; McNamara 2002). Geoff Mann (2013) and Jacqueline Best (2018) have therefore argued that central banks operate in a space of exception that affords the antidemocratic disposition undergirding monetary policy, with these institutions both straddling and assembling boundaries between states and markets, and politics and economics (Coombs & Thiemann 2022; Mitchell 1998). Moreover, the configuration of relations in central banks, with affiliations created with certain groups and estrangement from others, is part of a broader capitalist constellation (Jacobs & King 2016; Kirshner 2001; Mann 2013).

These independent central banks have been granted specific mandates. While the Fed has a dual mandate to consider inflation and employment, central banks such as the Bank of England have been given a primary mandate to prioritize price stabilization. The politics of the mechanisms and measurements of inflation targeting have been contested. The specific target for inflation has usually been set at 2 percent Consumer Price Index (CPI), despite a paucity of empirical or theoretical research justifying this number (Ferguson & Lahiri 2023; Rochon 2024). The CPI includes some measures while excluding others. Notably, it eclipses the significant rise in asset prices during the decade following the financial crisis, which had been characterized by the rise of the asset form including real estate (Birch & Muniesa 2020), aided by quantitative easing programs administered by central banks (Braun 2016; Dietsch et al. 2018; Moschella 2024). The scale, opacity, and lack of clarity about the transmission mechanisms of central bank asset purchase programs create concerns about central banks' exacerbation of inequalities. This in turn has intensified concerns with the democratic control of monetary policy, leading scholars to question the depoliticization of independent central banks (Downey 2025; Dietsch et al. 2018; Jacobs & King 2016; Monnet 2024; Moschella 2024; Tucker 2018).

I build on these approaches by unpacking how technologies of imagination in central banks permit, facilitate, and foreclose certain types of political and economic claims, in particular how economic models in monetary policy shape how central banks "pick winners" (Jacobs and King 2016). Specifically, in this chapter I follow historians of economics who have traced which forms of knowledge and evidence are produced, mobilized, and presented within the Bank of England (e.g., Acosta et al. 2023; hereafter "the Bank"). Unpacking how economists assemble understandings of "the economy," I ask how macroeconomic models of inflation have rendered legible, legitimate, or invisible particular dynamics, which correspond to forms of governance (Braun 2014). Focusing on the device of the Phillips Curve, I trace how this emphasizes a threat of wages and eclipses profits, while showing how these economic models are not stable and exact but emerge instead through a combination of discourses, practices, and negotiations.

They are thus not merely technical instantiations of precise knowledge that are either implemented or refuted, but bricolage artifacts from in a series of contentions and commitments. I argue their multiplicity is generative, as it allows the threat of labour to be de- and subsequently reemphasized through equivocation between categories, eliding critiques and curtailing appeals to empirical refutation (see also Pearson 2024). I reveal an epistemological ambiguity within economics, where the invisibility of dynamics economists posit is instead taken as a marker of policy success. The apparent empirical obsolescence of models they mobilize is therefore taken as indicator of their enduring necessity.

2. The Stories of Macroeconomic Models

The discursive and analytical device of the Phillips Curve posits an inverse relationship between unemployment and inflation, and I argue that this tool has given traction to instrumental concerns with wages and unemployment. Wages and employment are not themselves primary mandates of monetary policy in the Bank of England, but are instrumental variables existing in a trade-off in pursuit of price stability. Within architectures of inflation targeting, the Phillips Curve retains an ambiguous and ambivalent status. The Curve has been heavily critiqued but is still used, both theoretically and empirically disavowed yet the centrality of employment in concerns about inflation endures. This is despite the use of the Phillips Curve as analytical device increasingly diverging from the material realities that it assumes. Wages remain the specter of inflation.

A Phillips Curve is one component of the Dynamic Stochastic General Equilibrium (DSGE) models that are the workhorses of central banks. Both scholars and central bankers themselves have noted how these models can be mobilized in economic storytelling to policymakers and wider publics. In tracing the history of economic expertise in the Bank of England, Acosta et al. (2023) note that a modeling team within the Bank itself argued that DSGE models should be evaluated not only through correspondence with empirical data, but also on capacity to "communicate outputs" and "tell economic stories": the team explained that BEQM "can tell a story about how much weight to put on a purist, textbook explanation, and how much to put on short-run factors that, while ad hoc, have exhibited plausible correlations" (Acosta et al. 2023:21; see also Alvarez-Lois et al. 2008). Meanwhile,

Matthew Watson starts from the prompt of Varadarajan Chari's claim to a congressional hearing on the oversights of macroeconomics after the crisis, that "if you have an interesting and a coherent story to tell you can do so within a DSGE model" (Chari 2010:32; see Watson 2024). Watson argues that "a storytelling strategy then informs policymakers of where the solution to the system of equations positions the outer limits of both political desirability and political possibility" (Watson 2024:844). Following this emphasis on the political affordances of economic models in central banks, I argue that the Phillips Curve gives traction to stories centering on the specter of wages and full employment as threat to price stability when focus might have shifted elsewhere, such as profits, and sets the horizons for the economic imaginaries that animate inflation targeting.

By interrogating the relationship between assumptions of models and their mobilization within central banks, the chapter elucidates architectures of monetary policy to ask what is at stake in the logics and logistics of central banking. Seeking to control inflation through the problematization of labor aligns central banks with owners of capital in several respects, including that price rises are conceptualized through the threat of wage rises. This problematization of wages instantiates a "capitalist realism" (Fisher 2009), which animates practices of monetary policymaking (Mann 2013), as well as genres of austerity enacted by economists concerned with the control of labor (Blyth 2013; Mattei 2022). Economics inhabits a view from capital, with the technocratic apparatuses of central banks enmeshed with the extractive capacities of contemporary capitalism (Bear 2020; Mann 2013, 2019).

The problematization of labor and the positioning from capital reflect broader impetuses in economics to categorize wages as "cost" and capital as "investment." This lends itself to a characterization of wages as waste, to be reduced in "efficiency-enhancing" measures enacted in broader genres of austerity. The notion of wages as waste, opposed to investment in "assets," has characterized the era of austerity enacted since the 2008 financial crisis, with liquidity channeled towards certain economic objects and diverted away from others. Wages are imbued with notions of decay, loss, and the threat of unproductiveness, whereas profits are conceived as potentially productive and generative sources of fecundity. Margins were marginalized in inflation targeting: while wages animated anxieties, profit margins assuaged them.

The chapter proceeds in four parts. Firstly, I trace a brief history of the Phillips Curve in the second half of the twentieth century. Secondly, I probe how the Phillips Curve has endured in the twenty-first century despite the demise of labor power, by revealing how the device has been adapted to enfold multiple variables, which can subsequently be substituted for the singular category of employment. Thirdly, I show that, by contrast, profits margins have remained at the margins of concern in monetary policy. Finally, while elucidating how economic models are inscribed with a capitalist realism, I conclude by arguing their circulation is sustained in part through genres of capitalist unrealism, with a capitalist configuration that ascribes inflation to wage rises maintained through a willful blindness to the complexity of socioeconomic dynamics. While the empirical focus of the chapter centers on the United Kingdom, the analytical insights have broader purchase for unpacking macroeconomic models and the relations through which they are mobilized in governmental and financial institutions globally.

3. Assembling the Phillips Curve

Inflation has been a central concern of 20th-century economics, and inflation-targeting the primary mandate of 21st-century independent central banks. Monetary policymakers have been preoccupied with inflation, and the macroeconomic models they assembled to address the issue have distinct assumptions and relations inscribed in their foundations.

Historians and philosophers of economics have suggested that diagrammatic and mathematical formulations in economics make legible and legitimate certain analyses and narratives (Morgan 2012; Watson 2024). In particular, the marginalist aesthetics of a curve denoting an inverse relationship between two variables that are mapped on horizontal and vertical axes accelerated in economics during the marginalist revolution in the late nineteenth century, when economics became increasingly purified apart from its previous incarnation as political economy by figures who sought to model the discipline on the science of Newtonian physics (Mirowski 1989; Morgan 2012). The usually convex curves that populated their diagrams allowed mathematical analysis of marginal rates, and through drawing an inverse relationship between the two axes formalized the concern with trade-offs that came to characterize neoclassical economics. This aesthetic took hold in economics, and allowed use of similar mathematical and diagrammatic tools to tackle diverse concerns. A simple two-dimensional curve has been mobilized in different ways and imbued with distinct political imaginaries. In macroeconomics, the device of the Phillips Curve mapped a trade-off between unemployment and inflation, and served to increasingly render singular the focus on wages and employment in inflation targeting.

Wages have been the specter of inflation targeting in macroeconomics over the latter half of the twentieth century. Discussions of links between employment and inflation were present prior to the 1950's, but the relationship was subsequently formalized in a series of steps through its inscription in the Phillips Curve. Bill Phillips was an economist housed at LSE, where he had initially arrived to study sociology but subsequently moved to economics. In "*The Relation Between Unemployment and the Rate of Change of Money Wage Rates in the United Kingdom, 1861–1957*" (Phillips 1958), he posited a negative relationship between employment and wage rises. This was derived from historical data that was abstracted into a two-dimensional curve: as unemployment fell, wages increased. Yet the Phillips Curve was later transposed into a relationship between inflation and employment—as opposed to merely wages and employment—in stages following Phillips's intervention, particularly in a 1960 paper by Solow and Samuelson, who were colleagues at MIT, titled "*Analytical Aspects of Anti-Inflation Policy*." This formalized the inverse relationship that placed the two problems as existing in a trade-off, in the aesthetics of the mathematical economics flourishing in the postwar United States: as unemployment fell, prices increased. Full employment presented as inflationary threat.

While this relationship had already been discussed by economists, the Phillips Curve became an instrument animating debates in the discipline in subsequent decades, and afforded relations between employment and inflation a special status. Prior to the formalization of the Phillips Curve, wages had constituted one element of a heterogenous set of supply-side dynamics contributing to inflation. While the Phillips Curve is often posited as indexing inflation to employment, Phillips's original formalization instead indexed wages to employment: wages switched into the wider category of inflation. This translation from wages to prices would recur in later oscillations between the categories: implying wage rises meant price rises.

An abstraction into the purified concern between wages and inflation was not immediate. In Solow and Samuelson's paper formalizing the device, they discussed multiple possible causes of inflation and challenged the notion that wage-push was the authoritative diagnosis (1960:184; see Forder 2010). "What geographical, economic, sociological facts account for the difference between the two countries?" (1960:187), they asked when noting the differences between the empirical relationships between wages and employment that Phillips had observed for the UK versus Samuelson and Solow's focus on the US. Wages were thus placed amid multiple possible dynamics in cost-push and demand-pull inflation, which were posited as potentially socially, historically and geographically specific. Solow and Samuelson did not posit the Phillips Curve as a clear policy instrument, instead formalizing a potential relation amidst several contributing to inflation (Braun 2014:58; Forder 2014:33–49).

The precise theoretical and policy exercises that have been imbued in the Phillips Curve have been contested (Forder 2014). The Phillips Curve emerged during an era of the dominance of a Keynesian neoclassical synthesis that also exercised fiscal levers to calibrate the level of employment (Braun 2014). It was subsequently suggested that the Curve had been approached in the 1960's as a menu of possible monetary policy options (e.g., Haldane & Quah 1999; Mankiw & Reis 2018). Milton Friedman critiqued this apparent use of the Phillips Curve in his 1968 American Economic Association address and 1976 lecture for the Sveriges Riksbank Prize in Economic Sciences. Friedman aimed his critique at "cheap money policies" (1968:2), which he argued had characterized the postwar period, and the notion that low interest rates could be justified by seeking to raise employment (Friedman 1968, 1976). The stagflation of the 1970s suggested instead that unemployment and inflation could coexist. In 1968, Friedman characterized the contemporary moment: "today, primacy is assigned to the promotion of full employment with the prevention of inflation a continuing but definitely secondary objective" (1968:5). Friedman thus asserted that within a menu of policy options economists had prioritized lowering unemployment by increasing inflation, known as "exploiting the Phillips Curve" (e.g., Mankiw & Reis 2018:84).

However, historian James Forder has labeled this "the Phillips Curve myth" (Forder 2010, 2014): contra Friedman's narrative, pursuing inflationary policies to promote employment had rarely been posited as a desirable path by economists (Forder 2010). As such, Forder argues that instead "the prominence of the Phillips Curve (or a like relation) in the discussion of inflation policy emerges when it is deployed to describe the requirements of price stability" (Forder 2010:344). Rather than different combinations between employment and inflation being pursued, he argues that inflation was foregrounded as a concern. This prefigured the era of independent central banks pursuing price stabilization. While some have dual mandates to balance inflation with other considerations such as employment, inflation is enshrined as the primary target of monetary policy in central banks such as the Bank of England, and implicitly prioritized in independent central banks across other contexts, such as the Federal Reserve.

Friedman posited an expectations-augmented Phillips Curve, emphasizing how agents' expectations of inflation may shift the Curve up in the longer term, although an awareness of the difference between the short and long run and the role of expectations had already been offered by economists such as Solow and Samuelson. He critiqued a Keynesian approach to unemployment as "explained by rigidities or imperfections, not as the natural outcome of a fully operative market process" (1968:3). In the long run, Friedman sought instead to naturalize a certain level of unemployment in order to bolster a monetarism that would remain focused on inflation: this "Natural Rate of unemployment" (Friedman 1968) later became transposed into the Non-Accelerating Inflation Rate of Unemployment (Modigliani & Papademos 1975), or NAIRU, formalized in models as $U*$. Friedman also focused attention away from cost-push dynamics, whereby prices increased because the cost of inputs to the production of goods and services increased. He shifted instead toward demand-pull inflation, whereby prices increased because increasing wages increased demand and producers were thus able to rise prices. The implication of the latter is that targeting inflation operates through tempering demand: wage increases enable workers to afford more, which enables producers to raise prices, and inflation occurs through excess demand. Friedman foregrounded demand with an implied orientation to an austere management of desire.

Friedman's critiques formed part of a collective criticism in the late 1960s and 1970s (e.g., Friedman 1961; Fisher 1977), when several economists sought to disarm Keynesian economics through the notion of "expectations." While Friedman had focused on adjusted expectations, economists such as Robert Lucas and Thomas Sargent foregrounded rational expectations. The expectations critiques across fields of economics mobilized similar logics: that representative agents within an economy would anticipate the moves of policymakers, and in turn respond in ways that ultimately neutralized a policy intervention. This disarmed the careful calibration of monetary and fiscal levers in the economy by Keynesian economists (Braun 2014). Economists instead operated through anticipating the "expectations" of agents, who may in turn act by anticipating the expectations of policymakers.

Despite such critiques, a focus on wages and employment in discussions of prices endured. Inflation continued to be apprehended through wage-price spirals, with revived analysis of these dynamics offered by authors such as Olivier Blanchard, who in a 1986 *Quarterly Journal of Economics* paper "rehabilitates the old wage price spiral" (Blanchard 1986:543). These posited that increases in wages provoke increases in prices, either through increasing demand or through increasing costs of production, which in turn lead workers to press for further increases in wages. The Phillips Curve was reincarnated in emerging Dynamic Stochastic General Equilibrium (DSGE) models that became the workhorses of central banks, and inscribed in economics textbooks such as Blanchard's. The "New Keynesian Phillips Curve" was revised in particular in papers by Taylor (1980), Rosemberg (1982), and Calvo (1983), which focused on the temporality of adjustments in prices and wages, particularly with sticky prices that may adjust in different periods. This Phillips Curve assuaged Friedman's critiques by including both backward- and forward-looking expectations (e.g., Clarida et al. 1999; Gali & Gertler 1999). The revised Phillips Curve was deployed by central banks including the Bank of England in analysis of monetary policy in the 1990's and 2000's (e.g., Bakhshi et al. 2003; Barkbu et al. 2005).

However, the rehabilitation of the Phillips Curve was accompanied by the demise of trade unions. While the Phillips Curve rested on the assumption that workers were able to respond to inflation by pushing for wage increases, this assumed worker power for such negotiations was declining. The assumptions that undergirded the Phillips Curve therefore increasingly diverged from the actual experiences of workers, who lacked the bargaining power that had enabled organized labor to negotiate wage rises. In the twenty-first century, particularly following the 2007–2009 financial crisis, the endurance of the Curve as analytical tool was increasingly in tension with the empirical evidence that policymakers sought to apprehend.

4. The Multiplicity and Endurance of the Phillips Curve

While it has been argued that Friedman's narrative that the Phillips Curve dominated policymaking as a menu of available options for unemployment and inflation in the 1960's is a "myth" (Forder 2014), I suggest that the narrative that the Phillips Curve then died a distinct Friedmanite death itself obscures its ongoing discursive and material role in analysis and policy persuasion in central banks. In 2018, despite wages and inflation being delinked during a decade of low inflation during low unemployment, prominent macroeconomists could proclaim that "[a]s a scatter plot, the Phillips Curve has shifted so often that no one takes it to be anything other than a transitory, reduced-form empirical relation. Yet as a synonym for nominal rigidities, in the sense of a structural two-way causal relation between nominal and real variables in the short run, the Phillips Curve is as alive as ever" (Mankiw & Reis 2018:92).

The Phillips Curve has continued to preoccupy macroeconomists and policymakers in central banks. Central bankers have retained the place of the Curve as a core analytical model in academic papers and as a key explanatory device in speeches to broader publics. In the 2000's, the Bank's analysts estimated recent New Keynesian Phillips Curves in the United Kingdom, the United States, and Eurozone (e.g., Barkbu et al. 2005; Bakhshi et al. 2003; Groen & Mumtaz 2008). At the Bank of England, such analyses fed into presentations to the Monetary Policy Committee (MPC) before their meetings, and into associated Inflation Reports that had been introduced in the 1990's, shortly prior to the addition of a specialized Bank staff to aid external MPC members in analysis and speeches (Acosta et al. 2023). Members of the Monetary Policy Committee continued to account for their individual decisions on interest rates through narratives regarding wages and employment in the 2010s (e.g., Haldane 2017a; McCafferty 2016), even as they articulated how the Phillips Curve had begun to "break down."

During this period, attention shifted to the lack of visibility of the Curve, yet its role endured. In 2015, despite low inflation concurrent with low unemployment, the Chief Economist of the Bank of England, Andrew Haldane, emphasized that the "short-term relationship between unemployment or the output gap and wage growth or inflation—the Phillips Curve—is one of the most intensively studied in macro-economics" (Haldane 2015:7). Haldane's reference to "wage growth or inflation" mirrors the earlier move from Phillips's original focus on wages to Solow and Samuelson's centering of inflation. His use of the term reveals that this was not a linear historical shift from wages to inflation in uses of the Curve, but rather these two categories remained in an oscillation. As such, wage growth continued to be encoded as inflation, with the implication that inflation targeting was wage tempering.

Yet the relationships that the Phillips Curve depicted increasingly diverged from the realities that economists wrestled with. In the decade following the 2007–2009 financial crisis, the Phillips Curve was presented as a "wage puzzle" (e.g., Haldane 2015, 2017a). As Sir Jon Cunliffe, MPC member, put the puzzle in a speech to the Oxford Economics Society in November 2017: "the unemployment rate in the UK today is 4.3 percent. The last time it was that low was 1975." He recounted how he had emerged from university at the time, emphasizing "[t]hat year, average wages grew by 24 percent. 42 years later, with unemployment at the same level, whole economy average weekly earnings grew by 2.2 percent" (Cunliffe 2017:2). By official figures in the 2010's employment was high, and yet inflation remained low. This generated contention over whether the relation between unemployment and inflation was "broken," with uncertainty how to calibrate and predict the relationship. Low unemployment, as measured by macroeconomists, did not appear to be provoking anticipated increases in wages and was concurrent with low inflation, which was frequently below the 2 percent target.

However, this did not lead to a simple move away from concerns with wages and unemployment in inflation targeting to recenter other dynamics. Rather than merely abandoning the Curve, macroeconomists became occupied by how these dynamics changed its aesthetics. At the Bank of England analysts and policymakers contemplated whether contemporary conditions shifted the shape or slope of the Curve, in a series of papers and speeches entitled: "Long-term unemployment and convexity in the Phillips Curve" (Speigner 2014); "Drag and drop" (Haldane 2015); "The Phillips Curve: lower, flatter or in hiding?" (Cunliffe 2017); "Optimal Inflation and the Identification of the Phillips Curve" (McLeay & Tenreyo 2019). This genre of analysis persisted after the Covid-19 and invasion of Ukraine rises in inflation, with a Staff Working Paper in January 2025 still asking "How curvy is the Phillips Curve?" (Bunn et al. 2025). These were echoed by other central banks, such as the ECB, where economists asked "What's up with the Phillips Curve?" (Del Negro et al. 2020).

Many of these papers attempted to unpack the "wage puzzle" by questioning different contemporary dynamics in labor markets, such as whether measures of the category of employment captured the rise of informalized labor regimes in the gig economy and participation rates, and if worker expectations or capacity for bargaining had altered (e.g., Haldane 2015, 2017a). They traced how these dynamics flattened, shifted downwards or decreased the slope of the Curve. For example, Andrew Haldane outlined during a speech in Bradford how "recent trends in wages, alongside further falls in unemployment, reinforce the impression of an exceptionally weak relationship between wages and employment, a pancake-like Phillips Curve. Indeed, it is testimony to the flatness of the Phillips Curve that wage growth is at similar levels today to when unemployment was at its recent peak back in 2011" (Haldane 2107a:10). Yet economists did not simply shift attention away from the preoccupation with employment as threat to price stability—instead the centrality of the device of the Curve gave traction to an ongoing concern with unemployment and wages in inflation targeting when attention might have otherwise moved elsewhere, such as onto profit margins. These attempts at manipulating, moderating, and modeling shifts in the Phillips Curve mirror a strategy for dealing with "uncomfortable knowledge" identified by Jacqueline Best, where central bankers "displace uncomfortable knowledge by governing their models rather than the messier empirical world" (Best 2022:565). Economists retreated into speculating on shifts in the increasingly invisible Curve.

Meanwhile, some attempts to tackle the puzzle of the Phillips Curve situated the problem not within increasing informality in the workforce or the inability of economic categories to capture the nuances of these contemporary labor regimes, but as a reflection of the success of monetary policy itself by independent central banks. As MPC member Silvana Tenreyo and Monetary Policy Advisor Michael McLeay argued in the first iteration of a column that would later become a paper:

> The Phillips curve—a positive relationship between inflation and economic slack – is one of the building blocks of the standard macroeconomic models used for forecasting and policy advice in central banks. On the face of it, recent findings of a breakdown in this relationship would therefore have major implications for monetary policy. This column argues that these findings are perfectly consistent with a stable underlying Phillips curve. The reason is simple: monetary policy will typically seek to reduce output whenever inflation is set to rise above target, blurring the identification of the Phillips curve in the data.
>
> (Tenreyo & McLeay 2018)

They clarified that the relationship is the precondition for their analysis: "in our paper the Phillips Curve always holds—inflation depends positively on the output gap *by assumption*" (Tenreyo & McLeay 2018, emphasis original). Their epistemological project thus displaced the straightforward empiricist appeals of econometrics with attempts to analytically uncover structural relations through the practice of modeling. Similarly, MPC member Catherine Mann later stated: "[t]his relationship may not be immediately visible from a simple scatterplot. Just as correlation does not imply causation, causation does not imply correlation. In fact, if one were to simply fit a line through the scatter in Chart 3, which plots UK unemployment against CPI inflation in quarterly frequency [in the UK since 1971], there would be no detectable relationship" (Mann 2022). Despite the historical demise of the correlation between unemployment and inflation, policymakers were able to recover the relevance of the relationship through a shift to the device of the Phillips Curve as an analytical tool in modeling.

Through these moves, policymakers suggested that the Phillips Curve was only visible when monetary policy failed: if monetary policy were able to offset demand shocks, the correlation would not be visible, as "successful monetary policy will make the Phillips Curve harder to see in the data" (Tenreyo & McLeay 2018). They argued that the invisibility of the relationship indicated the success of central bank inflation targeting and its ability to anchor inflation expectations. Rather than unwinding an interest in wages and employment, the invisibility of the Phillips Curve was enrolled as a sign of its importance in monetary policymaking. This reveals an epistemological ambivalence in economics, where the empirical invisibility of the relationships that economists posit is itself deemed an indicator of the efficacy of their policy infrastructures, and critiques can be refuted as instead markers of success.

Ultimately, the Phillips Curve endured as a singular object that enfolded multiple variables. The erosion of worker power could be elided by discussions of the Phillips Curve that substituted different dynamics for the strict category of unemployment. The Office for National Statistics reported that the Curve's flattening caused the Bank of England by 2019 to use a variant of the Phillips Curve relationship that replaced the unemployment rate with the output gap (the difference between 'actual' and 'potential' gross domestic product [GDP]) (ONS 2019). The axis of unemployment was replaced by the more nebulous category of "slack" (e.g., Mann 2022). Slackness in the labor market was therefore substituted by slackness in general. Yet this break from slack in the labor market to slack in general was not clear-cut. Instead, it gave space for equivocation between categories. In later speeches policymakers continued to posit the Phillips Curve as the relationship between unemployment and inflation (e.g., Haskel 2023).

While previously an oscillation between wages and inflation had taken place on the vertical axis, this was supplemented by a bait-and-switch between unemployment and slack on the horizontal axis.

While slack in the labor market and slack in general substituted for one another, this latter category of slack was itself composed of multiple dynamics that have often been inadequately unpacked. There was a rise following the 2007–2009 financial crisis of attempts by macroeconomists in central banks to enquire into these diverse dynamics, including at the Bank of England, such as through heterogeneous agent models (e.g., Meeks & Monti 2019); a "globe-centric" Phillips Curve rather than those of atomized nations (e.g., Aquilante et al. 2024; Boris & Filardo 2007; Carney 2017); or a focus on disaggregating regional dynamics. These gestured towards different aspects of cost components; regional disaggregation; and a heterogeneity of firms, workers, and sectors. Yet, the default analyses of representative agents, standardized industries, and national aggregates remained standard, with the nuances of individual, sectoral, and regional differences obscured. In particular, the distinction between the extravagant rises in executive pay in recent decades and the minor rises in lower wages is obscured. The complexity of these dynamics was often not unpacked in the general use of the Phillips Curve, which posits simplified relationships. "Slack" in general became composed of disparate dynamics that could subsequently be substituted back to slack simply in the labor market.

This hybrid Phillips Curve amalgamated approaches to expectations, cost-pushes, and slack as the difference between supply and demand, which in turn comprised a composite of different variables that could be inadequately unpacked. In Andrew Haldane's terms, "[i]f you consider the traditional determinants of inflation, there are at least three plausible sources of disinflationary 'drag': slack in the economy, a weaker relationship between slack and wages, and lower levels of inflation expectations." (Haldane 2015:6). Haldane emphasized that these components were interrelated, thus integrating analyses of wages into further consideration of slack and expectations. Moreover, while economists increasingly noted the weakening relationship between slack and wages, the emphasis on wages was recovered by an emphasis on the "second round," when workers may observe inflation that emerged from other variables and in turn press for an increase in wages. Even when inflation was acknowledged to emerge from elements such as energy prices, the specter of the second round loomed large. Therefore, rather than simply abandoned, the Phillips Curve was given traction by substituting and translating between different categories at different moments to various audiences, and these categories could be inadequately unpacked. As one macroeconomist who acted as a consultant to central banks framed it, this was "the unbearable lightness of the Phillips Curve."

"Strategic ambiguity" has been a feature of central banking, with analysts and policymakers tailoring narratives to different audiences to generate continuity and legitimacy amidst shifting economic circumstances and political goals (van't Klooster 2022). Adam Leaver has noted how devices in economics can form "mutable mobiles" (Leaver 2015), extending Latour's analysis of immutable mobiles as scientific tools to account for how these devices are adapted in order to be adopted in different contexts. In central banks, the Phillips Curve has been rendered in multiple forms to accommodate changing labor regimes. Despite the demise of trade unions, the Phillips Curve endured. The analytical tool of the Curve gave traction to a focus on wages and unemployment in inflation targeting, when attention may simply have shifting onto other variables, such as profits. The ambiguity of its specific components and equivocation between categories enabled wages and unemployment to be de- and subsequently reemphasized. The multiplicity of the category of the Phillips Curve thus paradoxically reinforces the singularity of the focus on wages: while economists may be aware that multiple dynamics feed into the Curve, which sustain its validity, these complex dynamics can become synonymous with wages and unemployment through reference to the Curve. The specter of wages as threat to inflation remains paramount.

In particular, despite an appreciation of various variables leading to inflation, there is a focus on second round responses of workers, with the concern that upon seeing inflation they may subsequently push for a rise in wages: reflected in comments such as Governor Bailey's that upon witnessing inflation workers ought to restrain from asking for wage rises. Yet, their capacity to do so has been eroded by lack of bargaining power, and real wages have shown an average decline even in inflationary periods such as Covid-19 as they have not followed increases in prices. Wage increases have not caught up with price increases, and workers have in real terms taken pay cuts. While in theory the New Neoclassical Synthesis (Goodfried & King 1997) models have sticky prices and possibly sticky wages, the notion that wages react sensitively retains discursive force through such appeals to temper the responsiveness of workers. This is despite the lack of empirical evidence for renewed wage bargaining in the past two decades. As such, the Phillips Curve retains a discursive power that continues to place wages as the specter of inflation, and wage-price spirals remain a core concern in inflation targeting despite the demise of trade unions.

The enduring status of the Phillips Curve is ambiguous. While it has been problematized both theoretically and empirically, it remains used in analysis of monetary policy in many central banks. At times this use is explicit, but at others the relations that the Phillips Curve foregrounds remains implicit in assumptions and discourses regarding inflation. The Phillips Curve was refuted but remains used; disavowed yet endures. Meanwhile, even when economic models posit precise relationships between entities, the practices of inflation targeting instead rely on more nebulous narratives, assumptions, and forms of persuasion. Moreover, in practice economists do not use singular models, but rather assemblages of different models forming a bricolage with multiple dynamics. The Phillips Curve is not a simple singular model, but a set of discourses, dynamics, and threats that are evoked in analysis of monetary policy. The multiplicity of the model itself gives traction to the specter of wages and unemployment in concerns about inflation.

These concerns with wages reveal the economic imaginaries that animate macroeconomics and are enrolled in its genres of policy persuasion. Within inflation targeting, wages are scrutinized for their productivity and imbued with implications of wastefulness. The "productivity" of labor was another key "puzzle" amongst analysts and policy-makers in the Bank during this period, who problematized stagnant productivity in the population (e.g., Abel et al. 2016; Barnett et al. 2014; Haldane 2017b; McCafferty 2014; Weale 2014). Concerns with wages and productivity were entangled in inflation targeting, as wage rises without concomitant increases in productivity were considered the source of inflationary dynamics. Wage rises were therefore only deemed legitimate if accompanied by productivity increases, yet the measurement and delineations of these categories from capital are beset by problems. The "marginal return to labor" and "marginal return to capital" are foundational categories in the mathematical and geometric manipulations of marginalist economic models, which legitimize and naturalize returns to these apparently partible components. Yet the complex enmeshment of these relations and the social and political implications of extraction it produces is obscured.

This imaginary of wages as waste has larger traction in economics. The austerity programs implemented across Europe following the financial crisis took as their target wasteful public expenditure particularly on wages, often approached through discourses of excessive incomes or employee benefits. In these imaginaries of managing "the economy," a central concern is the parsimonious use of public funds. A focus on efficiency that is engendered by an austere labor force supplanted an earlier Keynesian focus on stimulating demand and raising tax revenue. While increases in GDP have been conceived as a relatively benign good, increases in wages have thus been approached with ambivalence in multiple fields of the discipline, which have often been animated by an imaginary of wages as waste. The generativity of livelihoods for the lives they make possible is either obscured or problematized in the terms of "excess" demand that threatens inflation.

5. At the Margins

By contrast to the enduring concern with wages and unemployment, profit margins have been marginalized in discussions of inflation. "Profits" featured only fleetingly in Bank of England speeches before 2020. In 2017, they were mentioned in the context of the impact of Brexit on the pound and in the context of regulatory policy (Woods 2017), as the Bank of England also houses the UK's Prudential Regulation Authority. During the period of 1997–2020, profits were given primary attention vis-a-vis monetary policy in a single Bank speech addressing whether low interest rates had tempered the profits of pension funds (Vlieghe 2016); yet this considered the impact of monetary policy on profits, rather than the impact of profits on inflation and thus monetary policy. Profits as a potential factor in inflation were eclipsed. Profit margins were marginalized until their recent revival (e.g., Weber & Wasner 2023).

By 2023, with such critiques accompanied by Covid-19 and the invasion of Ukraine, economists were pressed to respond to the question of profits. Jonathan Haskel, who was recruited as an external member of the MPC for his work on productivity, gave a speech titled "What's driving inflation: wages, profits, or energy prices?" at the Peterson Institute for International Economics, Washington, DC. He rebuffed the significance of profits by arguing that these constitute a small component of inflation through the accounting principles outlined above that "let us equate labor income to the return of workers, and capital income to the return of capital owners" (Haskel 2023:5), and reemphasizing the role of wages: "Looking forward, the labor market is still very tight in an absolute sense" (Haskel 2023:2). Similarly, external MPC member Megan Greene tried to estimate the appropriate shares of labor and capital in productivity when suggesting that "excess labour hoarding was a regular occurrence in the post-pandemic period, as labour shortages led to recruitment difficulties" (Greene 2024). This discursive register of "labor hoarding" again appealed to logics of excess and stagnancy in labor markets.

While analysis of the causes of inflation foregrounded some dynamics while eclipsing others, so did analysis of the mechanisms through which it was addressed. The elisions, erasures, and anxieties of policymakers involve class, gender, racial, geographical, and generational politics. In particular, there is an almost blanket silence in UK monetary policy on the implications of student loans. In the UK, there has been an unprecedented increase in student debt since the 2011 rise in tuition fees by the Conservative led coalition to £9000, leaving graduates in England with £27,000 in loans for tuition fees or English graduates in Scotland with £36,000, plus a potential additional £18,000 in maintenance loans. These are formally tagged to base rate and paid as a 10 percent additional tax above a certain income band, which if accruing interest faster than being paid off may last throughout their lives. The rapid increases in interest rates generated an unprecedented rise in this debt, which would create persistent pressure in the UK's population in the future. In January 2025, a search for "mortgage" in the publications and speeches of the Bank of England returned 185 results; "student loan" returned one, from a 2024 Financial Stability Report. The stark silence on the implications of monetary policy for student loans constitutes a considerable blindspot, inscribing a generational politics that compounds the distributive implications of transmission mechanisms of central banks. Similarly, despite the acknowledged role of mortgages as a transmission mechanism in monetary policy, inflation in the housing market itself was relatively neglected in discussions of inflation overall. This silence is striking given the rapid rise in real estate prices in the UK during the period.

In 2023, Andrew Bailey went on an outreach event to talk with "citizens" about what the Bank of England does. He spoke of disruption to supply chains as drivers of inflation as he gave examples of women doing care work or burdened by illness struggling to pay for food and heating, framing the problem: "more people in employment facing difficult choices and having to turn to food banks for help." Yet, while empathetically addressing the concerns of rising energy and food costs amidst his audience, he shifted focus when presenting solutions: "[b]ut what monetary policy can—and must—do is to make sure that the inflation that has come to us from abroad does not become lasting inflation generated at home... That is why we have increased Bank Rate. This works through the cost of living in a different way, of course: by increasing the cost of credit, including rates on many mortgages." He elaborated on the additional costs this would present for renters and home owners, before concluding on this raise in interest rates:

> It is having an impact. Let me say two things about that.
>
> First, with the external shocks that have hit the economy, there is no easy way out. People on lower incomes are struggling to make ends meet. We must ensure that the situation does not get worse through homemade inflation taking hold.
>
> The UK labour market remains very tight. Since the start of the Covid pandemic, we have seen a large increase in the number of people who do not take part in the labour market in this country. The UK labour force has shrunk. While not the focus of my remarks today, this feature of the UK labour market is an important backdrop to our monetary policy decisions.
>
> (Bailey 2023)

The Bank of England's page where the speech was uploaded included a picture of a banner from such an event, with the title "Thank you for listening." The banner itself was embossed with the Bank of England logo, and stated "We're listening to your community." The speech empathized with the difficulties inflation presented to workers, who are often hit hard by increases in prices. Yet in the measurement, modeling, and mechanisms of inflation targeting, tempering wages remained a core concern. Solutions to the "cost of living crisis" were presented as suppressing wages and further squeezing the cost of living.

6. Capitalist (un)realism

Macroeconomics adopts a technocratic view, which assumes the position of a subject who erases their own subjectivity (Mann 2019); yet economics acquires specific subject positions through both how models are assembled and how they are subsequently mobilized. Economists assemble models using categories of labor and capital, positing relations between these categories and problematizing specific questions. This enables the abstractions of macroeconomic modeling by situating economists in a technocratic outside to the indicators they assemble and assess. But rather than a view from nowhere, central banks are embedded in a set of relations that create affinity and alterity, positioning economics from the perspective of capital (Mann 2013); capital becomes subject position while labor becomes analytical object. Capitalist relations are inscribed both in the foundations of economic models and in how they are mobilized in central banks.

A "capitalist realism" (Fisher 2009) animates economic models, from Keynesian characterizations of unemployment (Mann 2019), to genres of austerity concerned with the control of labor (Blyth 2013; Mattei 2022). Yet, this capitalist realism itself constitutes a form of capitalist unrealism. Wilful blindness sustains projects of modeling, which are based on assumptions that foreground some dynamics while eclipsing others. Commitments to the epistemic modalities of modeling and the assumptions that undergird them gave traction to certain problematics and eclipsed others. Wage rises remained a primary concern through their formalization in the Phillips Curve, while margins continued to be marginalized. Some realities were sanctioned by unseeing them.

Economics has ambiguous and ambivalent relationships with the "real," with models simultaneously appealing to epistemic prowess and partitioning apart from empiricism (Pearson 2024). While it called for a reconsideration of socioeconomic dynamics driving inflation, Isabella Weber's 2021 Guardian article acquired a social life of its own. Paul Krugman called it "truly stupid", and Weber's analysis was implicitly referenced in a Chicago Economics exam asking how a "real economist" would instead address inflation, leading Weber to self-identify as the "unreal economist." In this contestation, the presence of profits in inflationary dynamics was thus designated not a concern of a "real economist," yet the term "real" acquired ambiguous meaning. Rather than an empirical appeal to the irrelevance of profits, the "unreal" consisted of a divergence from a profession that practices the manipulation of standardized mainstream models, many of which assumed the benevolence or irrelevance of profits. It was not characteristic of a "real economist" as it departed from the a-realism of certain mainstream economic models. The "real economist" was to be identified by using these surrealist models. The "real" referred to belonging in a profession, with its epistemological and analytical commitments, rather than the empirical accuracy of the profession's representations.

Central banks "represent" capitalism in dual senses. Their models act as representations of capitalist dynamics, depicting economic relations. Meanwhile, economists form relations that align them disproportionately with representatives of certain socioeconomic groups. While representative agents are abstract figures in economics, economists establish relations with specific representatives of social, historical, and cultural institutions. This occludes certain economic dynamics while foregrounding others. Rebalancing these representations entails acknowledging the presence of disparate dynamics in inflation, highlighting which relations models foreground and eclipse. This includes recovering "margins" from their marginalization in economics, and destabilizing assumptions regarding the uniquely reified relations employment and inflation have historically held in macroeconomics.

References

Abel, W., R. Burnham, and M. Corder. 2016. "Wages, productivity and the changing composition of the UK workforce". Quarterly Bullentin Q1, Bank of England.

Acosta, J, B. Cherrier, F. Claveau, C. Fontan, and A. Goutsmedt. 2023. "Six Decades of Economic Research at the Bank of England." *History of Political Economy* 56 (1): 1–40.

Alvarez-Lois, P., R. Harrison, L. Piscitelli, and A. Scott. 2008. "On the Application and Use of DSGE Models." *Journal of Economic Dynamics and Control* 32(8): 2428–2452.

Aquilante, T., A. Dogan, M. Firat, and A. Soenarjo. 2024. "Global Value Chains and the Dynamics of UK Inflation." Bank of England, Staff Working Paper No. 1060.

Bailey, A. 2023. "The Cost of Living." Speech given at Brunswick Group's Cost of Living Conference, London. Bank of England.

Bakhshi, H., P. Burriel-Llombart, H. Khan, and B. Rudolf. 2003. "Endogenous Price Stickiness, Trend Inflation, and the New Keynesian Phillips Curve." Bank of England, Staff Working Paper No. 191.

Barkbu, B., V. Cassino, A. Gosselin-Lotz, and L. Piscitelli. 2005. "The New Keynesian Phillips Curve in the United States and the Euro Area." Bank of England, Staff Working Paper No. 285.

Barnett, A., A. Chiu, J. Franklin, and M. Sebastia-Barriel. 2014. "The Productivity Puzzle: A Firm-Level Investigation into Employment Behaviour and Resource Allocation over the Crisis." Bank of England, Working Paper No. 495.

Barro, R. J., and D. B. Gordon. 1983. "Rules, Discretion and Reputation in a Model of Monetary Policy." NBER Working Paper 1079.

Bear, L 2020. "Speculation: A Political Economy of Technologies of Imagination." *Economy and Society* 49 (1): 1–15.

Bear, L., K. Ho, A. L. Tsing, and S. Yanagisako. 2015. "GENS: A Manifesto for the Study of Capitalism." *Society for Cultural Anthropology*, Theorizing the Contemporary, *Fieldsights*, March 30.

Best, J. 2018. "Technocratic Exceptionalism: Monetary Policy and the Fear of Democracy." *International Political Sociology* 12: 326–345.

Best, J. 2022. "Uncomfortable Knowledge in Central Banking: Economic Expertise Confronts the Visibility Dilemma." *Economy and Society* 51: 559–583.

Best, J. 2024. "Central Banks' Knowledge Controversies." *New Political Economy* 29(6): 857–871.

Birch, K., and F. Muniesa 2020. *Assetization: Turning Things into Assets in Technoscientific Capitalism.* Cambridge, MA: MIT Press.

Blanchard, O. 1986. "The Wage Price Spiral." *The Quarterly Journal of Economics,* 101(3): 543–566.

Blinder, A. S. 2004. *The Quiet Revolution: Central Banking Goes Modern.* New Haven: Yale University Press.

Blinder, A. S., M. Ehrmann, J. de Haan, and D.-J. Jansen. 2024. "Central Bank Communication with the General Public: Promise or False Hope?." *Journal of Economic Literature,* 62(2): 425–457.

Blyth, M. 2013. *Austerity: The History of a Dangerous Idea.* Oxford: Oxford University Press.

Borio, C., and Filardo, A. 2007. Globalisation and inflation: New cross-country evidence on the global determinants of domestic inflation. Monetary and Economic Department, BIS Working Papers, No. 227.

Bovensiepen, J., and M. Pelkmans. 2020. "Dynamics of Willful Blindness: An Introduction." *Critique of Anthropology* 40(4): 387–402.

Braun, B. 2014. "Why Models Matter: The Making and Unmaking of Governability in Macroeconomic Discourse." *Journal of Critical Globalisation Studies* 7: 48–79.

Braun, B. 2016. "Speaking to the People? Money, Trust, and Central Bank Legitimacy in the Age of Quantitative Easing." *Review of International Political Economy* 23(6):1064–1092.

Braun, B. 2020. "Central banking and the infrastructural power of finance: the case of ECB support for repo and securitization markets." *Socio-Economi Review,* 18(2): 395–418.

Braun, B., and M. Düsterhöft. 2025. Noisy Politics, Quiet Technocrats? Central Banking in Contentious Times. *Regulation and Governance,* 1–23.

Bunn, P, L. Anayi, N. Bloom, et al. 2025. "How Curvy is the Phillips Curve?" Bank of England, Staff Working Paper No. 1107.

Callon M. 1998. *The Laws of the Markets.* London: Blackwell.

Callon M., and F. Muniesa 2005. "Economic Markets as Calculative Collective Devices." *Organization Studies* 26 (8): 1229–1250.

Calvo, G. 1983. "Staggered Prices in a Utility-Maximizing Framework." *Journal of Monetary Economics* 12(3): 383–398.

Carney, M. 2017. "[De]Globalisation and inflation". IMF Michel Camdessus Central Banking Lecture. Bank of England.

Chari, V. 2010. Testimony. Hearing before the Committee on Science and Technology, US House of Representatives, July 20, 2010.

Clarida, R., J. Gali, and M. Gertler. 1999. "The Science of Monetary Policy: A New Keynesian Perspective." *Journal of Economic Literature* 37(4): 1661–1707.

Coombs, N., and M. Thiemann. 2022. "Recentering Central Banks: Theorizing State-Economy Boundaries As Central Bank Effects." *Economy and Society* 51(4): 535–558.

Cunliffe, J. 2017. "The Phillips Curve: Lower, Flatter or In Hiding?" Speech Given at Oxford Economics Society. Bank of England.

Davies, W. and L. McGoey. 2012. "Rationalities of Ignorance: On Financial Crisis and the Ambivalence of Neo-Liberal Epistemology." *Economy and Society* 41(1): 64–83.

Del Negro, M., M. Lenza, G. Primiceri, and A. Tambalotti. 2020. "What's up with the Phillip's Curve?". ECB Working Paper, No. 2435.

Dietsch, P., F. Claveau, and C. Fontan. 2018. *Do Central Banks Serve The People?* Hoboken, NJ: Wiley.

Downey, L. 2021. "Delegation in Democracy: A Temporal Analysis." *The Journal of Political Philosophy* 29(3): 305–329.

Downey, L. 2025. *Our Money: Monetary Policy As If Democracy Matters.* Princeton: Princeton University Press.

Ferguson, R. W., and U. Lahiri. 2023. "The History and Future of the Federal Reserve's 2 Percent Target Rate of Inflation". Council on Foreign Relations.

Fisher, M. 2009. *Capitalist Realism: Is There No Alternative?* Zero Books, John Hunt Publishing.

Fisher, S. 1977. "Long-Term Contracts, Rational Expectations, and the Optimal Money Supply Rule." *Journal of Political Economy* 85(1): 191–205.

Forder, J. 2010. "Friedman's Nobel Lecture and the Phillips Curve Myth." *Journal of the History of Economic Thought* 32(3): 329–348.

Forder, J. 2014. *Macroeconomics and the Phillips Curve Myth.* Oxford: Oxford University Press.

Friedman, M. 1961. "The Lag in Effect of Monetary Policy." *Journal of Political Economy* 69(5): 447–466.

Friedman, M. 1968. "The Role of Monetary Policy." Presidential Address Delivered at the 80th Annual Meeting of the American Economic Association. *American Economic Review* 58(1): 1–17.

Friedman, M. 1976. Inflation and Unemployment. Nobel Memorial Lecture, December 13, 1976.

Gali, J., and M. Gertler. 1999. "Inflation Dynamics: A Structural Econometric Analysis." *Journal of Monetary Economics* 44(2): 195–222.

Gibson-Graham, J. K. 1996. *J.K Gibson-Graham, The End of Capitalism (As We Knew It): A Feminist Critique of Political Economy.* Oxford: Blackwell Publishers.

Greene, M. 2024. "Two puzzles: recent UK labour market dynamics." Speech given at Make UK. Bank of England.

Groen, J, and H. Mumtaz. 2008. "Investigating the Structural Stability of the Phillips Curve Relationship." Bank of England, Staff Working Paper No. 350.

Haldane, A. 2015. "Drag and Drop." Speech given at BizClub lunch, Rutland. Bank of England.

Haldane, A. 2017a. "Work, Wages and Monetary Policy." Speech given at National Science and Media Museum, Bradford. Bank of England.

Haldane, A. 2017b. "Productivity Puzzles." Speech given at London School of Economics and Political Science. Bank of England.

Haldane, A., and Quah, D. 1999. "UK Phillips curves and monetary policy," *Journal of Monetary Economics, Elsevier* 44(2): 259–278.

Haskel, J. 2023. "Implications of Current Wage Inflation." Speech given at Bank of England Watchers' Conference. Bank of England.

Holmes, D. 2013. *Economy of Words.* Chicago: University of Chicago Press.

Holmes, D. 2018. "A Tractable Future: Central Bankers in Conversation with their Publics." In eds. Jens Beckert and Richard Bronk. *Uncertain Futures: Imaginaries, Narratives and Calculation in the Economy*, 173–193. Oxford: Oxford University Press.

Jacobs, L. and D. King. 2016. *Fed Power: How Finance Wins.* Oxford: Oxford University Press.

Jessop, B, and S. Oosterlynck. 2008. "Cultural Political Economy: On Making the Cultural Turn Without Falling Into Soft Economic Sociology." *Geoforum* 39: 1155–1169.

Kirshner, J. 2001. "The Political Economy Of Low Inflation." *Journal of Economic Surveys* 15(1): 41–70.

Krippner, G. 2012. *Capitalizing on Crisis: The Political Origins of the Rise of Finance.* Cambridge, MA: Harvard University Press.

Leaver, A. 2015. "Fuzzy knowledge: an historical exploration of moral hazard and its variability". *Economy and Society*, 44(1): 91–109.

Lucas, Robert E. 1972. "Expectations and the Neutrality of Money." *Journal of Economic Theory* 4(2): 103–124.

MacKenzie D. 2008. *An Engine Not A Camera: How Financial Models Make Markets.* Cambridge, MA: MIT Press.

MacKenzie D., F. Munieasa, and L. Siu. 2007. *Do Economists Make Markets? On the Performativity of Economics.* Princeton, NJ: Princeton University Press.

Mankiw, G., and R. Reis. 2018. "Friedman's Presidential Address in the Evolution of Macroeconomic Thought," *Journal of Economic Perspectives* 32(1): 81–96.

Mann, C. 2022. "Inflation expectations, inflation persistence, and monetary policy strategy." Speech given at 53rd Annual Conference of the Money Macro and Finance Society, University of Kent. Bank of England.

Mann, G. 2013. "The Monetary Exception: Labor, Distribution and Money in Capitalism." *Capital & Class* 37(2): 197–216.

Mann, G. 2019. *In The Long Run We're All Dead: Keynesianism, Political Economy and Revolution.* Verso, London.

Mattei, C. 2022. *The Capital Order: How Economists Invented Austerity and Paved the Way to Fascism.* Chicago: University of Chicago Press.

McCafferty, I. 2014. "The UK productivity puzzle—a sectoral perspective." Speech. Bank of England.

McCafferty, I. 2016. "Wages, Inflation and Current Monetary Policy." Speech. Bank of England.

McGoey, L. 2012. "Strategic Unknowns: Towards a Sociology of Ignorance". Economy and Society, 41(1):1–16.

McLeay, M., and S. Tenreyo. 2019. "Optimal Inflation and the Identification of the Phillips Curve." *NBER Macroeconomics Annual* 34(1): 199–255.

McNamara, K. 2002. "Rational Fictions: Central Bank Independence and the Social Logic of Delegation." *West European Politics* 25(1): 47–76.

McPhilemy, S. and M. Moschella. 2019. "Central Banks Under Stress: Reputation, Accountability and Regulatory Coherence." *Public Administration* 97(3): 489–498.

Meeks, R., and F. Monti. 2019. "Heterogeneous Beliefs and the Phillips Curve." Bank of England, Staff Working Paper No. 807.

Mirowski, P. 1989. *More Heat than Light.* Cambridge University Press.

Mirowski, P., and Nik-Khah, E. 2007. Markets Made Flesh: Callon, Performativity and a Problem in Science Studies, Augmented with Consideration of the FCC Auctions. In MacKenzie et al. (eds.) *Do Economists Make Markets?* Princeton University Press.

Mitchell, T. 1998. "Fixing the Economy". *Cultural Studies* 12(1): 82–101.

Mitchell, T. 2005. "The work of economics: how a discipline makes its world". *European Journal of Sociology* 46(2): 297–320.

Modigliani, F., and L. Papademos. 1975. "Targets for Monetary Policy in the Coming Year". *Brookings Papers on Economic Activity* 1: 141–165.

Monnet, E. 2024. *Balance of Power: Central Banks and the Fate of Democracies.* Chicago: University of Chicago Press.

Morgan, M. 2012. *The World in the Model.* Cambridge University Press.

Moschella, M. 2024. *Unexpected Revolutionaries. How Central Banks Made and Unmade Economic Orthodoxy.* Ithaca, NY: Cornell University Press.

Moschella, M. and L. Pinto. 2019. "'Central Banks' Communication As Reputation Management: How the Fed Talks Under Uncertainty." *Public Administration* 97(3): 513–529.

Muniesa, F. 2021. "Finance: Cultural or Political?" *Journal of Cultural Economy* 17(5): 1–4.

Ortiz H. 2021. "A Political Anthropology of Finance: Studying the Distribution of Money in the Financial Industry as a Political Process." *Anthropological Theory* 21(1): 3–27.

Pearson, A. 2024. "The Discipline of Economics: Ambivalent Epistemologies and the Foreclosure of Critique in Elite Economics Education." *Journal of the Royal Anthropological Institute* 30(4): 932–952.

Phillips, A W. 1958. "The Relation Between Unemployment and the Rate of Change of Money Wage Rates in the United Kingdom, 1861–1957." *Economica* 25(100): 283–299.

Rochon, L.-P. 2024. The damning truth about the UK's 2% inflation target: it's completely made up. *The Guardian*, February 1, 2024.

Samuelson, P, and R. Solow. 1960. "Analytical Aspects of Anti-Inflation Policy." *The American Economic Review*, 50(2): 177–194.

Scott, J. 2024. "Special Section Introduction: Epistemic Politics in International And Comparative Political Economy." *New Political Economy* 29(6): 835–843.

Speigner, B. 2014. "Long-term Unemployment and Convexity in the Phillips Curve." Bank of England, Staff Working Paper No.519.

Taylor, J. (1980). "Aggregate Dynamics and Staggered Contracts". *Journal of Political Economy*, 88(1): 1–23.

Tenreyo, S, and M. McLeay. 2018. "Optimal Inflation and the Identification of the Phillips Curve." VoxEU Column, CEPR.

Tucker, P. 2018. *Unelected Power: The Quest for Legitimacy in Central Banking and the Regulatory State*. Princeton, NJ: Princeton University Press.

van 't Klooster, J. 2022. "Technocratic Keynesianism: A Paradigm Shift without Legislative Change." *New Political Economy* 27(5): 771–787.

Vlieghe, G. 2016. "Umbrellas Don't Cause Rain." Speech given at Sheffield University. Bank of England.

Watson, M. 2024. "'Let me tell you a story': The Politics of Macroeconomic Models." *New Political Economy* 29(6): 844–856.

Weale, M. 2014. "The UK productivity puzzle: an international perspective". Speech Given at Queen Mary University of London. Bank of England.

Weber, I. M. 2021. "Could Strategic Price Controls Help Inflation?" *The Guardian*.

Weber, I. M., and E. Wasner. 2023. "Sellers' Inflation, Profits and Conflict: Why can Large Firms Hike Prices in an Emergency?" Economics Department Working Paper Series, 343.

Woods, S. 2017. "Looking Both Ways." Speech at Building Society Association (BSA) Annual Conference. Bank of England.

6

To Whom Do Central Banks Listen?

Reputation, Public Contestation, and the Strategic Use of Economic Imaginaries

Manuela Moschella

1. Introduction

Central banks and financial regulators are far from neutral arbiters of economic policy. While often portrayed as technocratic institutions operating above the political fray, they are in fact deeply embedded in—and actively contribute to—the shaping of domestic political conflict. Through the design and implementation of monetary and regulatory policies, these institutions help structure the distribution of economic risks and rewards, reinforcing existing inequalities and reshaping the political economy of advanced capitalism (Jacobs and King 2025).

Central banks exemplify these dynamics with particular clarity. As the guardians of the value of money in domestic political systems, they have occupied a privileged institutional position within the contemporary capitalist regime. In particular, by consistently prioritizing low inflation over employment or growth by adhering to the logic of credibility, central banks have systematically favored capital and financial actors over wage earners and the broader public (Grabel 2003; Kirshner 2003). Central banks have also influenced the balance of power among different societal groups through asset purchases and liquidity injections during periods of financial market turmoil. These interventions have disproportionately benefited financial actors and wealthy asset holders, reinforcing the structural asymmetries of financialized capitalism (Dietsch et al. 2018; Jacobs and King 2016; Thiemann 2023).

Manuela Moschella, *To Whom Do Central Banks Listen?*. In: *Picking Winners*. Edited by: Lawrence R. Jacobs and Desmond King, Oxford University Press. © Oxford University Press (2026).
DOI: 10.1093/9780197831823.003.0006

This chapter builds on these insights but introduces an important refinement. It argues that while central banks remain deeply aligned with financial interests, they cannot advance those interests unmediated. As public institutions, they must maintain legitimacy across multiple and sometimes competing audiences—including elected officials, expert communities, and, increasingly, the broader public. In this context, reputation becomes a central currency of authority (Moschella 2024). According to Daniel Carpenter's widely used definition, bureaucratic reputation refers to "a set of symbolic beliefs about the unique or separable capacities, roles, and obligations of an organization, where these beliefs are embedded in audience networks" (Carpenter 2010, 45). This definition underscores that a central bank's authority does not rely solely on its economic performance. Instead, its reputation is sustained by a shared set of symbolic beliefs—or, as framed in this volume, by a dominant economic imaginary: a publicly circulating vision of the economy and of the central bank's role within it. This imaginary casts central banks as apolitical guardians of price stability, immune from distributional conflict and guided solely by economic logic. It supports the perception that central banks are technical institutions rather than political actors.

Crucially, central banks tend to cling to this imaginary even when their policies falter or come under intense public scrutiny—for instance, when inflation rises despite their interventions or when their close ties to financial elites become too evident to dismiss (Best 2018). Rather than rethinking their policy orientation in such moments, central banks respond through symbolic recalibrations. Specifically, they adjust their imaginaries—not by abandoning the core tenets of inflation control and market credibility, but by selectively broadening their discursive remit. These adaptations allow them to acknowledge public concerns and maintain legitimacy without undermining their authority or altering the institutional logic of central banking, while still falling short of truly democratizing central banking (see Downey 2024). This pattern mirrors a broader political dynamic: like elected officials, central bankers craft public narratives that simulate responsiveness, signaling attentiveness to societal demands while preserving the status quo (see, for instance, Jacobs and Shapiro 2000). In short, when contested, central banks manage their reputations by adjusting the stories they tell about themselves.

The post-2020 responses of the US Federal Reserve and the European Central Bank illustrate this dynamic. In the face of intensifying public contestation, the Fed revised its monetary strategy to emphasize "broad-based and inclusive" employment, explicitly recognizing the benefits of tight labor markets for historically disadvantaged groups. The ECB, for its part, incorporated climate considerations into its monetary policy framework, pledging to align its operations with the EU's broader green transition agenda.

Yet in both cases, the new social goals were carefully framed within the existing imaginary of technocratic, market-centered governance. Neither the Fed nor the ECB redefined their institutional objectives or challenged their foundational commitments to price stability and financial market confidence. Instead, they reframed those commitments in ways that gestured toward inclusivity and responsiveness. The goal was twofold: to respond symbolically to public pressure while preserving core institutional authority.

This reputational strategy has clear limits. As the inflationary pressures of 2021–2022 mounted, both the Fed and the ECB quickly reversed course. The Fed abandoned its dovish tone and launched a rapid tightening cycle. The ECB sidelined its climate roadmap and returned to its traditional inflation-fighting posture. These reversals reveal the fragility of symbolic adaptation. Central banks' engagement with public concerns is conditional, contingent, and constrained by the imperative to maintain credibility in the eyes of markets.

Taken together, the case studies offer three key findings. First, they show that public contestation can shape central bank behavior, not by producing policy reversals but by prompting discursive recalibration. Central banks may not democratize their goals but adapt their public narratives to deflect critique. Second, these adaptations are strategically conservative. They expand the institutional imaginary just enough to acknowledge societal expectations and demands—but not enough to disrupt the existing hierarchy of policy priorities. Third, the durability of these shifts is limited. When crisis conditions give way to inflationary pressure or renewed market volatility, central banks revert to the orthodoxy of inflation control and reputational insulation.

By foregrounding the politics of reputation and the strategic deployment of economic imaginaries, the chapter thus contributes to the volume's broader argument: that institutions like central banks do not merely reflect distributional conflict—they help to structure it. In moments of political contestation, they adapt—but they do so in ways that preserve their role as arbiters of a financial order that remains deeply unequal. Understanding how they navigate this tension is central to understanding the contemporary governance of money, markets, and the public good.

The chapter proceeds in three steps. First, it situates central banks within the broader literature on financial governance and introduces the concept of economic imaginaries as tools of reputational maintenance. Second, it examines how the Fed and ECB revised their public narratives and strategy frameworks in the early 2020s, selectively incorporating social goals in response to contestation. Third, it considers the implications of these developments for democratic responsiveness, central bank independence, and the politics of symbolic adaptation in financialized capitalism.

2. Whose Interests Do Central Banks Listen To?

There is now ample evidence that central banks maintain a structurally privileged relationship with financial markets—one that consistently tilts the policy playing field in favor of capital. This is not simply a functional by-product of monetary policy implementation or an unintended outcome of technocratic decision making. Rather, it reflects a deeper political-economic logic: Central banks and financial markets are mutually constitutive components of a governance architecture that underpins financialized capitalism. As Coombs and Thiemann (2022) argue, central banks occupy a nodal position in a dense network of public and private institutions that collectively sustain the production and circulation of credit-money. In this system, monetary authority is not exercised in isolation from markets but through a recursive relationship with them. Central banks rely on financial markets not only as transmission mechanisms for monetary policy, but also as the institutional terrain on which their legitimacy and effectiveness is continually negotiated.

This entanglement has profound implications for the distribution of authority and influence. The credibility of central banks—their ability to guide expectations and anchor inflation—is tightly coupled with the confidence of financial actors. In practice, this means that central banks must continuously signal responsiveness to market sentiment, stabilize financial conditions, and avoid policies that might unsettle them. This dependency grants financial markets a form of "infrastructural" power, as Braun (2020) argues: a form of indirect yet pervasive influence that stems from central banks' embedded reliance on financial institutions for policy efficacy.

Unlike traditional forms of political pressure, infrastructural power does not require direct lobbying or coercion. Instead, it operates through structural interdependence—a condition in which central banks can act only to the extent that markets validate and operationalize their actions.

But this power is not merely material; it is also profoundly ideological. Central bankers and financial elites often emerge from similar institutional backgrounds. They attend the same elite universities, participate in the same transnational policy circles, and move between public and private sector roles through revolving doors. This shared epistemic environment fosters a convergent worldview among central bankers rooted in the axioms of neoliberal economic governance (Baker 2006; Marcussen 2006). McNamara (2002) explores the social construction of central bank independence and the formation of a shared professional culture among central bankers, where economic principles like price stability are internalized as apolitical goals. In this context, central bankers adopt a common understanding that focuses on low inflation, fiscal restraint, and the minimization of distributive conflict. Johnson (2016) similarly highlights how the socialization and professional networks within the central banking community reinforce these shared norms, which prioritize macroeconomic discipline over social inclusion and financial stability over democratic responsiveness. This process of transnational socialization and the reproduction of policy paradigms is central to understanding how the power of finance is not just influenced by external actors like investors but is embedded within the very conceptual framework of central banking.

The political alignment between central banks and financial interests became deeply entrenched with the rise of inflation targeting and the institutionalization of central bank independence in the 1990s. These developments did not arise in a vacuum. Rather, they were the culmination of a profound transformation in the theory and practice of monetary policy that began in the aftermath of the Great Inflation of the 1970s and crystallized under the disinflationary regime led by Paul Volcker at the US Federal Reserve. Volcker's decisive break with the employment-oriented policy of the 1960s and 1970s established a new macroeconomic orthodoxy: that central banks should prioritize price stability above all else, and that their effectiveness depends on cultivating a reputation for inflation aversion.

This "Volcker moment" reshaped not only how central banks operated but also how they understood their role in the political economy. Indeed, the Fed's painful but ultimately successful disinflation of the early 1980s was interpreted—by economists, policymakers, and financial actors alike—as proof that credibility and conservatism were the cornerstones of monetary effectiveness (see Moschella 2024, Chapter 2). Volcker's example fostered a new policy consensus in which the central bank's capacity to act depended on its perceived independence from politics and its commitment to a low-inflation regime (Goodfriend 2007). The rise of rational expectations theory reinforced this shift: If economic agents form expectations based on antic-ipated policy, then monetary credibility—anchored in a clear, rule-based commitment to price stability—would reduce inflationary pressures at lower economic cost.

These insights laid the groundwork for a dramatic global shift in cen-tral banking. From the early 1990s onward, countries across advanced and emerging economies adopted formal inflation-targeting regimes and granted legal independence to their central banks (Gilardi 2007; Mas-ciandaro and Romelli 2015; Wasserfallen 2019). This transformation was not limited to a handful of countries—it became a global policy script (McNamara 2002) that redefined the central banker's role as that of a conser-vative guardian of monetary discipline (Moschella 2024) diffusing rapidly through international financial institutions, policy networks, and epistemic communities (Johnson 2016).

In institutionalizing this new orthodoxy, central banks increasingly came to embody what Feygin (2021) aptly terms the "deflationary bloc"—a transnational coalition of actors, particularly in the financial sector and export-oriented industries, whose interests are best served by low infla-tion, tight monetary control, and fiscal restraint. This coalition did more than shape central bank mandates; it succeeded in embedding a specific economic imaginary into the very architecture of modern central banking—namely one in which inflation is framed as the principal threat to prosperity, the achievement of price stability should be taken away from elected policy markets and assigned to independent institutions, and market confidence is equated with macroeconomic soundness (Grabel 2003; Kirshner 2003; McNamara 2002). In other words, the new orthodoxy cast inflation as the ultimate economic threat and positioned central banks as uniquely capable—and uniquely obligated—to prevent it. This shift marginalized competing policy goals such as full employment, social investment, or redis-tribution, which had animated the Keynesian order of the postwar decades. This (re)orientation has been most visible during moments of crisis. In 2008, 2010, and again in 2020, central banks intervened decisively to stabilize markets (Thiemann 2023)—but often in ways that reinforced asset-based inequality and protected incumbent financial actors, with minimal regard for broader distributive consequences (Dietsch et al. 2018; Jacobs and King 2016).

Yet this alignment with financial interests does not fully define the political position of central banks. While markets are central to the operational logic of monetary policy, they are not the only audience to whom central banks are accountable. As Moschella (2024) reminds us, central banks are political institutions—not in the partisan sense, but in the sense that their authority depends on their legitimacy within democratic polities. That legitimacy requires more than market credibility; it also rests on public trust and political acceptance. In other words, central banks' authority ultimately rests on political foundations. Indeed, central banks are not isolated technocratic actors; they operate in politically contested environments where legitimacy derives from broader public support and political acceptance. Governments and legislators retain the authority to revise or repeal central bank mandates (Keefer and Stasavage 2003), and citizens, while often perceived as a diffuse and less powerful audience, can nonetheless exert influence—particularly in moments of crisis when monetary policy decisions are perceived as unjust or unresponsive (Jones 2009; Moschella et al. 2020).

To navigate these intersecting pressures, central banks rely on a crucial symbolic resource: reputation. Reputation is the public image that central banks project of themselves and that defines who they are and how actors read them (Moschella 2024). It is built, sustained, and defended through the mobilization of economic imaginaries that define what the economy is, how it works, and what role central banks should play in it. These imaginaries revolve around the goal they pursue and the means through which central banks claim neutrality, insulate themselves from political interference, and maintain the authority to act.

Economic imaginaries are thus not simply interpretive frameworks. They are foundational to how central banks construct and protect their legitimacy. They offer a vision of central banking as objective and neutral. They naturalize policy priorities—such as inflation control and financial stability—as the only appropriate course of action rather than political choices with distributive implications. In short, they constitute the ideological core of monetary orthodoxy: a set of taken-for-granted assumptions that depoliticize central banking by casting its goals and tools as technically necessary. When those priorities are challenged—whether by crises, inflation surges, or growing demands for climate and social justice—central banks turn to these imaginaries as tools of reputational adaptation.

This chapter argues that the strategic recalibration of economic imaginaries has become especially salient in the post-2020 era. Confronted with heightened public contestation, both the US Federal Reserve and the ECB revised their policy strategies—not to break with orthodoxy, but to reframe it in ways that resonated with evolving societal expectations. The Fed, under pressure to address racial inequality and labor market exclusions, adopted a new emphasis on "broad-based and inclusive" employment. The ECB, facing mounting activism around climate change, incorporated environmental considerations into its monetary operations and assessments. These shifts were not random policy adjustments. They were deliberate moves designed to preserve central bank authority by recalibrating the imaginaries through which legitimacy is performed.

Importantly, these recalibrations were selective and symbolic. The new social goals were carefully positioned within the dominant imaginary of market credibility and price stability. Central banks did not depart from their foundational logic. Instead, they adjusted its discursive boundaries to accommodate new pressures. This suggests a reputational strategy that is responsive but not transformative—one that seeks to preserve institutional authority by appearing adaptive, rather than by enacting substantive change. In doing so, central banks deploy economic imaginaries not as reflections of changing economic realities but as instruments of political navigation. They update the stories they tell about themselves and their role not to transform monetary governance but to sustain its existing power structures under conditions of strain.

3. Central Banks Go Social

To decide how to respond to changing economic conditions, central banks usually rely on a monetary policy strategy. Specifically, a monetary strategy is the *framework* through which a central bank defines its monetary policy objectives, selects appropriate instruments, and communicates its policy intentions to the public and markets. It usually includes a specification of goals (such as inflation targets), the analytical tools and indicators used to assess economic conditions, and the rules or principles that guide policy decisions over time.[1] As such, the strategy is not just a technical manual: it

---

[1] For an overview of monetary policy frameworks and what they see, for instance, Bank for International Settlements (BIS). 2022. "Monetary Policy Frameworks and Central Bank Market Operations," https://www.bis.org/mc/compendium.htm. Accessed April 3, 2025.

is also a key component of how central banks construct and defend their authority in the public sphere.

The revision of the monetary strategies by the US Federal Reserve and the European Central Bank in 2020–2021 occurred against the backdrop of two major structural shifts that had begun to unsettle the conventional monetary policy playbook. First, following the 2008 global financial crisis— and further intensified by the COVID-19 pandemic—both institutions faced persistent difficulty in meeting their inflation targets. Despite prolonged and aggressive interventions, inflation in both economies remained stubbornly below the 2 percent benchmark (with a brief exception in the United States in 2017–2018). Second, the empirical foundations of the Phillips Curve, which posits a stable trade-off between unemployment and inflation, appeared increasingly tenuous. The breakdown of this relationship weakened the rationale for preemptive monetary tightening and prompted calls for a broader reassessment of central bank strategy.

These macroeconomic developments provided a compelling technical rationale for reviewing existing frameworks. However, this chapter contends that they are insufficient to explain the particular direction and content of the strategic adjustments introduced. In both cases, the embrace of new social goals—"broad-based and inclusive" employment in the United States and climate action in the eurozone—was not merely a technocratic response to evolving macroeconomic conditions. It was also a reputational maneuver designed to manage growing political contestation and to recalibrate central banks' public standing amid heightened scrutiny.

The US Fed and Inclusive Employment

In August 2020, Federal Reserve Chair Jerome Powell used the prestigious Jackson Hole symposium to unveil a revised monetary policy framework. At the center of this shift was the adoption of flexible average inflation targeting, allowing inflation to run "moderately above 2 percent for some time" to compensate for prior undershooting (Powell 2020). Equally notable was the Fed's reframing of its reading of the labor markets. Rather than responding to "deviations" from maximum employment, the Fed would now focus on "shortfalls."[2] Though seemingly minor, this change marked a meaningful

---

[2] "Federal Open Market Committee announces approval of updates to its Statement on Longer-Run Goals and Monetary Policy Strategy." Press release, August 27, 2020. https://www. federalreserve.gov/newsevents/pressreleases/monetary20200827a.htm.

rhetorical pivot—suggesting that the Fed would not tighten preemptively in response to falling unemployment unless inflationary pressures actually materialized.

More striking still was the explicit invocation of "broad-based and inclusive" employment. Powell emphasized the benefits of tight labor markets for historically marginalized groups, including racial minorities and low-income workers—an unusual move for an institution long sought to distance itself from explicitly social or distributive concerns. The revised framework thus appeared to signal a significant rebalancing of the Fed's dual mandate, prioritizing employment not just as a macroeconomic aggregate, but as a socially embedded objective with distributional consequences.[3]

Taken at face value, these changes suggested a progressive turn in US monetary governance. Yet a closer reading reveals that the 2020 framework did not represent a fundamental transformation of the Fed's policy paradigm. Instead, it functioned as a symbolic recalibration of the economic imaginary underpinning the Fed's authority—a reputational maneuver aimed at restoring legitimacy in the face of growing political and social contestation.

The official rationale for the review emphasized structural economic shifts: persistently low inflation, a flattening Phillips curve, and declining estimates of the natural rate of interest.[4] These developments had indeed weakened the case for preemptive tightening and highlighted the limits of conventional policy tools. But the technical explanation alone cannot account for the timing, content, and framing of the Fed's new strategy.

The broader context was one of reputational strain. After more than a decade of crisis management, the Fed faced mounting criticism for exacerbating inequality. Its post-2008 interventions had fueled asset price inflation, disproportionately benefiting the wealthy while doing little for wage earners or small businesses. During the COVID-19 pandemic, this disconnect became even more pronounced. The Fed's rapid and massive support for financial markets triggered one of the fastest rebounds in Wall Street history, even as unemployment soared and small enterprises shuttered. The perceived imbalance—between a central bank that catered to investors and

---

[3] On the increased attention the US Fed devoted to social inequalities, see the conference organized by the Board of Governors of the Federal Reserve System on September 26–27, 2017, titled "Disparities in the Labor Market: What Are We Missing?" The conference proceedings are available on the Board of Governors official webpage at https://www.federalreserve.gov/conferences/disparities-in-the-labor-market-about-2017.htm.

[4] See, among the others, Galí and Gambetti, 2019; Hooper, Mishkin and Sufi, 2020; Ratner and Sim, 2022.

one that neglected Main Street—undermined public trust and amplified calls for greater accountability.

For instance, public opinion surveys in the aftermath of the post-2008 crisis period revealed widespread mistrust in the Fed's ability to act in the interests of ordinary citizens.[5] These views have coalesced in a growing negative assessment of the central bank by US citizens.[6] The changes in public attitudes toward the central bank are also reflected in the growing attacks of policymakers from across the political spectrum. Indeed, ever since the start of the global financial crisis, the number of Congress proposals made that aim to curb the Fed's powers has increased markedly (Binder and Spindel 2017). Even former President Donald Trump repeatedly criticized the Fed for being insufficiently supportive of economic recovery—a populist line of attack that found considerable resonance.[7]

In this context, the Fed's embrace of "inclusive employment" was not merely technocratic; it was also performative. As one Financial Times reporter noted at the time, "Narrowing Wall Street's lead…has become more than simply a matter of financial stability. It is also about the Fed's reputation."[8] Through initiatives like "Fed Listens"—a series of nineteen public engagement events held in 2019 and 2020—the Fed solicited input from a wide range of social groups, including labor unions, minority organizations, and small business owners (see Federal Reserve 2021), also with the view to project an image of institutional openness and societal responsiveness. Participants emphasized that economic gains were not evenly distributed and that historically disadvantaged groups had only recently begun to benefit from tight labor markets (Sablik 2021). In response, the Fed articulated a more socially attuned interpretation of its employment mandate.

---

[5] Harris Interactive. 2009. Monthly Opinions of Adults from Five European Countries and the United States. http://www.harrisinteractive.com/news/datatables/HI_FT_HarrisPoll_July2009.pdf July and Ipsos/Axios survey, *Americans do not trust the Federal Reserve to look out for them*, May 20, 2020.

[6] For instance, a 2014 Pew Research Study found that 37 percent of American citizens have an unfavorable view of their central bank. The survey also found that negative attitudes toward the Fed are significantly affected by political orientation, with Republican voters being more likely to declare a negative opinion about the Fed. See Pew Research Center. 2015. "Americans' views of Fed depend on their politics." December 16. https://www.pewresearch.org/fact-tank/2015/12/16/americans-views-of-fed-depend-on-their-politics/.

[7] Between 2019 and 2020, former US President Trump repeatedly demanded that the Fed take a series of actions such as decisive interest rate reductions and the restart of crisis-era policies in order to stimulate economic growth.

[8] Smith and Colby, 2020. "The Fed's quest for higher inflation looks doomed without Congress." *Financial Times*, September 4.

This rhetorical shift allowed the Fed to appear attentive to public concerns. At the same time, however, the new framework did not define what "inclusive" employment would entail in operational terms, The new framework did not define what "inclusive" employment would entail in operational terms, nor did it establish concrete metrics for achieving average inflation and in what time frame (see also English and Sack 2024; Romer and Romer 2024 for a critical analysis of the 2020 monetary strategy). It retained significant ambiguity, which ultimately enabled the Fed to pivot away from the revised strategy when macroeconomic conditions changed.

Indeed, the fragility of this symbolic recalibration was exposed almost immediately. As inflation surged in 2021, the Fed abandoned its dovish posture and initiated one of the fastest tightening cycles in recent history (Moschella and Polyak 2022). The 2020 strategy—barely a year old—was effectively sidelined. By 2022, the institution had reverted to its foundational imaginary: credibility equated with inflation control, not employment inclusiveness.

In short, the Fed's 2020 strategy review exemplifies how central banks mobilize economic imaginaries as instruments of reputational management. By adopting the language of equity and inclusion, the Fed sought to navigate a politically volatile moment without conceding substantive change. It adjusted its narrative, not its priorities. The revised imaginary was symbolic, not transformative—an effort to square the political need for legitimacy with the enduring institutional imperative to maintain market confidence.

The ECB and a Green Monetary Strategy

In July 2021, the European Central Bank released its first comprehensive monetary policy strategy review since its establishment. The review introduced three key changes: a shift to a symmetric 2 percent inflation target; the formal incorporation of crisis-era policy tools into the ECB's standard monetary arsenal; and, most notably, the integration of climate change into the ECB's policy framework. Though framed as a necessary adaptation to evolving macroeconomic conditions, this strategy review was equally a reputational intervention—a symbolic recalibration of the ECB's economic imaginary aimed at restoring legitimacy in an increasingly contested political and social environment.

The first transformation involved the redefinition of the ECB's inflation objective. The previous target—"below but close to 2 percent"—was replaced with a symmetric 2 percent target, implying that undershooting inflation was now regarded as equally problematic as overshooting it.[9] As the 2021 policy statement reads, "The Governing Council considers that price stability is best maintained by aiming for two percent inflation over the medium term." (European Central Bank 2021c). This change signaled a rhetorical shift: a greater willingness to tolerate temporary inflation overshoots in pursuit of sustained economic recovery. As the ECB's statement put it, "In the presence of an adverse supply shock, the Governing Council may decide to lengthen the horizon over which inflation returns to the target level in order to avoid pronounced falls in economic activity and employment, which, if persistent, could themselves jeopardize medium-term price stability" (European Central Bank 2021d). Though price stability remained the ECB's sole legal mandate, this discursive adjustment gestured toward a more flexible approach—one that recognized the dangers of premature tightening in a low-inflation, low-growth context.

Second, the strategy normalized the expanded monetary policy toolkit the ECB had relied on since the euro crisis. While reiterating that interest rates remained the primary instrument, the review formalized the use of forward guidance, asset purchases, and long-term refinancing operations (European Central Bank 2021c). These tools—once justified as emergency measures—were now institutionalized, and the ECB explicitly reserved the right to develop new instruments in the future. Importantly, the emphasis on "flexibility" allowed the ECB to preserve discretion while retroactively legitimizing its crisis response. This move did not signal a transformation in how the ECB conceives of monetary authority; it affirmed that the ECB would continue to act decisively when needed—but on its own terms.

The third change was the ECB's climate turn. For the first time, the Bank committed to integrating climate-related risks and sustainability considerations into its monetary assessments and operations. The 2021 policy statement pledged that "within its mandate," the ECB would take account of the implications of climate change and the carbon transition. In particular, the ECB committed "to ensuring that the Eurosystem fully takes into

---

[9] The target of inflation below but close to 2 percent had been agreed upon by the Governing Council in 2003.

account, in line with the EU's climate goals and objectives, the implications of climate change and the carbon transition for monetary policy and
central banking" (European Central Bank 2021c). A roadmap followed, out-
lining planned adjustments to disclosure standards, collateral frameworks,
and corporate asset purchases (on the "green turn" within the ECB see also
Deyris 2023; Di Leo et al. 2023).

At first glance, this appeared to mark a major institutional evolution. For
an organization long committed to a narrow interpretation of price stability, the inclusion of climate goals suggested an expanded conception of the
ECB's role, aligned with broader EU efforts to green the economy. However,
as with the Fed's "inclusive employment" rhetoric, a more critical reading
reveals this move as a symbolic recalibration of the ECB's economic imaginary. The integration of climate considerations was tightly circumscribed.
The ECB did not claim a new mandate, nor did it challenge the institutional
hierarchy that places inflation control at the top (van't Klooster and Boer
2023). Rather, climate risk was redefined as a potential threat to price and
financial stability—thus justifying limited intervention without altering the
core logic of monetary governance (also Quorning 2024).

This reputational maneuver was shaped by significant external pressures.
Over the previous decade, the ECB had been subject to intensifying politicization and declining public trust. The euro crisis, followed by a prolonged
period of low inflation and controversial bond purchases, eroded elite consensus and invited both legal and popular challenge. The 2020 ruling of the
German Constitutional Court, which questioned the legality of the ECB's
Public Sector Purchase Programme, was a particularly stark indicator of
eroding legitimacy.[10] Meanwhile, the ECB became the target of civil society mobilization—from Blockupy's anti-austerity protests to climate activists
who criticized the Bank for indirectly financing fossil fuel firms through its
asset purchase programs.[11]

Public trust in the ECB fell dramatically between 2008 and 2014, as surveys conducted by Eurobarometer and academic studies show. Importantly,
this loss of trust occurred even as support for the euro remained relatively

---

[10] Whereas German public and political elites had traditionally supported the independence of
the ECB since its creation (Brunnermeier, James and Landau, 2017; Hayo, 1998; Howarth and Rommerskirchen, 2013) the German constitutional court ruled in May 2020 that the ECB had acted
beyond its competences with respect to the bond buying program.

[11] Treeck, Johanna. 2021. "Greenpeace lands on ECB tower in climate finance protest." *Politico.*
https://www.politico.eu/article/greenpeace-protest-european-central-bank-paraglider-climate-fin
ance-carbon/.

stable—revealing a growing disconnect between citizens' support for European integration and their views of the ECB as its monetary guardian. This legitimacy deficit was especially troubling for a central bank operating in a multinational polity, where trust must be earned across diverse national publics (see also Bergbauer et al. 2020; Dotti and Magistro 2016; Foster and Frieden 2017; Roth et al. 2014).

ECB officials were acutely aware of this challenge. A 2020 survey of former Governing Council members revealed that trust and credibility were viewed as the most important goals of central bank communication (Ehrmann et al. 2021). Internal publications and research increasingly emphasized the dangers that public distrust posed to both monetary effectiveness and institutional independence (Angino and Secola 2022; Christelis et al. 2021; Ioannou et al. 2015). In response, the ECB embarked on a transformation of its communicative practices. It began publishing summaries of Governing Council deliberations in 2015, expanded its appearances before national parliaments, strengthened ties with the European Parliament, and increased outreach through social media and "listening events" (Fraccaroli et al. 2018; Moschella and Romelli 2022; Tesche 2018).

The 2021 strategy review must be seen within this broader context. It was not simply a response to technical concerns about inflation or macroeconomic stability. It was a reputational strategy designed to rebuild legitimacy by adapting the ECB's public image to shifting societal expectations. The review process included public consultation and outreach events across the eurozone, where civil society organizations—especially NGOs, youth groups, and climate activists—called on the ECB to address broader economic and social concerns.[12] Many of these groups explicitly asked the Bank to incorporate climate considerations and promote inclusive growth (European Central Bank 2021b).

In summarizing these consultations, the ECB acknowledged that "the costs of climate change and possible future economic and financial crises were mentioned prominently across all listening channels" (European Central Bank 2021b). Although not all policymakers within the ECB were enthusiastic about expanding the Bank's role in this direction, the decision

---

[12] During the strategy review period, the ECB listened to the views of EU citizens and social organizations through ad hoc listening events and a web survey conducted from February to October 2020. According to the ECB, approximately four thousand respondents answered questions on four topics relevant to the monetary policy strategy review: (1) price stability, (2) economic issues, (3) global challenges, and (4) central bank communication. See European Central Bank, 2021b and European Central Bank, 2021a.

to include climate objectives reflected an effort to respond to public contestation without triggering legal or political backlash. By framing climate risk as a threat to financial and price stability, the ECB was able to act without formally expanding its mandate or altering its primary objective.

This strategy mirrors the Fed's approach: Both central banks recalibrated their economic imaginaries to signal responsiveness while preserving autonomy. In the ECB's case, climate action became a reputational device—a way to appear engaged with pressing societal concerns without undermining the institutional foundations of the Bank's authority. As ECB Chief Economist Philip Lane (2022) explained, the revised strategy served two purposes: to provide a coherent analytical framework for policy and to make "it easier for the ECB to be held accountable and for it to build trust among the general public."

However, as with the Fed, the limits of this symbolic adaptation became visible when inflation returned in 2022. The ECB decidedly shifted back to orthodox inflation-fighting mode, raising interest rates to reaffirm its credibility. While the climate roadmap was not formally rescinded, it has been largely sidelined in public communication and policy action. Price stability has once again asserted itself as the dominant principle—underscoring the durability of the ECB's core economic imaginary, where legitimacy flows from market confidence, not public inclusion.

In sum, the ECB's 2021 strategy review exemplifies how central banks manage contestation through reputational recalibration. Rather than fundamentally altering their purpose, they adjust the language and framing of their actions to accommodate political pressure and deflect criticism. Climate risk, like inclusive employment at the Fed, became a symbolic means through which central banks engaged with societal concerns without changing their underlying orientation.

4. Conclusions

Central banks have long been designed as institutions insulated from public pressures. Their autonomy (and authority) is premised on the idea that monetary policy should remain above the fray of electoral politics and short-term demands, with credibility measured by financial market confidence rather than societal approval. Yet, as this chapter—and the broader contributions in this volume—make clear, central banks are not apolitical technocrats simply executing neutral mandates. They are deeply embedded in contested political and economic landscapes. Far from being inert guardians of macroeconomic stability, they actively shape the large distributional politics that define financial governance.

This chapter contributes to the volume themes by showing how central banks respond to public pressure not by transforming the foundations of monetary policy, but by recalibrating the *economic imaginaries* that underpin their authority. The cases of the US Federal Reserve and the European Central Bank reveal how, under conditions of post-crisis legitimacy strain and politicization, central banks engaged in strategic adaptations of their public narratives. The Fed embraced the language of "inclusive employment" in response to rising inequality and social protest; the ECB incorporated climate concerns following legal and activist challenges to its role in financing carbon-intensive sectors.

These responses were not transformative shifts in the politics of distribution. They were reputational maneuvers—namely symbolic recalibrations that aimed to manage political risk and sustain institutional autonomy. In both cases, the social goals adopted were framed in ways that aligned with, rather than disrupted, the dominant imaginary of central banking as a guardian of price stability, market confidence, and technocratic neutrality. In short, the two central banks responded to contestation by selectively expanding their discursive repertoires while preserving their underlying distributional commitments.

This dynamic raise two major sets of questions. First, it invites a rethinking of when and how central banks become responsive to the public. The evidence here suggests that crisis moments—when the legitimacy of monetary authorities is in question—create openings for reputational recalibration. But these windows are narrow and conditional. The Fed's rhetorical commitment to inclusive employment unravelled rapidly once inflation returned in 2021–2022. The ECB, while not formally abandoning its climate orientation, has significantly downplayed its green initiatives amid renewed inflation concerns. In both cases, the revised imaginaries proved fragile and reversible—subordinate to the enduring priority of anti-inflationary credibility. In short, outside specific crisis contexts, central banks are more likely to retreat into their conventional role, with financial markets regaining prominence as their primary constituency. Future research should further explore how different types of crises and forms of public mobilization shape central banks' receptiveness to societal claims.

Second, this chapter raises normative and conceptual questions about the meaning of central bank independence in the face of public demands. At first glance, responsiveness to citizen concerns might appear to challenge central bank autonomy or authority over policy. However, as the cases above suggest, such responsiveness often functions symbolically—not to alter the core tenets of monetary policy, but to sustain central bank legitimacy in times of crisis. In this view, public engagement is less about genuine policy change and more about strategic recalibration: an effort to appear attentive while ultimately preserving the institutional logic and autonomy of central banking. Rather than diluting independence, this selective engagement reinforces it by helping central banks adapt reputationally without yielding ground on substantive policy decisions. The challenge, then, is not simply to democratize monetary policy (Downey 2022) but to understand how central banks construct and defend their authority through carefully managed forms of symbolic accountability—and what this means for democratic oversight of powerful, unelected institutions.

In sum, this chapter reinforces one of the key insights of this volume: monetary and financial authorities do not merely manage the economy. They shape societal conflict and influence the balance of power among social groups. They do so not only through policy instruments, but also through the deployment of economic imaginaries. These imaginaries are not neutral frameworks or simple cognitive maps; they are tools of power that are integral to the legitimation and reproduction of authority within technocratic institutions. When contested, central banks do not revise these imaginaries to redistribute power. Rather, they recalibrate them symbolically to deflect criticism and manage political risk. The long-term significance of these adaptations will depend on whether they remain instrumental or become institutionalized—whether symbolic responsiveness opens the door to structural change or simply forestalls it. For now, central banks continue to adjust the image while preserving the substance of a financial order that, as this volume shows, continues to choose its winners carefully yet unequally.

References

Angino, S., and S. Secola. 2022. "Instinctive versus Reflective Trust in the European Central Bank." *ECB Working Papers* 2660.

Baker, A. 2006. *The Group of Seven: Finance Ministries, Central Banks and Global Financial Governance*. London, Routledge.

Bergbauer, S., N. Hernborg, J.-F. Jamet, and E. Persson. 2020. "The Reputation of the Euro and the European Central Bank: Interlinked or Disconnected?" *Journal of European Public Policy* 27(8): 1178–1194.

Best, J. 2018. "The Inflation Game: Targets, Practices and the Social Production of Monetary Credibility." *New Political Economy* 24(5): 623–640.

Binder, S. and M. Spindel. 2017. *The Myth of Independence: How Congress Governs the Federal Reserve*. Princeton, NJ: Princeton University Press.

Braun, B. 2020. "Central Banking and the Infrastructural Power of Finance: The Case of ECB Support for Repo and Securitization Markets." *Socio-Economic Review* 18(2): 395–418.

Brunnermeier, M.K., H. James, and J.-P. Landau. 2017. *The Euro and the Battle of Ideas*. Princeton, NJ: Princeton University Press.

Carpenter, D. P. 2010. *Reputation and Power. Organizational Image and Pharmaceutical Regulation at the FDA*. Princeton, NJ: Princeton University Press.

Christelis, D., D. Georgarakos, T. Jappelli, and M. van Rooij. 2021. "Trust in the Central Bank and Inflation Expectation." *ECB Working Paper Series* 2375.

Coombs, N. and M. Thiemann. 2022. "Recentering Central Banks: Theorizing State-Economy Boundaries as Central Bank Effects." *Economy and Society* 51(4): 535–558.

Deyris, J. 2023. "Too Green To Be True? Forging a Climate Consensus at the European Central Bank." *New Political Economy* 28(5): 713–730.

Di Leo, M., G. Rudebusch and J. V. T. Klooster. 2023. "Why the Fed and ECB Parted Ways on Climate Change: The Politics of Divergence in the Global Central Banking Community." *Brookings Institution, Hutchins Center Working Paper No. 88*.

Dietsch, P., F. Claveau, and C. Fontan. 2018. *Do Central Banks Serve the People?* Hoboken, NJ: John Wiley & Sons.

Dotti, G. M., and B. Magistro. 2016. "Increasingly Unequal? The Economic Crisis, Social Inequalities and Trust in the European Parliament in 20 European Countries." *European Journal of Political Research* 55(2): 246–264.

Downey, L. 2024. *Our Money: Monetary Policy as if Democracy Mattered*. Princeton, NJ: Princeton University Press.

Ehrmann, M., S. Holton, D. Kedan, and G. Phelan. 2021. "Monetary Policy Communication: Perspectives from Former Policy Makers at the ECB." *ECB Working Paper Series* 2627.

English, W., and B. P. Sack. 2024. "Challenges Around the Fed's Monetary Policy Framework and Its Implementation." *Brookings Papers on Economic Activity*.

European Central Bank. 2021a. "ECB Listens—Summary report of the ECB Listens Portal responses." *ECB*. Available at https://www.ecb.europa.eu/mopo/strategy/strategy-review/html/ecb.strategyreview002.en.html.

European Central Bank. 2021b. "ECB Listens—Midterm Review Summary Report." *ECB*. Available at https://www.ecb.europa.eu/mopo/strategy/strategy-review/html/ecb.strategyreview001.en.html.

European Central Bank 2021c. "The ECB's Monetary Policy Strategy Statement." *ECB*. Available at https://www.ecb.europa.eu/home/search/review/html/ecb.strategyreview_monpol_strategy_statement.en.html.

European Central Bank 2021d. "Overview note of the ECB's monetary policy strategy statement", *ECB* Available at https://www.ecb.europa.eu/home/search/review/html/ecb.strategyreview_monpol_strategy_overview.en.html.

Federal Reserve 2021. "Federal Reserve Board—Fed Listens," *Board of Governors of the Federal Reserve System*. Available at *https://www.federalreserve.gov/monetarypolicy/review-of-monetary-policy-strategy-tools-and-communications-fed-listens-events.htm*.

Feygin, Y. 2021. "The Deflationary Bloc." Phenomenal World. January 9, https://www.phenomenalworld.org/analysis/deflation-inflation.

Foster, C. and J. Frieden. 2017. "Crisis of Trust: Socio-Economic Determinants of Europeans' Confidence in Government." *European Union Politics* 18(4): 511–535.

Fraccaroli, N., A. Giovannini, and J.-F. Jamet. 2018. "The Evolution of the ECB's Accountability Practices during the Crisis." *ECB Economic Bulletin* 5: 47–71.

Galí, J. and L. Gambetti. 2019. "Has the US Wage Phillips Curve Flattened? A Semi-Structural Exploration." National Bureau of Economic Research Working Papers 25476.

Gilardi, F. 2007. "The Same, But Different: Central Banks, Regulatory Agencies, and the Politics of Delegation to Independent Authorities." *Comparative European Politics* 5(3): 303–327.

Goodfriend, M. 2007. "How the World Achieved Consensus on Monetary Policy." *Journal of Economic Perspectives* 21(4): 47–68.

Grabel, I. 2003. Ideology, Power, and the Rise of Independent Monetary Institutions. In *Monetary Orders. Ambiguous Economics, Ubiquitous Politics*, edited by J. Kirshner. Ithaca, NY, Cornell University Press, 25–53.

Hayo, B. 1998. "Inflation culture, central bank independence and price stability." *European Journal of Political Economy* 14(2): 241–263.

Hooper, P., F. S. Mishkin, and A. Sufi. 2020. "Prospects for inflation in a high pressure economy: Is the Phillips curve dead or is it just hibernating?" *Research in Economics* 74(1): 26–62.

Howarth, D. and C. Rommerskirchen. 2016. "Inflation aversion in the European Union: exploring the myth of a North–South divide." *Socio-Economic Review* 15(2): 385–404.

Ioannou, D., J.-F. o. Jamet, and J. Kleibl. 2015. "Spillovers and Euroscepticism." *ECB Working Paper Series* 1815.

Jacobs, L., and D. King. 2016. *Fed Power: How Finance Wins*. New York: Oxford University Press.

Jacobs, L. R., and D. King, eds. 2025. Picking Winners: Citizenship, Central Banks, and Consumer Finance.

Jacobs, L. R. and R. Y. Shapiro. 2000. *Politicians Don't Pander: Political Manipulation and the Loss of Democratic Responsiveness*. Chicago: University of Chicago Press.

Johnson, J. 2016. *Priests of Prosperity: The Transnational Central Banking Community and Post-Communist Transformation*. Ithaca, NY: Cornell University Press.

Jones, E. 2009. "Output Legitimacy and the Global Financial Crisis: Perceptions Matter." *JCMS: Journal of Common Market Studies* 47(5): 1085–1105.

Keefer, P. and D. Stasavage. 2003. "The Limits of Delegation: Veto Players, Central Bank Independence, and the Credibility of Monetary Policy." *American Political Science Review* 97(3): 407–423.

Kirshner, J. 2003. "Money is Politics." *Review of International Political Economy* 10(4): 645–660.

Lane, P. R. 2022. *The Monetary Policy Startegy of the ECB: The Playbook for Monetary Policy Decisions*. Speech delivered at the Hertie School, Berlin, March 2.

Marcussen, M. 2006. "The Transnational Governance Network of Central Bankers. In eds. M. L. Djelic and K. Sahlin-Andersson, *Transnational Governance: Institutional Dynamics of Regulation*. Cambridge, UK: Cambridge University Press, 180–240.

Masciandaro, D. and D. Romelli. 2015. "Ups and Downs of Central Bank Independence from the Great Inflation to the Great Recession: Theory, Institutions and Empirics." *Financial History Review* 22(3): 259–289.

McNamara, K. 2002. "Rational Fictions: Central Bank Independence and the Social Logic of Delegation." *West European Politics* 25(1): 47–76.

Moschella, M. 2024. *Unexpected Revolutionaries. How Central Banks Made and Unmade Economic Orthodoxy*. Ithaca, NY: Cornell University Press.

Moschella, M., L. Pinto, and N. Martocchia Diodati. 2020. "Let's Speak More? How the ECB Responds to Public Contestation." *Journal of European Public Policy* 27(3): 400–418.

Moschella, M. and P. Polyak. 2022. "Managing Global Monetary Spillovers. How the Fed's Interest Rate Hikes and Uncoordinated Tightening Affect the Euro Area." *Monetary Dialogue Papers*.

Moschella, M., and D. Romelli. 2022. "ECB Communication and Its Post-Pandemic Challenges." *Monetary Dialogue Papers.*

Powell, J. H. 2020. "New Economic Challenges and the Fed's Monetary Policy Review." Speech delivered at the Federal Reserve Bank of Kansas City Economic Symposium, Jackson Hole, Wyoming, August 27.

Quorning, S. 2024. "The 'Climate Shift' in Central Banks: How Field Arbitrageurs Paved the Way for Climate Stress Testing." *Review of International Political Economy* 31(1): 74–96.

Ratner, D. and J. W. Sim. 2022. "Who Killed the Phillips Curve? A Murder Mystery." Finance and Economics Discussion Paper Series 028.

Romer, C. D. and D. H. Romer. 2024. "Did the Federal Reserve's 2020 Policy Framework Limit Its Response to Inflation? Evidence and Implications for the Framework Review." *Brookings Papers on Economic Activity* September.

Roth, F., D. Gros, and F. Nowak-Lehmann. 2014. "Crisis and Citizens' Trust in the European Central Bank—Panel Data Evidence for the Euro Area, 1999–2012." *Journal of European Integration* 36(3): 303–320.

Sablik, T. 2021. "The Fed's New Framework. With a Revised Strategy, the Fed Responds to Challenges Facing Central Banks Today." Econ Focus, Federal Reserve Bank of Richmond. https://www.richmondfed.org/-/media/richmondfedorg/publications/research/econ_focus/2021/q1/federal_reserve.pdf.

Tesche, T. 2018. "Instrumentalizing EMU's Democratic Deficit: the ECB's Unconventional Accountability Measures during the Eurozone Crisis." *Journal of European Integration* 41(4): 447–463.

Thiemann, M. 2023. *Taming the Cycles of Finance? Central Banks and the Macro-Prudential Shift in Financial Regulation*, Oxford: Oxford University Press.

Van't Klooster, J., and N. D. Boer (2023) "What to Do with the ECB's Secondary Mandate." *Journal of Common Market Studies* 61(3): 730–746.

Wasserfallen, F. 2019. "Global Diffusion, Policy Flexibility, and Inflation Targeting." *International Interactions* 45(4): 617–637.

Index

For the benefit of digital users, indexed terms that span two pages (e.g., 52–53) may, on occasion, appear on only one of those pages.

Tables, figures, and boxes are indicated by an italic *t*, *f*, and *b*.